THORSTEIN VEBLEN

" ProCASTINATiON is the ArT / KEEpING
up w/ yesTerday."
—Don Marquis —

In his latest book, scholar-historian Murray G. Murphey exhaustively explores the life and theory of Thorstein Veblen (1857–1929), whom, many scholars agree, remains one of the leading social theorists of all time, if not also one of the more confounding. Murphey's account begins with a brief economic history of nineteenth-century America, wherein he examines the conditions that formed Veblen's ideology. With that understanding, the author studies Veblen's personal history and brings to the fore his foundational ideas on human psychology, race, his theory of knowledge, and his analysis of social evolution. In the book's later chapters, Murphey considers Veblen's writing through the scope of his major volumes – *The Theory of the Leisure Class*, *The Theory of Business Enterprise*, and *Imperial Germany and the Industrial Revolution*, among others.

Spanning the latter stages of the nineteenth century into the first several decades of the twentieth century, Murphey traces Veblen's radical economics and thinking within the broader context of America's economic theory. In so doing, he upholds Veblen's influence on the canons of economics and social science, and importantly, he attempts to resolve the lingering mystery behind one of America's more puzzling and influential theorists.

Murray G. Murphey is Emeritus Professor of American Civilization at the University of Pennsylvania. He is the author of *Philosophical Foundations of Historical Knowledge*, *The Development of Peirce's Philosophy*, co-author of the two-volume *A History of Philosophy in America*, and co-editor of *Values and Value Theory in Twentieth Century America*.

THORSTEIN VEBLEN

Economist and Social Theorist

Murray G. Murphey

NEW YORK AND LONDON

First published 2018
by Routledge
711 Third Avenue, New York, NY 10017

and by Routledge
2 Park Square, Milton Park, Abingdon, Oxon OX14 4RN

Routledge is an imprint of the Taylor & Francis Group, an informa business

© 2018 Taylor & Francis

Library of Congress Cataloging-in-Publication Data
A catalog record for this title has been requested

ISBN: 978-1-138-06906-0 (hbk)
ISBN: 978-0-8153-7185-4 (pbk)
ISBN: 978-1-351-24439-8 (ebk)

Typeset in Bembo
by Taylor & Francis Books

"The price/wisdom is ABOVE rubies."
— Job 28:18 —

CONTENTS

PREFACE

Thorstein Veblen (1857–1929) Veblen is one of the most puzzling figures in American intellectual history. He has won extraordinary accolades from a variety of major scholars. Geoffrey Hodgson writes:

> It may take one hundred years from Veblen's death in 1929 for him to be recognized by social scientists as one of the leading social theorists of all time.[1]

Douglas Dowd writes:

> There can be little doubt that Thorstein Veblen was and remains the most eminent and seminal thinker in the area of social analysis yet to emerge in America.[2]

Similar comments are numerous. Yet even today Veblen remains a somewhat mysterious figure. This is not because he has failed to receive scholarly attention. But most of those who have written about Veblen have done him less than justice. There are several reasons for this. First, some who admire Veblen have been embarrassed by what they consider to be his racism and have not felt comfortable with this aspect of his work. We are so used to the pejorative use of racial terms that we find it difficult to recognize the non-pejorative use when we meet it. Veblen does consider race (as he defines it) a significant factor, but he is not a "racist" in the sense of Adolf Hitler or Theodore Bilbo. Second, some have thought that Veblen's fundamental ideas are archaic and have concluded that that fact invalidates his work as a whole. There is something to this objection, but not much. What is out of date in Veblen's work does not contaminate the whole of it. Indeed, some of what Veblen wrote is strikingly up to date. Third, the standard tools of intellectual history have been difficult to apply to Veblen. He does not often cite his sources or the authorities for what he says so source hunting is largely futile, and Veblen left no body of unpublished manuscripts behind him where gems of exotic wisdom might be discovered. Fourth, there have been a number of people who have found it difficult to accept Veblen's apparent originality and have set out to prove that he was really a closet Marxist. He was not, and this line of inquiry has led to less than nothing.

There are also critics who have objected to Veblen's prose, claiming that it is tortuous and obscure. But Veblen's writing is neither tortuous nor obscure; his writing is straightforward and remarkably clear. Veblen was a penetrating observer of the culture of his time, and the conclusions he drew from his observations were often radically different from those that others drew. It was not that his readers could not understand what he said; it was rather that they could not believe that he meant what he said. So they missed his message and then blamed his style for their confusion. This was most famously the case with *The Theory of the Leisure Class*, a beautifully crafted treatise in economic theory that his readers could only interpret as a satire, thereby missing the whole point of the work. Veblen was a radical in the original sense of the term – he went to the root of things. Those happy with a more superficial approach found him difficult to understand. For these and similar reasons, Veblen's thought has remained something of a mystery. It is time that the mystery was resolved, and that is the aim of this work.

INTRODUCTION

The world in which Thorstein Veblen came of age was one of rapid, profound, and disturbing change. In spite of, or because of, his marginal position in American society, Veblen was a close and keen observer of that world, and his hopes, fears, and thoughts were molded by the context in which he lived. A brief description of that context is therefore necessary.

In 1800, the United States was a nation 95 percent of whose population was rural. By 1900, it was an industrial powerhouse. What brought this transformation about was a series of changes that affected almost every aspect of American life. One of the most important factors in making this transformation possible was the policies of the federal government with respect to land. Land tenure, from the beginning of the republic, was ownership in fee simple, which enabled individuals to buy and sell land and to exercise almost complete control over the land they owned. Furthermore, the federal government set the price of the public land low enough so that ownership of land was relatively easy. And by imposing on the public lands the rectangular survey, the land was packaged in easily saleable lots of quarter sections, half sections, and sections. The government used the public lands to subsidize the settlement of the West, and the policy succeeded. Even today, if one flies over the Midwest, one can look down on a checkerboard agricultural landscape, quarter section after quarter section.

For that rural population farming was the chief occupation. In 1800, the methods used were traditional and the farm technology was primitive. The Industrial Revolution transformed agriculture as it did industry. A variety of new tools were introduced, of which the reaper was the most important. Before the introduction of the reaper in 1834, a good man using a grain cradle could harvest two to four acres a day; with a McCormick reaper, he could harvest twelve to twenty acres in a day. There were other innovations too: iron and steel plows, threshing machines, fanning mills, seed drills, the spring-toothed harrow, and many more. By 1900, one man properly equipped could produce what it had required four men to produce in 1800.

The transformation of the farm had profound consequences. It meant that a quarter of the population could feed the rest, and so made possible rapid urbanization. It offered a market for factories producing agricultural machinery, and created a demand for transportation that could carry bulky farm produce to markets. It created agricultural surpluses that could be sold abroad. And it stimulated the settlement of the Midwest and West, where immigrants like the Veblens found homes.

The growing population of the Midwest, with its rapidly increasing agricultural production, needed access to the markets of the East Coast. The topography of the United States did not make this easy. The United States has splendid water transportation routes in the Atlantic Ocean and the Mississippi River system, but these ran north and south whereas what was needed was transportation between west and east. For this, the Appalachian mountain chain posed what appeared to be an insuperable barrier. There was one break in the Appalachian mountain chain north of Atlanta where a canal appeared possible: the route from Buffalo to Albany, a distance of over three hundred miles. The state of New York, realizing what such a canal could mean to its economy, undertook the venture, and in 1825 the Erie Canal opened. The impact of the canal was enormous. For the first time, goods from the Great Lakes area of the Midwest could be direct shipped east, first to Albany and then down the Hudson River to New York City. The canal solidified New York City's position as the dominant US port on the East Coast. It also set off a flurry of canal building to connect more areas of the Midwest to the Great Lakes system. Farmers would no longer have to turn their grain into whisky in order to have an exportable product; now they could ship the grain itself.

Such canals were not possible for Philadelphia and Baltimore. For these cities, the railroad was the only hope. Both set out to build east–west rail lines. In 1854, the Summit Tunnel was opened and the Pennsylvania Railroad was through to the Ohio River. At about the same time, the Baltimore and Ohio also reached the river. In 1853, the New York Central Railroad reached Buffalo, giving New York City rail access to the West.

Railroads quickly spread across the country. They played an essential part in the Civil War, making possible armies of a size inconceivable before. They created a national market where before there had been only regional markets. They were themselves huge markets for heavy industry; the Baldwin Locomotive works in Philadelphia was the pre-eminent heavy industrial plant in America. Because they affected regional economies, the railroads were heavily involved in politics at the local, the state, and the national levels. They were the largest businesses of the time. America would never be the same.

Industrialization had begun in the United States before the railroad with the development of textile manufacturing in New England, based on wooden machinery and water power. Steam powered industry was not far behind. The steam engine provided a moveable generator of power, and power far beyond what human or animal muscle could supply. Industries grew in the major port cities on the East Coast, geared to regional markets. But as the railroad expanded their markets, these cities began to specialize, New York City and Philadelphia emerging as the centers of heavy industry. By 1860, sectional economies had developed with the South specializing in commercial agriculture and the North specializing in industry and family farming. The Civil War came at an economically plausible time.

Industrialization and integration accelerated after the Civil War. Rail lines were pushed to the West Coast, creating the possibility of a single national market. Government policy encouraged these developments. The Homestead Act of 1862 gave public lands to settlers free on the condition of settlement and improvement. Federal land grants helped to finance railroad construction. As rail lines multiplied, land companies brought immigrants to the West where population growth created business for the railroads. Tariffs helped to protect the home markets from European competition as "infant industries" grew to maturity.

And how they grew! The railroads were the first really large businesses, with operations spanning the continent and huge investments in rails, rolling stock, and terminals. Wherever rail lines went, they converted subsistence farming into commercial farming by giving the farmers access to markets. For towns and cities, having rail connections was the difference between being a commercial center or a dying backwater. Where the railroads entered cities, they needed terminals, which required city rights of way, which required lots of money to persuade the city fathers of the virtues of connection with a particular railroad company. Corruption was built into this process as local politicians sought to exploit the railroads and the railroads sought to buy local cooperation. In 1850, the US had ten thousand miles of first-line track; in 1900 it had two hundred thousand.

As businesses scrambled to take advantage of the opportunities of the continental market, the increasing population and the virgin natural resources, new forms of business were created to deal with these opportunities. The corporate form of organization, with its ability to raise capital, became increasingly the dominant form of business. Industrial production boomed to feed the rapidly expanding market. But in the later nineteenth century, even the rapid expansion of the market was not enough to absorb the increasing production of new industries. How to deal with that problem was made clear by John D. Rockefeller when in 1882 he founded the Standard Oil Company – the first great trust. So successful was Standard Oil that by the early years of the twentieth century it had established a virtual monopoly over the American oil industry, and where Rockefeller led, others followed. Trusts soon operated in tobacco, meatpacking, flour, and a number of other industries.

American cities had always been located to take advantage of transportation possibilities. Before 1850, that meant water transport; the major American cities were river ports, lake ports, or ocean ports. Naturally enough, the railroads' major lines connected the major cities and so increased their populations and commerce. Immigrants coming to America usually landed in the port cities where many stayed, though others moved further inland. Before 1880, the major sources of immigration were the British Isles and Northern Europe, particularly Ireland and Germany. But after 1880, these immigrant streams were swamped by a flood of immigrants from Italy and Eastern Europe – a flood that continued until the Great War interrupted it. This massive immigration furnished cheap labor for the rapidly expanding industries and swelled the population of the cities. New York City went from a city of a few thousand in 1800 to a city of over a million by 1900. Chicago went from nothing in 1800 to over a million in 1900. Other cities also bloomed, though few so spectacularly.

American cities were hopelessly unprepared for these changes. The pre-Civil War American city had been a walking city; people lived near their places of work, retail stores were within walking distance, and there was little need for in-city transport. As industries grew in the cities, they located where the railroads offered transportation or by the harbor if the city was a port. Immigrants crowded into the areas around the factories. But the cities lacked the housing for the flood of newcomers and could not build new housing fast enough to meet the demand. Overcrowding and congestion followed, and combined with low wages to create slums of a sort not previously seen in American cities. The need for in-city transportation became critical as the borders of the city expanded, and electric streetcars were introduced to try to provide it. Problems of water supply, fire protection, police protection, sewage disposal, and disease grew with the cities' size. But the governmental structure of the city was still the traditional mayor and council system; the cities offered few services and had little money to finance such activities. Given the incapacity of the legal structure of the city to deal with its growing problems, extra-legal structures developed to take their place. So-called political machines, such as Tammany Hall in New York City, may have been corrupt, but they provided essential services that the legal government could not.

These radical transformations of American life between the Civil War and the Great War provoked dismay. Most people, caught in the midst of the flood of changes, were bewildered by it. Few understood what was happening, or could imagine where the flood was taking them. Their city's streets were filled with strange people and a babble of unintelligible languages. New industries poured smoke into the air and paved the streets with soot. Their city governments, once a source of pride, were now said to be corrupt, and they were plagued by fears of disease and crime. There was an overwhelming sense that things had gone wrong, but no one seemed to know what to do about it or how to fix it. Accordingly, efforts to deal with the host of new problems were disorganized and usually ineffective. But the sense of unease was palpable.

Farmers reacted to this situation by the establishment of the Patrons of Husbandry, or the Grange, in the 1870s. A particular grievance of the farmers was the rates railroads charged for carrying their crops to market. Led by the Grange, the farmers succeeded in getting some states to pass laws regulating railroad rates, but these victories turned to ashes when the Supreme Court declared such laws unconstitutional. The failure of the Grange led to the formation in the 1880s of the Farmers' Alliances. Their program called for the regulation of the railroads by the federal government, cooperative buying and marketing to break the hold of the middle men on the farm economies, commodity credit for farmers, and a federal income tax, and some even demanded federal ownership of the railroads. Inevitably, the Alliances turned to political action; much of their program called for government action and they saw no other way to get it. The result was the formation of the People's Party (Populists). In the elections of 1890 and 1892, the Populists did well, electing some of their men to Congress. When the depression of 1893 broke upon the nation, the Populists thought they had a real chance to take the presidency in 1896. But the Democrats, well aware of the growing strength of the Populists, nominated William Jennings Bryan of Nebraska in 1896, knowing that he would draw many Populist votes. He did, but Bryan could not win the urban labor vote. Bryan's defeat in the 1896 election broke the back of the Populist movement, and the rise in agricultural prices after 1896 prevented it from rebuilding.

Not surprisingly there was also a strong reaction to industrialization from labor. The depression of 1873 hit the nation, and labor, very hard, and such unions as there were proved ineffective in dealing with it. Between 1875 and 1877 there were a number of uncoordinated strikes accompanied by rioting and violence. This militancy helped to found the Knights of Labor in 1879. By 1885, the Knights had 110,000 members. In that year also a competing organization, a federation of craft unions, was formed. The Knights achieved great prestige when they won a strike against three of Jay Gould's rail lines. Not to be outdone, the federation thereupon called a general strike for May 1, 1886, demanding the eight-hour day. The Knights had little choice but to support the strike, and it did succeed in bringing out 340,000 workers – the largest strike in US history up to that date. But on May 4, a bomb exploded in Haymarket Square in Chicago during an anarchist rally, killing seven and injuring twenty-seven. Played up by the press, the event was used to discredit unions, and had some significant effect on public opinion. But also in 1886, the federation became the American Federation of Labor (AFL), which over the next few years steadily gained in strength as the Knights declined. The Knights had never fully accepted the realities of the new business system; they wanted a return to the industrial system of an earlier time. The AFL did accept the realities of the new system and concentrated on issues like wages and hours that had immediate appeal to workers. By 1900, the AFL was clearly the dominant American labor union.

But labor radicalism did not end in 1900. In 1905, the International Workers of the World – the IWW – was founded in Chicago; it was an international union with a broadly syndicalist (socialist) program. The IWW called for "One Big Union" that would include all workers; it professed to be non-violent and to wage its campaigns by the use of "sabotage," which it defined as "the deliberate withdrawal of efficiency" – a phrase Veblen translated as "slacking and malingering." It was considered radical by American businessmen and politicians, and was fought by the AFL; the AFL promoted craft unions whereas the IWW advocated industrial unions. The IWW gained strength, particularly among migrant workers, up to the beginning of the Great War, when it probably had about one hundred thousand members. But then, acting under wartime legislation, the government imprisoned many of the IWW leaders and effectively crushed the organization.

While the labor organizations jockeyed for position, the fight against the bosses went on. In 1892, the Carnegie Homestead Plant was struck. During the strike, a riot broke out in which several men were killed and others wounded. The governor of Pennsylvania called out the militia and the borough was put under martial law. The company won the strike. Two years later, the Pullman strike occurred. Eugene Debs had organized an industrial-type union – the American Railway Union. When the Pullman Company instituted pay cuts, Debs called a strike. A federal judge, responding to the company's claim that the strike interfered with the US mail, issued a sweeping injunction against the strike. President Cleveland sent in federal troops, despite the objection of Illinois Governor Altgeld, but the strike was broken and Debs was sent to jail. So clear was it that the courts and the political leaders would support the companies. So did the press, and so too, usually, did the public.

Although the local, state, and federal governments had usually supported big business, the general anxiety about the direction of the country was percolating through the political system. Political reform began to gather steam. By 1900, the "muckrakers" – what today would be called "investigative journalists" – were publishing accounts that caught the public's interest. Ida Tarbell's exposure of Rockefeller's practices, Lincoln Steffens's exposures of urban corruption, and Jacob Riis's descriptions of the appalling living conditions faced by immigrants were drawing attention to the social costs of industrialization. Political reformers like Theodore Roosevelt were attacking trusts and advancing what was called a "progressive" program of reform. At the local, state, and national levels, reform movements were growing. And even the Supreme Court showed signs of responding to the changing times. In 1911, the Court dissolved the Standard Oil Trust. This was hailed as a great victory by the reformers, although in fact all it did was to substitute the holding company for the trust.

There was however another political development suggesting more extreme opposition to the course being followed by American business culture. Socialism had proven to have slight appeal in the United States in the nineteenth century. It had been widely viewed as an immigrant ideology and had attracted few American followers. The protest movements of the 1880s and 1890s were not inspired by socialism, nor were their objectives socialistic. But their opponents – particularly the business leadership – labeled them as socialistic to mobilize public opinion against them.³ Secular socialism remained a minor movement associated particularly with immigrants from central Europe. But around 1900, this situation began to change. New Socialist leaders – notably Eugene Debs and Victor Berger – were able to present socialism in a way that connected with current concerns. In 1904, Debs headed the Socialist ticket for president of the United States and received four hundred thousand votes. Much more impressive was the outcome of the 1912 election. Wilson got six million votes, Roosevelt four million, Taft 3.5 million, and Debs just under a million – nearly 7 percent of the total. And Debs did this running against the nations two leading progressives – Roosevelt and Wilson. Who could say what the future might hold for socialism?

Given how bewildering and disturbing Americans found their situation in the post-Civil War era, one might have expected them to turn to religion for guidance. The world view of most Americans before the Civil War was an amalgam of Protestant theology, Scottish Common Sense Realism, Newtonian science, and Natural Law political theory. But the publication of Darwin's *The Origin of Species* in 1859, followed by his *The Descent of Man* in 1871, challenged this world view. The picture of human origins presented by Darwin contradicted with that of the Bible. But the problem posed by evolution went deeper. If the evolutionary theory is true, human beings are descended from non-human animal ancestors. Nowhere in that process of descent does Darwin suggest the need for a soul; all of man's attributes are derived from our pre-human ancestors. But Christians have always believed that humans have a dual nature – half animal and half angel. If there is no angel, no soul, there is no immortality, no post-mortem reward or punishment, no divine spark. Many of the religious saw such claims as equivalent to saying that Christianity was false. This was the fundamental issue.

The churches divided in their response to Darwin. Some flatly denied evolution, some sought to find a compromise with evolution, but all of them had to deal with Darwin's theory and its implications. And some of these compromises had profound implications for society. Perhaps the most persuasive of these was that of Herbert Spencer, whose "Synthetic Philosophy" proposed a scheme of cosmic evolution that was providentially ordained to lead mankind to a state of perfection. For Spencer, the economic and social turmoil of the late nineteenth century was the struggle for existence that would lead to the survival of the fittest, and attempts to remedy the evils of industrialism would perpetuate the unfit. Thus evolution as developed by Spencer provided a system that was deterministic, mechanical, and providential all at the same time, and which gave to the events of the time a certain intelligibility.

Faced with the problems raised by Darwin, and his interpreters such as Spencer, many American philosophers turned to Idealism. If all nature and all history are simply the mind of God in action, then human contact with the divine is guaranteed and the dire implication of Darwinian evolution are aborted. Accordingly, there was a great vogue of Hegel in the United States; Hegelian Idealism, with its thesis that history is the process by which the World Spirit realizes itself, provided a providential interpretation of evolution. But some of the philosophers, repelled by the determinism of the Idealists as well as Spencer, developed a different view that came to be called Pragmatism. Led by William James and John Dewey, the pragmatists emphasized human freedom and creativity while also embracing Darwinian science. One result of this was the publication in 1890 of William James's *The Principles of Psychology*, which became the dominant psychological work of the next generation. For James, human beings have free will and the ability to respond to their environment with spontaneity and creativity.

While this was happening in psychology, Darwinian theory as interpreted by Spencer found application in other social sciences. Spencer drew from his cosmic philosophy the conclusion that the evils of industrialism were part of the pre-determined march to perfection. This "Social Darwinist" position became a rationale for laissez-faire economics and implied that efforts at social reform were actually dangerous to the pre-ordained course of social evolution. As propounded by William Graham Sumner, who was one of Veblen's teachers at Yale, this view championed unrestricted individualism. But although Social Darwinism attracted wide support, it was not the dominant position in American economics.

But these developments were all part of a broader movement – one that was less obvious at the time but far more important. Before the Civil War, Protestant religion dominated the lives of most Americans and Protestant theology dominated American thought. Catholic minorities like the Irish were reviled, atheism was unheard of, and science was interpreted as supporting religion. But in the era from the Civil War to the Great War, this changed.

First, there had been conflicts between science and religion before, but in the post-Civil War period the churches found themselves facing a much stronger challenge than they had faced previously. Darwinian evolution, backed by geology, made some tenets of the prevailing theologies untenable. The course of this conflict can be indicted by the titles of two widely influential books. In 1873, William Draper published *A History of the Conflict between Science and Religion*. In 1895, Andrew Dickson White published *A History of the Warfare of Science with Theology in Christendom*. As the great historian Perry Miller pointed out, the change from "religion" to "theology" indicates the nature of the compromise that was made. The churches largely abandoned theology to concentrate on religion, understood as a matter of ethics and social reform. On these matters, at least at first, the sciences had little to say. But that would change with the development of the social sciences.

Second, the huge influx of non-Protestant groups – of Italian Catholics and Polish and Russian Jews – undermined the dominance of Protestantism. Further, the enormous problems of industrialism – poverty, crime, slums, corruption – led the churches to focus on social issues. Doctrinal issues were put aside to focus on social reform. The Social Gospel movement was the leading expression of this thrust, but other churches followed too.

Third, revivalism continued to hold the devotion of many, not just in rural areas but in urban areas as well. Its emphasis on religious experience continued to satisfy many people but its teachings remained largely orthodox. Accordingly, it failed to satisfy those who were concerned with the more complex issues the changing times presented.

But religion remained for many people in the form of Christian morality, Christian ethics, and a belief in an overall divine superintendence of events, even though there was no longer a coherent theological system backing such beliefs. Dewey and Spencer, pragmatists and Idealists, were still religious men, at least in this sense. And nowhere was this more painfully evident than in the developing social sciences.

Given the part played by business in the turbulent post-Civil War era, one might have expected that the group best qualified to deal with the issues of the day would be the economists. One would be wrong. As a distinct discipline, economics did not exist in the United States when the Civil War ended. One should recall that Adam Smith was a Scottish moral philosopher. The *Wealth of Nations*, now regarded as the founding work in economics, was for Smith the second part of his course on moral philosophy, of which the first part was published as *The Theory of the Moral Sentiments*. Scottish moral philosophy was standard in nearly all American colleges, with the emphasis on the "moral." The required course on moral philosophy was usually taught in the senior year by the college president, who was invariably a minister, and was intended to send the college graduate out into the world fully armed against sin and temptation. American textbooks in moral philosophy were usually either Scottish texts or directly derived from Scottish works. Even when economics was given a separate treatment, as in Francis Wayland's *Elements of Political Economy* (1843), it was labeled as "Political Economy," not "Economics," and did not deviate from the Scottish models. In the period before 1870, those Americans who considered economics their primary concern were largely self-educated.

It was common in the 1870s for American students who wanted advanced training in their subjects to go to Germany. The German universities emphasized advanced work – something that was rare in the United States – and their famous seminar system encouraged research. Of the leading American "economists" of the post-1870 period, nearly all studied in Germany and a number of them received German PhDs.[4] The first chair in political economy in the United States was established at Harvard in 1871, and was held by Charles Dunbar. Yale was second, where Francis Walker held the chair. And interestingly the third was Carelton College in 1875 with a chair occupied by John Bates Clark, just back form Heidelberg and Zurich.[5] In the 1870s and 1880s, there was a dramatic expansion in American universities – Cornell, Johns Hopkins, Clark, Stanford, and the University of Chicago were all free of church control and were well endowed.

In such schools, courses on political economy multiplied. In 1886, the American Economic Association was established. And by 1900 there were fifty-one chairs of political economy in the United States.[6] Economics had achieved a secure place in the American academic institutions.

The economics taught in the United States in the post-Civil War era was classical economics as it had developed in England. There were important deviations from the classical canon, particularly on the question of free trade. Protectionism, as championed by Henry C. Carey, had many adherents in America where the argument that tariffs were necessary to protect fledgling American industries from European competition found strong support in and out of Congress, and the tariff became a standard feature of American policy. But by and large American economists hewed closely to the classical position.

But post-Civil War America presented problems for which classical economics offered no simple solutions. One was the issue of monopoly. The railroads posed this issue in stark form. In many cases, towns were served by only one railroad company that could set its rates as it pleased. Farmers with no other way to get their crops to market had to pay these rates or go broke. Nor did competition offer a solution to such problems. A return that would make one railroad profitable could mean bankruptcy if it were divided between two. Having left the railroads in private hands rather than nationalizing them, American political leaders were unable to control them. The growth of trusts in many industries made the issue more pressing as the century wore on. Were trusts conspiracies? Should they be regulated? And if so, how? These were burning issues of the time.

Equally an issue was labor. The notion that employment represented a contract freely entered into by employer and employee became absurd when the contracting parties were Standard Oil and the individual worker. The attempt to remedy the helplessness of the worker by organization baffled the economists. Were unions monopolies? Were strikes justified? If so, under what conditions? Should the government regulate wages? Hours? Working conditions? What about working conditions for children? Or for women? Should the government impose an eight-hour limit on the workday? Or set a minimum wage? These were questions to which neither the economists nor anyone else had simple answers, yet the urgency of the problems forced decisions, wise or not.

In the 1880s, a new cohort of young economists appeared on the scene. It included John Bates Clark, Richard Ely, Simon Patten, J. Laurence Laughlin, Frank Taussig, and Arthur Hadley, among others, and Thorstein Veblen. All of them were born between 1847 and 1859. But there the resemblance stopped. Laughlin, Taussig, and Hadley were sons of successful businessmen and were, by and large, content with the prevailing economic system. Clark, Ely, and Patten were "sons of evangelical families of New England heritage that valued moral conscience in social and political as well as personal life," and who were bent on reform.[7] And then there was Veblen, who fit neither pattern.

Of the reformers, the most fervent was Richard Ely. Born in Fredonia, New York, in 1854, he was raised in a strict Presbyterian family on a diet of orthodox Calvinism. He began his college career at Dartmouth, but after two years transferred to Columbia in New York City. It was here that Ely abandoned the Presbyterian church for the Universalist church. He rejected the doctrines of election and predestination, although he kept some of his childhood religion, particularly the moral teachings. He continued to believe in the sacraments, and later in life he joined the Episcopal church, drawn by its sacramentalism. In 1876, he went to Germany where in due course he landed at Heidelberg, came under the influence of Karl Knies, and found in the German historical approach an emancipation from classical economics. He adopted Knies's view that an adequate economic theory must be a theory of the whole society: understanding anything required understanding the whole. In 1880, Ely returned to the United States, only to find the country embroiled in bitter conflicts between the workers and the owners. As Everett says:

> Something had to be done at once. The classical economist could give answers deduced from his *a priori* principles regarding the "iron law of wages" or the "sanctity of private property." But Ely had no such system of economics. It was therefore most natural that he took the responsibility for solving the problem out of the hands of the economists and placed it at the door of religion.[8]

This was to be Ely's approach throughout his career. He was a Christian missionary to economics who believed that the problems of the economy could be solved by Christian reformation. He was also a tireless promoter of Christian causes. He led the formation of the American Economic Association in 1885 which at its founding contained most of the more radical young economists rather than the more conservative ones. As professor of economics at Johns Hopkins University, Ely had a pulpit and he used it. He considered classical economics obsolete and argued for the approach of the German historical school.[9] Ely believed that the Christian religion was the answer to all the problems facing society. Repeatedly, he called upon the churches to assume the leadership of American society and to deal with the economic problems facing the country, calls that went largely unanswered. If only men could be reformed and the fervor of Christianity restored, Ely thought all the current problems could be solved. For him, the brotherhood of men as children of God was the fundamental fact of the social order. Ely believed in social solidarity, but it was the Christian solidarity of the brotherhood. He emphasized the importance of the sacraments as means for bringing believers together. Social conduct, he said, should be judged by its contribution to social welfare. It was Christianity that would solve the conflicts of society.

For Ely, laissez-faire was an evil system. As he saw it, capitalism unrestricted would become a war of all against all, each man striving to get the better of his rivals, until the strong had devoured the weak and the economy consolidated into giant corporations that had monopoly power. Competition did not preserve free enterprise; it destroyed it by leading to massive consolidations. To Spencer's and Sumner's claims that competition was the present form of the struggle for the survival of the fit, Ely replied that indeed social evolution involved natural selection, but, he asked, what was the meaning of "fit." According to Ely, "fit" may have meant "the strong" in barbarism, but today, "It can be said that competition increasingly comes to mean worthy struggle, and true progress implies that that success will be secured hereafter by conformity to higher and ever higher, nobler and ever nobler ideas."[10]

The alternative to capitalism in Ely's time was taken to be socialism. But the term "socialism" had many meanings, ranging from Marxist socialism to the various forms of religious socialism. Ely opposed Marxist socialism which he considered materialistic and irreligious and which he thought ignored the religious factor in social evolution. Further, Marxism was deterministic and denied the free will of men who it held were governed by an inflexible and inevitable process. But there were other forms of socialism. Ely was a Christian socialist; his fundamental doctrine was the brotherhood of men and his fundamental principle was the law of service to others. Although he recognized that monopolies can be socially benevolent as well as malevolent, he believed that they should be either socialized or regulated. But unlike most socialists, he was not opposed to private property, since he believed in the stewardship theory of property – that property is entrusted to individual men on the condition that it is be used in socially benevolent ways. Thus in the 1880s and 1890s, to say that someone was a socialist was only to say that he was opposed to laissez-faire capitalism and rampant individualism.[11]

The most outstanding economist among the young reformers was John Bates Clark. He was born in 1847 and grew up in Providence, Rhode Island, in a devout Congregationalist family. Religion was thus a basic part of his life from the beginning and shaped his thoughts and ambition. He entered Amherst College in 1867, but his education was interrupted by a stint in Minneapolis assisting his father in business. His father died of tuberculosis and Clark thereupon returned to Amherst to complete his education.[12] He had planned to become a minister, but in his senior year he was persuaded by Amherst's president Julius Seelye to devote himself to economics instead.[13] This was not as radical a change as one might think. Seelye was a moral philosopher of the Scottish school who regarded economics as a domain that ought to be governed by moral laws, a view that was entirely congenial to Clark. In turning to economics, Clark was not abandoning religion but was turning to a new field of religious endeavor.[14]

Clark graduated from Amherst in 1872, and went to Germany to pursue advanced studies. He chose Heidelberg, where he came under the influence of

Karl Knies, one of the leading German economists of the historical school. What he seems to have absorbed from his studies in Germany was the view of society as an organism, which became a fundamental part of his system of belief.[15] Upon his return to the United States, he accepted a position at Carleton College, where he remained until 1882.[16] It was here that he met Veblen who entered Carleton in 1880.

Clark began publishing in 1877 and in his articles he developed a set of ideas that came together in his *The Philosophy of Wealth* in 1886. Clark was a Christian Socialist. The emphasis should be on "Christian," for he was no advocate of Marxist socialism or of the other varieties then current in America. What Clark meant by "socialism" was the coming together of all men as children of God, and therefore as brothers due to their common parentage, in common worship and in Christian love.

> True socialism appears to say, "Here is the world; take it as a family domain under the common father's direction. Enjoy it as children, each according to his needs; labor as brethren, each according to his strength. Let justice supplant might in the distribution, so that, when there is abundance, all may participate, and when there is scarcity, all may share in the self-denial. If there is loss of independence, there will be gain of interdependence; he who takes less for himself will think more for his brother. If there is loss of brute force gained in the rude struggle of competition, there is gain of moral power, acquired by the interchange of kindly offices.[17]

The opposite of this was the isolated individual, devoid of the bonds of love. Accordingly, Clark regarded any organization of men united in a common endeavor as a step – likely a very small step – toward the realization of the ideal unity of the Kingdom of God. Clark seems to have been convinced that the attainment of the Kingdom of God on earth was inevitable – foreordained by God.[18] But our attainment of the Kingdom was dependent upon a general reformation of men, something that would not come quickly or by either the edicts of law or revolution. He therefore thought other socialists of his time were doing more harm than good. The chief example of state socialism at that time was in Germany, and Clark had spent enough time in Germany to know what the system was like. He opposed German state socialism, holding that the imposition of socialism had led to the loss of freedom by the people. The attempts to establish political and/or economic socialism by force violated the liberty of individuals and was the opposite of the loving communion that he thought characterized the Kingdom.[19]

Clark viewed classical economics as pitting every individual against every other individual. He found this doctrine repulsive, but he believed it was being overcome by the development of collective forms of organization, such as the corporation. Imperfect as the corporation was, it represented a step away from individual ownership to collective ownership – a step of which Clark approved.[20] Similarly, the organizations of labor, such as they were, represented similar substitutions of collective action for individual action. Clark held that unions would give labor strength that it could use to combat what he called the "strategic inequality" that prevailed between capital and labor. Once strong unions were formed, they would redress this inequality and create a more equitable situation.[21]

Clark was not in favor of strikes as a way of dealing with labor problems. He believed that labor disputes involved real issues; it was, he thought, "imbecile" to claim that capital and labor had no real differences, as apologists for wealth maintained.[22] He thought that disputes ought to be dealt with through arbitration. Competition, he held, led to nothing but conflict; arbitration offered a way to resolve disputes that was peaceful and could yield justice – something that was not a common outcome of labor settlements. But here as elsewhere much depended on the character of the arbitrators. Arbitration would work only if the arbitrators approached the issues in the proper religious spirit. It was as children of God that arbitration should be conducted.[23]

Obviously the evolution Clark was calling for involved a spiritual reformation of men. The material wants of men, he held, are finite; it is possible to produce goods in sufficient quantity so that the material needs of all people can be satisfied. But spiritual needs are infinite in number; the more that are satisfied the more that are created. There is therefore a spiritual economics superior to material economics, and it is the duty of men to work for such spiritual growth. In this work, the churches ought to be leading the way. But Clark considered institutional religion to be failing at this task. While Clark believed the churches ought to be taking the lead in reform, it was clear that they were not. Nevertheless, the sort of collectivization Clark believed in was happening. Corporations involved collectivism, but were commonly regarded as having no soul – a view born out by their conduct. But Clark said a corporation could be transformed into a cooperative businesses by simple changes, and doing so would restore a soul.[24] Cooperation on the Rochdale model he thought a superior form of organization to the standard corporation, particularly since it eliminated the distinction between owner and worker, but he was well aware of the problems cooperatives had faced in America.[25] He also praised such changes as profit sharing, where again the distinction between owner and worker was somewhat attenuated.[26]

Clark believed that "natural" laws were rules of the divine plan and were therefore just. So far as economics was concerned, Clark meant by "justice" that every person involved in the economic process was entitled to receive the full value of all that he personally produced. This notion appears to be based on the Lockean theory of property that held that whatever a man creates is therefore his property. The acceptability of any economic system depended on its being just. No economic system was tolerable if it was not a just system in this sense.[27]

Clark's socialism was clearly not the socialism of Marx or the other secular socialists that were agitating America in the 1880s. Clark was in fact opposed to those socialisms which he thought tried to reach the Kingdom before men were ready for it. The Kingdom will come, Clark believed; it will be the result of evolution, but the evolution will take time and must proceed slowly, for it can only be attained when men are sufficiently imbued with the spirit of Christian brotherhood, and that will not happen quickly.[28] So Clark is a Christian socialist of a sort, but a very special sort.

In the late 1880s, Clark's views began to change, apparently as a result of the increasing consolidation of American business. Corporations seeking monopoly power were hardly the benevolent institutions Clark had thought them. But it was the early Clark – the Clark of the early 1880s – that taught Veblen.

Among the younger economists who did not go to Germany to study was Thorstein Veblen. But it would be a mistake to think that he was not aware of the work of the German historical school. Veblen was fluent in German; of the reviews he wrote for the *Journal of Political Economy*, almost half were of books in German. And the Germans had much to offer Veblen. Emerging in 1843 with the publication of Wilhelm Heinrich Roscher's *Grundriss*, the movement presented an alternative to the classical English tradition but one that was free of Marxist influence. The German economists rejected the claims of the classical economists to have discovered economic laws true everywhere and in all times; they adopted the relativist view that different countries have different economies and therefore require different economic theories. They also rejected the laissez-faire claim that the state should not interfere in economic matters. The German state was not the limited state of British and American political theory but a dominating force in German life, necessarily concerned with the treatment of German workers, working conditions, health, and similar matters. The German economists were early welfare economists. They also rejected the classical theory's narrow definition of the field of economics to purely economic institutions; they held that economic issues involved the whole culture and could only be properly dealt with on that basis. And they rejected what they saw as the deductive approach based on premises of questionable validity. The Germans believed that economics should be an inductive science that would formulate a German economics from the study of German history. Veblen took these early German economists – Roscher, Bruno Hildebrand, and Knies – as neo-Hegelians and their economics as too metaphysical for his taste.

But after 1870, the younger German economists, led by Gustav Schmoller, gave the historical school a new direction. Veblen says that with Schmoller the historical details became data for a scientific inquiry.

> For the distinguishing mark of Professor Schmoller's work, that wherein it differs from the earlier work of the economists of his general class, is that it aims at a Darwinian account of the origin, growth, persistence and variation of institutions, in so far as these institutions have to do with the economic aspect of life either as cause or as effect.[29]

Clearly Veblen found in Schmoller a kindred spirit. But when Schmoller came to deal with contemporary German culture, Veblen found that he abandoned the scientific approach and turned to homiletics, defending contemporary institutions such as the family against change. Veblen took this not only as a failure but as a betrayal by Schmoller of the scientific standards he had preciously endorsed. But leaving aside Schmoller's contemporary apostasy, Veblen had high regard for Schmoller's work and drew on some of the findings of the younger German economists such as Werner Sombart in his own work.

The inadequacy of the response to the problems facing the nation by professional economists opened the way for the amateurs. The most impressive of these was Henry George. Having lived through the depression of 1873, his focus was on the paradox of poverty in the midst of plenty. Why, George asked in *Progress and Poverty* in 1879, should the rapidly advancing productivity of industry lead to widespread poverty?[30] George had the courage of his convictions. He took on classical economic doctrine, arguing that the standard excuses for the poverty of labor – the wages fund theory and the population theory of Thomas Robert Malthus – were false. He did not hesitate to propose new definitions of capital, interest, and rent. From his basic equation:

$$\text{Produce} = \text{rent} + \text{wages} + \text{interest}^{31}$$

George argued that it is rent that keeps wages and interest low. This left him with the choice: confiscate land or confiscate rent. He chose the latter – a single tax that would eliminate rent would, he believed, end land speculation and result in rising wages and production. If George's remedy was too simple, his argument was nevertheless persuasive and won widespread support among the people – far more support than was accorded to any doctrines of the professional economists.

A second book that captured a wide public following was Edward Bellamy's *Looking Backward* which appeared in 1887.[32] In this utopian novel, Bellamy used the device of a man of 1887 falling into a trance and awakening in 2000, when his existence is discovered by workmen excavating on the site of the house in which he had lived. Thus transplanted from the social and economic horrors of the late nineteenth century, the man finds himself in a society in which all the problems of the earlier time have been solved, and the book describes in some detail how this magic world has come to pass. The society of 2000 is a socialist society – the government is the sole employer – but one in which the freedom of the individual is carefully guarded. The book is encumbered by a rather dreadful love story, but the real love story is that of the protagonist becoming enamored of the new society in which he finds himself. The book was very popular, and included among its enchanted readers Veblen and his wife, Ellen Rolfe.

The 1890s were very far from Bellamy's utopia. Problems of monopoly became worse as consolidation proceeded apace in business, reaching a new high with the creation of US Steel in 1901 – the first billion-dollar corporation. Labor problems, farm problems, and money problems all got worse with the depression that began in 1893. Various reforms were urged, but to little effect. And where reforms made it from proposal to enactment, they were usually cut down by the courts.[33]

Notes

1 Geoffrey Hodgson, *The Evolution of Institutional Economics* (London: Routledge, 2004), 9.
2 Douglas Dowd, *Thorstein Veblen: A Critical Appraisal* (Ithaca: Cornell, 1958), vii.
3 Dorothy Ross, *The Origins of American Social Science* (Cambridge: Cambridge University Press, 1991), 98–99.
4 John Parrish, "The Rise of Economics as an Academic Discipline: the Formative Years to 1900," *Southern Economic Journal* 34 (1967): 13–16.
5 Parrish, "Rise of Economics," 6.
6 Parrish, "Rise of Economics," 11.
7 Ross, *Origins of American Social Science*, 102–103.
8 John R. Everett, *Religion in Economics* (New York: King's Crown, 1946), 81.
9 Ross, *Origins of American Social Science*, 111.
10 Everett, *Religion in Economics*, 87.
11 Everett, *Religion in Economics*, 75–98.
12 Everett, *Religion in Economics*, 75–98.
13 John F. Henry, *John Bates Clark* (New York: St. Martin's Press, 1995), 1–2.
14 Everett, *Religion in Economics*, 29–31.
15 Everett, *Religion in Economics*, 29–33.
16 Everett, *Religion in Economics*, 34.
17 John Bates Clark, "The Nature and Progress of True Socialism," *The New Englander* 38 (July 1879): 580.
18 Everett, *Religion in Economics*, 51.
19 Everett, *Religion in Economics*, 37–57.
20 Clark, "True Socialism," 566, 572.
21 Everett, *Religion in Economics*, 40–42.
22 Clark, "True Socialism," 569.
23 Everett, *Religion in Economics*, 42.
24 Clark, "True Socialism," 573.
25 Clark, "True Socialism," 574.
26 Everett, *Religion in Economics*, 37–51.
27 Everett, *Religion in Economics*, 52.
28 Clark, "True Socialism," 580.
29 Thorstein Veblen, "Gustav Schmoller's Economics," in *The Place of Science in Modern Civilization*, intro. Warren J. Samuels (New York: Cosimo, 2007), 265.
30 Henry George, *Progress and Poverty* (New York: Modern Library, 1938).
31 George, *Progress and Poverty*, 171.
32 Edward Bellamy, *Looking Backward* (New York: Dover, 1996).
33 Emil Kaudwe, *A History of Marginal Utility Theory* (Princeton: Princeton University Press, 1965), Chaps. 5–17.

1

EARLY DAYS

Biographical Note

Thorstein Veblen was born on July 30, 1857, on a Wisconsin farm, the child of Norwegian immigrant parents. When he was eight, the family moved to a farm in Minnesota where he grew up in an immigrant community composed of Norse, Irish, German, and "Yankee" farmers. Thus Veblen was bilingual in Norwegian and English from an early age. Thomas Veblen, his father, believed in the importance of education and determined to send all his children to college.[1] In 1874, his father sent Thorstein to Carleton College in the hope that he might become a Lutheran minister. Veblen did not fit easily into the social life of the college, but he did capture the affections of Ellen Rolfe, a niece of the president of the college. She was an exceptionally bright woman, but one who, like Veblen, found the college atmosphere stultifying. They were subsequently married, although the marriage would prove difficult for them both.

Carleton College was a Congregationalist college that claimed to meet "the standard of scholarship maintained by the best New England colleges."[2] Like most American colleges of the time, it was thoroughly Christian and was heavily influenced by the Scottish philosophers, most notably Thomas Reid. The theory of natural law and natural rights was the backbone of the "intellectual philosophy" taught, where the key natural rights were those of life, liberty, and property. The theory of property was Locke's theory that men have a natural right to the products of their own labor. Property was held to be the foundation of individual freedom, since it provided individual economic security. The right to property came with the right to exchange property for the goods necessary to satisfy needs. The Scottish philosophy was held to provide a conclusive refutation to the skepticism of David Hume; there was no need to explore German philosophy for that purpose.

Carleton College had a chair of economics; it was the third such chair to be established in the United States. In Veblen's time, the chair was occupied by John Bates Clark, already recognized as one of the brightest young stars in economics in the US, and subsequently to become the outstanding American economist of his time.

Veblen graduated in 1880, and for his graduation oration chose as his subject John Stuart Mill's examination of the philosophy of Sir William Hamilton. Since its publication in 1865, Mill's attack on Hamilton's philosophy had been a subject of great controversy, especially among the followers of the Scottish philosophy, of which Hamilton was the last great exponent. This was a highly technical subject upon which Veblen acquitted himself admirably, to the wonder and delight of his parents who were in the audience.[3]

The interest in philosophy demonstrated in his graduation oration was genuine, and Veblen went to Johns Hopkins University where he intended to pursue postgraduate studies in philosophy. He spent only a term there. His formal application for a scholarship was to study economics, although the courses he took were chiefly in philosophy. These included a course with Charles Peirce, then a lecturer in logic, George Morris's course on Immanuel Kant, and a course with Richard Ely, whom he found unimpressive; apparently the feeling was mutual since Ely did not take to him. In any case, Veblen did not receive the scholarship for which he had applied, and decided to seek wisdom elsewhere.[4]

Veblen then went to Yale to study under Noah Porter, a distinguished philosopher of the Scottish school, and the president of Yale. At the time Veblen arrived, the university was convulsed by a controversy between Porter and William Graham Sumner over Sumner's insistence on using Herbert Spenser's *Study of Sociology* as a text for his class. Porter was impressed by Veblen's intelligence and the two became more friendly than was usual for a teacher–student relation at that time. But Veblen remained very short of money, and entered an essay contest in the hope of winning the $250 prize offered for the best essay. He won. Sumner was so impressed with his paper that he suggested Veblen use it for his doctoral dissertation in economics, but Veblen remained focused on philosophy.[5] It was with Porter that Veblen studied Immanuel Kant and under whose direction he wrote his dissertation on "Ethical Grounds for a Doctrine of Retribution." Veblen received his PhD in 1884,[6] and in that year he published his first article, "Kant's Critique of Judgment," in the *Journal of Speculative Philosophy*, then the leading philosophical journal in the country.[7] How this article was related to his dissertation, we do not know. No copy of the dissertation is known to have survived. It would be plausible to believe that an article written so soon after the dissertation was finished was drawn from it, but this remains a speculative conclusion.

Kant's Critique

Kant's *Critique of Pure Reason* was designed to provide a philosophic foundation for natural science, which he conceived on the model of Newtonian mechanics. His *Critique of Practical Reason* was designed to prove that human beings were free and to provide a foundation for morality. To these two, Kant added a third *Critique* that was designed to mediate between them. This was the *Critique of Judgment* – the last of the three to be written, and the one that has most puzzled his commentators.[8] Veblen's article is not simply an analysis of Kant's argument; it also presents an interpretation of Kant that was Veblen's own, and is his first public statement of his developing position. It therefore requires some careful analysis.

The *Critique of Judgment* is divided into two parts – the Critique of Aesthetic Judgment and the Critique of Teleological Judgment. Each of these is further divided into two parts labeled as an "analytic" and a "dialectic." In addition, there are two introductions to the volume – a longer one that was not published with the volume and a shorter one that was. The section on the Aesthetic Judgment is longer than that on the Teleological Judgment, and has received more attention among Kant scholars, but Kant obviously saw them as part of a single work. So did Veblen.

Why, Veblen asks, did Kant feel it necessary to introduce Judgment to mediate between Reason and Understanding? If as Kant held we can freely choose our acts, these must appear in the phenomenal world as determined by efficient causes. But that is not enough; if our freely chosen acts are to be rational, we must be able to foresee their consequences, and that requires inductive reasoning. This is provided by the Judgment, but only in its reflective use, not in its determinative use. For in its determinative use Judgment simply applies to particulars a universal drawn from another faculty, but in its reflective use, Judgment is under the obligation of ascending from the particular in nature to the universal. In other words, it is required to discover true universal statements by induction from particulars. This requires a principle that it cannot borrow from another faculty or from experience. As Kant sees it, the problem is not just one of finding some empirical generalizations that cover particulars but in showing that these generalizations will hold good in the future. That requires that there be some reason for empirical laws to be true, for even though they appear to us now as contingent, if they are not ultimately necessary then there is no reason why they should continue to hold in the future. Kant is not willing simply to assume that nature is uniform; he wants a reason for its being uniform.[9]

Veblen notes that scholars have disagreed over the interpretation of the *Critique of Judgment* "because," he says, "they have taken up the *Critique* wrong end foremost."[10] He then presents his own interpretation. "The reflective judgment passes beyond the simple data of experience and seeks a universal which is not given in empirical cognition; therefore it must proceed according to a principle not given to it from without."[11] The reflective judgment must seek for and find universals that can bring the manifold to unity.

Its office is to systematize, and to systematize is but another expression for reducing things to intelligent orders; that is, to think things as though they had been made according to the laws of an understanding, to think them as though made by an intelligent cause...that the things be thought as falling under a system of laws according to which they adapt themselves to the laws of our understanding. But to think things in a system as though they had been made by an intelligent cause is not the same as to think that they are made by such a cause. So much is not required by the principle. The principle of the reflective judgment is, therefore, primarily the requirement of adaptation on the part of the object to the laws of the activity of our faculties of knowledge, or, briefly, adaptation to our faculties.[12]

When the intellect finds its objects to be such that our faculties work upon them easily and without hindrance, we experience a "gratification such as is always felt upon the attainment of an end striven for."[13] The more closely the concept of the object matches what the mind itself would have created if it had worked freely without hindrance, the more fully will the requirements of the mind's activity be realized and the more intense the gratification felt will be in contemplating the object of thought which so employs the mind.[14]

What the feeling of gratification testifies to, is that the play of the faculties of the intellect is free, or but little hindered by the empirical element in its knowledge. It therefore indicates that the objects are, in the form in which they are present in thought, adapted to the faculties.[15]

There are two different ways in which adaptation to our faculties may occur. First, if what is apprehended is a simple datum, the concept of the datum, taken simply as such, may be pleasing or displeasing. If it pleases, then

The object corresponding to such a concept, which pleases in its simple apprehension, is said to be beautiful, and the reflective judgment, in so far as it proceeds on the simple adaptation of the data of apprehension to the faculties of cognition, is aesthetic judgment.[16]

Such a judgment is purely subjective. But, second, if the objects of our apprehension are conceived to be part of reality, the "objects are conceived to stand in such relations of dependence and interaction as corresponds to the logical relations of the concepts we have of them."[17] But this is to conceive the world as being made so as to harmonize with our understanding, and so to conceive it as made by an intelligent cause. Accordingly, the cause must have made the world according to a plan, and "the idea of what the world was to be precedes and conditions the world as it actually comes into existence – which is precisely what we mean when we say that the world was created by final cause."[18] But this whole argument rests on the principle of the reflective judgment, and that principle is purely subjective. "The principle guides us to an hypothesis, but it has nothing to say as to the validity of the hypothesis in the world of reality."[19]

Kant further believed that the mechanical laws of nature cannot account for organic beings. The characteristics of such a being are not, Kant held, explicable by mechanical laws, but require the use of final causes.

> In such a product of nature each part is conceived as if it exists only through all the others, thus as if existing for the sake of the others and on account of the whole, i.e., as an instrument (organ), which is, however, not sufficient (for it could also be an instrument of art, and thus represented as possible at all only as an end); rather it must be thought of as an organ that produces the other parts (consequently each produces the others reciprocally), which cannot be the case in any instrument of art, but only of nature, which provides all the matter for instruments (even those of art): only then and on that account can such a product, as an organized and self-organizing being, be called a natural end.[20]

In Kant's view, beauty is a property we attribute to objects when we experience a particular kind of pleasure. This aesthetic pleasure is not merely a sensory gratification, but the result of the fact that in the apprehension of the phenomenal object, the Imagination and the Understanding work together freely and harmoniously.[21] The attribution of beauty to the object, however, is an imputation; the aesthetic response is purely subjective, and may be aroused by fictions, our own creations, our perception of nature, or by the fitting of means to ends. Nevertheless, Kant holds that propositions of aesthetics can be universal because all men possess the same faculties of Imagination and Understanding, and will respond in the same way to aesthetic stimuli. Intersubjectivity here is the basis of universality. Veblen generalizes Kant's theory in making aesthetic gratification function as the mark of successful inductions, or perhaps it would be more accurate to say that he makes the gratifications that come from successful inductions aesthetic.

> Why then do we follow the principle of the Reflective Judgment? What is proved by the tenacity with which we cling to our teleological conception of the world is, that the constitution of our intellect demands this conception – that our faculties, in their normal action, must arrive at this before they can find any halting-place.[22]

This is the requirement of the mind to which our hypotheses must be adapted. The mind requires that we conceive the world as a teleologically ordered consistent whole and it therefore requires that the hypothesis contribute to that end. Veblen asserts that so far as the ordinary experiences of life are concerned, we could get along without teleology, but the principle of the Reflective Judgment, interpreted as the requirement of adaptation to our faculties, shows that we cannot get along without order. We are dissatisfied with a disorderly world and are driven to seek for order in it.

> What the principle of adaptation does is, "that it makes us guess, and that it guides our guessing … The principle guides us to an hypothesis but it has nothing to say as to the validity of the hypothesis in the world of reality."[23]

It is experience alone that can prove the validity of the hypothesis. Veblen reiterates, "So far as concerns the distinctive character of the reflective judgment – and, therefore, of inductive reasoning – it proceeds on subjective grounds entirely."[24] Moreover, the feeling of gratification resulting from adaptation to our faculties is the test of the application of the principle; it is "this feeling of gratification alone which can decide whether the principle has been applied successfully in any given case."[25] But since the gratification is aesthetic, it is subjective.

Veblen's objective in this article is on the one hand to offer an interpretation of the *Critique of Judgment* while on the other developing Kant's theory in ways of his own. Critical here is the contradiction between the conception of nature as a mechanical system governed by efficient causes and the conception of nature as a teleological system governed by final causes. Kant states this contradiction as the Antinomy of the Reflective Judgment.

> Thesis: All generation of material things is possible in accordance with merely mechanical laws.
>
> Antithesis: Some generation of such things is not possible in accordance with merely mechanical laws.[26]

As stated, the Antinomy concerns only the production of organic beings in nature, and Kant resolves it by appeal to the supersensible.[27] But in doing so he makes all of nature a teleological system, so that if the role of the supersensible is eliminated, the Antinomy remains in force and is more general. For Veblen, appeal to the supersensible was out of the question, and the Antinomy became a contradiction between how the world is and how we must conceive it.

But do we know how the world really is? In Kant's view, the world must form a complete and perfectly ordered whole, a teleological system that is perfectly harmonious. Accordingly, our knowledge of the world ought to form a perfectly consistent system. Those hypotheses should be preferred which best contribute to such a perfect order of the world. And it is these that best fit the needs of the mind, that are best adapted to the requirements of the mind.[28]

The system of the world, viewed in its entirety, may bespeak final causes but the connections within this system may be those of efficient cause. Furthermore, as far as the requirements of everyday life are concerned, the overall teleology of the system is irrelevant; what concerns us in our daily lives is the relations of efficient causality within the system. "The knowledge we need and can use can be got, and got in sufficient completeness for all purposes of utility, without any appeal to, or aid from, the developed principles of finality."[29] What the principles of adaptation require is that we organize our experienced world into a systematic whole founded on the principle of efficient causality. Component propositions of this system may turn out to be false; empirical knowledge is never more than probable. But that is a matter to be settled by testing our theory against experience. What the principle of adaptation requires is hypotheses that give coherence to our experience. And the underlying hypothesis is that those hypotheses that best contribute to a unified concept of the world are most likely to be true, i.e., are the most probable.

> Yet, singular as it might seem, hardly any part of our knowledge except that got by induction is of any immediate use for practical purposes. For by induction alone can we reduce things to system and connection, and so bring particular things and events under definite laws of interaction; therefore, by induction alone can we get such knowledge as will enable us to forecast the future; and knowledge which shall help us to forecast the future – to tell what will take place under given circumstances and as the result of given actions – is the only knowledge which can serve as a guide in practical life, whether moral or otherwise.[30]

Certain points should be noted here. First, Veblen puts no stock in inductive logic; he sees hypotheses as guesses made to bring order to experience, but the guesses can have only probable truth; they are not necessary. Second, he regards the antinomy of the Reflective Judgment as genuine. Human beings think in teleological terms, but the "mechanical" world works by efficient causes. Third, he offers what he calls a theory of "induction." But is this really a theory of "induction"?

The term "induction" is a mare's nest of conflicting meanings. The two that seem relevant here are (1) the deriving of a general rule from particulars, and (2) the testing of an hypothesis against empirical data. What Veblen apparently means by induction is not (2), for he explicitly says that "the principle guides us to an hypothesis but it has nothing to say as to the validity of the hypothesis in the world of reality." It is experience alone that can tell whether an hypothesis is true. What he is describing is not the testing of an hypothesis against empirical data but the formation of an hypothesis, and the question he is apparently seeking to answer is why some hypotheses are better than others. The test to which he calls hypothesis is whether or not they fit the mind, not experience, and the test of fitting the mind is the feeling of gratification that results from the hypothesis. Given the context it is clear that this feeling is aesthetic, it is the result of the faculties acting in harmonious concert, and is confirmed by the beauty of the result.

Scientists often talk about hypothesis as being beautiful or sweet – similar expressions are used. What this means is that the hypothesis appears to fit the data so well that it brings a new order and harmony into the domain. This is apparently what Veblen intends. That hypothesis is preferred that gives the maximum coherence to the data, that explains all the known facts in a simple and "elegant" way.

It is remarkable to find Veblen dealing with this issue in this way. In standard treatments of scientific method, the processes of deduction and induction (testing against the data) are clearly distinguished, but little guidance is given concerning the formation of hypothesis. There is general agreement that there is no mechanical procedure that can generate good hypotheses from given data; there is no "inductive logic" as it has been called. Carl Hempel used to tell the story of how August Kekulé discovered the benzene ring. Kekulé, having worked long and hard to find the correct structure for benzene, one night fell into a doze as he sat before his fire, and dreamed that he saw two snakes dancing in the flames. In due course, the snakes took hold of each other's tails. Kekulé awakened with the recognition that the structure he was seeking was in fact a ring structure. "Now what kind of process is that?" Hempel would ask, indicating that the question did not admit of reasonable answer. But the question requires an answer. The number of hypotheses that can be drawn from given data is truly infinite; testing each one of them would be impossible. There has to be some rule that guides our selection, since we do in fact find good hypotheses. And this appears to be the problem Veblen is trying to answer.

His answer is that the best hypothesis is the one that brings maximum coherence to the data, and the sign that this is achieved is the beauty of the result. Adaptation to our faculties does not show that our hypotheses are true; they may turn out to be false. What it shows is that the hypotheses fit the requirements of the mind.

Why does Veblen call this process "induction"? Apparently he is taking "induction" to mean the inference of a general rule from particulars without any assertion of its truth. But in the Kantian framework used here, it does mean that adaptation to the mind is a criterion for the probability of the hypothesis. That itself would be a major achievement.

Biographical Note

Having received his doctorate from Yale, Veblen looked for a job. It was a hopeless search. In American colleges of the 1880s, philosophers were employed, if at all, to teach Scottish moral sense philosophy. For so delicate a task, more was required than a PhD. Only someone who was a minister of a suitable denomination was deemed worthy of being entrusted with such a responsibility. Veblen had no chance at all of securing such a position. So he was forced to return to his father's farm where, under pretext of illness, he spent the next seven years. During this enforced sabbatical, he read everything he could get his hands on and watched the passing show. One book that he and Ellen read together and that we know had a profound influence on him was Bellamy's *Looking Backward*.[31] But Veblen was doing more than reading; he was thinking about the issues of the day. And, as noted in the Introduction, the years from 1884 to 1891 were years of growing protest against the rapidly evolving capitalist system by farmers and urban laborers alike. The products of these years of enforced "idleness" would become apparent when he returned to academic life.

That return occurred in 1891. Accepting the fact that he would never be hired to teach philosophy, Veblen decided to turn to economics – a field to which he had been introduced by Clark and in which employment did not require ministerial credentials. In 1891 he matriculated at Cornell as a graduate student in economics. Once again, money was a problem, but Veblen so impressed J. Lawrence Laughlin, Cornell's professor of economics, that he was given a grant. Laughlin was a relatively conservative economist; he refused to join the American Economic Association which he considered too radical. His own position was chiefly that of John Stuart Mill. But Laughlin encouraged young economists regardless of their views if he thought they were bright, and he helped many who, like Veblen, were just starting out.

Then in 1892, the University of Chicago was established with a large endowment given by John D. Rockefeller. Its president, William Rainey Harper, set out to make it the greatest university in the land, which he did by recruiting outstanding faculty from other schools by offering them salaries that they could not refuse. Among his recruits was Laughlin to head the economics department, and Laughlin took Veblen with him as a graduate student. Veblen was appointed a fellow and registered for courses, but he also found himself the *de facto* editor of the newly established *Journal of Political Economy*. It was in these circumstances that he began to publish the ideas that he had developed during his sabbatical on his father's farm.[32]

The Neglected Argument

In 1891, Veblen published an article entitled "Some Neglected Points in the Theory of Socialism."[33] Focusing on a paper by Spencer ("From Freedom to Bondage") that had attacked socialism, Veblen offered certain "suggestions" on matters that he said Spencer had overlooked. Veblen's statement that he was writing "in the spirit of a disciple"[34] has usually been taken to be tongue-in-cheek, but it should be remembered that he had studied Spencer's work under Sumner when he was at Yale and was indebted to both men. Veblen points out that although socialism has as yet made little headway in the United States, there is a rising amount of discontent in the country with the present state of economic affairs.

> There is a distinct unrest abroad, a discontent with things as they are, and the cry of injustice is the expression of this more or less widely prevalent discontent. This discontent is the truly socialistic element in the situation.[35]

Veblen takes this discontent as the problem to be explained. The source of the discontent is not, Veblen asserts, the impoverishment of the working class. A comparison of the standard of living of the present working class with that of workers at any past period shows that workers today are far better off than ever before. The trouble is not deprivation; it is relative deprivation. It is a "feeling of slighted manhood" of those who are currently not only poor but find themselves increasingly poorer than those others in society with whom they compare themselves.[36]

Poverty is never pleasant, but when everyone around you is as poor as you are, people find it endurable. But when those whose talents you know are not superior to your own rise in the world while you do not, poverty becomes intolerable. It is not the absolute amounts that matter; it is the difference. A rich man, whom most people would envy, may find his lot intolerable if many he considers no more capable than himself are moving up in the world while he is not. People judge themselves by comparison with others they know, and when the golden showers fall upon your neighbors and leave you untouched, you can easily become convinced of the injustice of it all. Note here Veblen's use of reference group theory long before Robert K. Merton.

Two factors are here involved. First, there is a feeling that the economy is increasingly dominated by monopolies whose practices confer advantages upon a few at the cost of the public at large. Second, in the present society economic success has become the index of personal worth to a greater degree than in the past. Doubtless a man's character is the basis of his worth, but the evaluation of a man's character requires considerable knowledge of him – knowledge that casual acquaintance does not provide. And in environments increasingly urban and among people increasingly mobile, contact with others whose esteem one wishes to acquire has become increasingly brief and casual. Economic success, however, can be judged by casual observation if it is suitably displayed. Hence economic attainment and its display have become the essential indicators of worth that command respect. Those who lack the necessary indicators of wealth are left with a feeling of envy.

Classical economics lumped together the goods people seek as "gains"; Veblen disaggregates this bundle by singling out esteem or prestige as the fundamental goal. Competition is a competition for prestige; goods – at least those beyond subsistence – are sought for their prestige value. The motive here is emulation, the desire to out-do one's fellows. Because emulative gains are purely relative, they are limitless; enough is never enough, if someone else has more.

The emulative struggle for esteem is made possible by the institution of private property. It is by owning more than others that one demonstrates one's superior worth. If the discontents arising from emulation are to be assuaged, the remedy of the nationalization of industry and property appears to be the most effective means available. Even if nationalization would result in a decline in the net pro-duct, Veblen argues that so much of current output is directed to wasteful display that the loss would have no significant bearing on the actual material welfare of the population.

In his *Principles of Sociology* Spencer argued that all social systems are either systems of status or systems of contract, and in the article Veblen addresses here, Spencer portrayed socialism as a system of status. Veblen disputes this; the bipolar typology is not exhaustive; there is another alternative – the system of modern constitutional government.

> The whole system of modern constitutional government in its latest developed forms, in theory at least, and, in a measure, in practice, does not fall under the head of either contract or status. It is the analogy of modern constitutional government through an impersonal law and impersonal institutions, that comes nearest to doing justice to the vague notions of our socialist propagandists.[37]

Nationalization in the United States would bring the economy under the direction of such a republican type of government.

Veblen does not claim that the record of constitutional government is one of complete success. "Our modern republics have hardly given us a foretaste of that political millennium whereof they proclaim the fruition."[38] It is not certain that mankind has arrived at that level of perfection necessary for self-government. But he holds that the record of modern republics is sufficient to justify trying the experiment.

This article is the product of Veblen's years of involuntary unemployment, and the conclusions he had reached form a basis for his further work. His view that emulation is the desire for esteem and drives the acquisitive behavior of mankind is a major departure from established economic theory and underlies all his subsequent work. His faith in constitutional representative government gave to his version of socialism a clarity concerning what would come "after the revolution" that was lacking among the socialists such as Marx. Veblen abandoned this view of constitutional government after the Great War, as we shall see.

Biographical Note

Veblen stayed at the University of Chicago for fifteen years. First appointed as a fellow, in 1895 he was promoted to instructor and in 1900 to assistant professor. Aside from teaching, his main activity was the editing of *The Journal of Political Economy* in which he published a number of book reviews, chiefly of books on socialism. The faculty Harper had recruited for the University contained a number of very able men, including John Dewey in philosophy, William I. Thomas in sociology, and Jacque Loeb in physiology. How much Veblen influenced, or was influenced by, his colleagues is not at all clear. What is clear is that he was working out his own theory of economics which appeared in *The Theory of the Leisure Class* in 1899 and in "Industrial and Pecuniary Employments" in 1900. He also succeeded in formulating his theory of business, which he published in 1904 in *The Theory of Business Enterprise*. These publications were major intellectual achievements. In addition, he published four important articles on the prevailing theories of economics which proved to have considerable influence on economists. He also published fourteen other articles and a number of book reviews. One would have thought that this record would certainly have merited his promotion to a full professorship. It did not. Why?

There appear to have been several reasons. First, Veblen was not a popular teacher, nor did he make any great effort to be one. The problem was not so much the content of his teaching but the style. He spoke in a monotone and so softly that students had to exert more effort to understand him than they were accustomed to doing. As Dorfman says, "His languid, conversational manner and the apparent irrelevancy of many of his disquisitions were not conducive to popularity."[39] Students found it nearly impossible to take notes on his lectures, and students' efforts had no effect on their grades; Veblen gave the same grade – a C – to all his students. Second, when *The Theory of the Leisure Class* appeared, a number of reviewers misinterpreted it as satire rather than a serious work in economic theory. It did receive some very good reviews by men able to understand it such as Lester Ward, and an interesting one by William Dean Howells, then regarded as the dean of American writers. Howells saw in the Leisure Class as described by Veblen a great field for novelists, particularly in the relation of the American upper class to the English upper class.[40]

Henry James was already exploring this situation. This was a period when upper class Englishmen whose funds were running low were seeking to recoup their fortunes by marrying American heiresses. But these serious reviews could not offset the popular verdict that the book was a satire on the Leisure Class. Veblen thus found himself acclaimed as an author for the wrong reasons. Finally, Veblen had marital problems. He was apparently very attractive to women and found it difficult to avoid such involvements. His wife objected, and the result was a series of separations, until finally Ellen left him. The university administration did not look kindly upon this situation. As Veblen wrote to a friend:

> As to my reason for leaving here, I have never stood well with the president, and have been kept on the staff rather as a concession to Professor Laughlin than by the president's own choice. Lately, since last spring, his aversion has grown more settled, if not stronger, so that I am now staying here on sufferance and have been given notice that I need look for no recognition or advancement, but may be departed whenever it can be done without inconvenience. The president's growing dislike in connection with the scandalous gossip which has apparently reached you, being the cause of it rather than the effect. You are right in assuming that the gossip comes from Chicago, the center of diffusion being apparently his office in Haskell.[41]

In 1891, Veblen was some variety of socialist; just what variety is unclear, and was probably unclear to him. He may even have been a "Nationalist" of the Bellamy sort. But to be any type of socialist implied the belief that the ownership of private property should be abolished. Such a position contradicted the established doctrine that the ownership of property was a natural right. It also contradicted classical economic theory that was built upon the thesis that the acquisition of property was the chief goal in life. If, as Veblen believed, what really motivated competition was the desire for prestige, classical economic theory would have to be revised. Nor was there any lack of evidence of the inadequacy of classical theory. The growth of monopolies, the increasing labor strife, the protest movements among farmers, the existence of poverty in the midst of plenty of which Henry George had made so much, and above all the periodic depressions which classical economic theory could neither explain nor remedy – there were abundant indictors that a new theory of economics was needed. This is what Veblen undertook to create, and to the exposition of his new theory we now turn.[42]

Notes

1 Rick Tilman, *The Intellectual Legacy of Thorstein Veblen: Unresolved Issues* (Westport, Connecticut: Greenwood Press, 1996), 8–9.
2 Joseph Dorfman, *Thorstein Veblen and His America* (Clifton, New Jersey: Augustus M. Kelley, 1972), 18.
3 Dorfman, *Veblen and His America*, 35–36, Chaps. 1–2.
4 Dorfman, *Veblen and His America*, 40–41.
5 Dorfman, *Veblen and His America*, 46.
6 Dorfman, *Veblen and His America*, Chaps. 1–3.
7 Thorstein Veblen, "Kant's Critique of Judgment," in *Essays in Our Changing Order*, ed. Leon Adzrooni (New York: The Viking Press, 1945) 175–193.
8 Immanuel Kant, *Critique of the Power of Judgment*, ed. Paul Guyer and trans. Paul Guyer and Eric Matthews (Cambridge: Cambridge University Press, 2000).
9 J. D. McFarland, *Kant's Critique of Judgment* (Edinburgh: University of Edinburgh Press, 1970), 74–75.
10 Veblen, "Kant," in *Changing Order*, 179.
11 Veblen, "Kant," in *Changing Order*, 178.
12 Veblen, "Kant," in *Changing Order*, 180–181.
13 Veblen, "Kant," in *Changing Order*, 181.
14 Veblen, "Kant," in *Changing Order*, 181.
15 Veblen, "Kant," in *Changing Order*, 181.
16 Veblen, "Kant," in *Changing Order*, 182–183.
17 Veblen, "Kant," in *Changing Order*, 184.
18 Veblen, "Kant," in *Changing Order*, 185.
19 Veblen, "Kant," in *Changing Order*, 190.
20 Kant, *Critique*, 245.
21 Paul Guyer, *Kant and the Claims of Taste* (Cambridge: Cambridge University Press, 1997), 65.
22 Veblen, "Kant," in *Changing Order*, 186.
23 Veblen, "Kant," in *Changing Order*, 189–190.
24 Veblen, "Kant," in *Changing Order*, 192.
25 Veblen, "Kant," in *Changing Order*, 192.

26 Kant, *Critique*, 258–259.
27 Kant, *Critique*, 260–261.
28 Veblen, "Kant," in *Changing Order*, 192.
29 Veblen, "Kant," in *Changing Order*, 191.
30 Veblen, "Kant," in *Changing Order*, 193.
31 Dorfman, *Veblen and His America*, 68–73.
32 Dorfman, *Veblen and His America*, Chaps. 3–6.
33 Thorstein Veblen, "Some Neglected Points in the Theory of Socialism," in *The Place of Science in Modern Civilization*, intro. Warren J. Samuels (New York: Cosimo, 2007), 387–408.
34 Veblen, "Socialism," in *Place of Science*, 387.
35 Veblen, "Socialism," in *Place of Science*, 389.
36 Veblen, "Socialism," in *Place of Science*, 390.
37 Veblen, "Socialism," in *Place of Science*, 403.
38 Veblen, "Socialism," in *Place of Science*, 406.
39 Dorfman, *Veblen and His America*, 119.
40 William Dean Howells, "An Opportunity for American Fiction," in Thorstein Veblen, *Essays, Reviews and Reports: Previously Uncollected Writings*, ed. Joseph Dorfman (Clifton, NJ: Augustus M. Kelley, 1973), 630–637.
41 Tilman, *Intellectual Legacy*, 22.
42 Dorfman, *Veblen and His America*, Chaps. 7–16.

2

BASICS

Psychology

The question of human nature – of man's psychic make-up – was fundamental for Veblen, as it is for any social scientist. His views on this subject evolved over a number of years and reached their final form in his 1914 book, *The Instinct of Workmanship*. Like all social scientists of his time, Veblen was greatly influenced by the "New Psychology" of William James and John Dewey. He refers repeatedly to James's *The Principles of Psychology* and its doctrines permeate his writings.[1] He was similarly influenced by Dewey, with whom he was associated at the University of Chicago, and cites his *Human Nature and Conduct* in his discussions of habit.[2] From James particularly, he early accepted the view that human beings are active, purposive beings constantly seeking satisfactions in the world. And here he confronted the fact that the psychological basis of classical economics was not consistent with the New Psychology. As he put it:

> In all the received formulations of economic theory, whether at the hands of English economists or those of the Continent, the human material with which the inquiry is concerned is conceived in hedonistic terms; that is to say, in terms of a passive and substantially inert and immutably given human nature … The hedonistic conception of man is that of a lightening calculator of pleasures and pains, who oscillates like a homogeneous globule of desire of happiness under the impulses of stimuli that shift him about the area, but leave him intact … When the force of the impact is spent, he comes to rest, a self-contained globule of desire as before.[3]

This is not the active purposive being of the New Psychology. Veblen therefore rejected the hedonistic view of classical economics and sought to fashion an adaptation of the New Psychology that could serve his own purposes.

Psychologically, Veblen held that human beings are composed of instincts and habits. But his view of instinct underwent significant development over the years. In his first use of the term in "The Instinct of Workmanship and the Irksomeness of Labor" in 1898, Veblen held that instincts, or "propensities" as he generally called them then, were hereditary traits of human beings that had been established through the inheritance of acquired characteristics.[4] A habit that has become established and approved within the group, and enforced by selection, becomes more than a habit.

> When this takes place, the acquired proclivity passes from the status of habit to that of aptitude or propensity. It becomes a transmissible trait, and action under its guidance becomes right and good, and the longer and more consistent the selective adaptation through which the aptitude arises, the more firmly is the resulting aptitude settled upon the race, and the more unquestioned becomes the sanction of the resulting canon of conduct.[5]

In 1898, Veblen's view of inheritance was Lamarckian, and the instinct of workmanship is taken to be the result of the habituation imposed by the regime of savagery under which primitive men lived.

This was however not a wholly satisfactory position for Veblen. He wanted to divide propensities into two classes, one of which was established earlier and was more fundamental than the other. The Instinct of Workmanship belongs to the former category; emulation to the latter. But if all propensities are the results of habituation, there would seem to be no basis for holding one group to be more entrenched in human nature than the other. The Lamarckian theory does not provide the justification for the view that Veblen wanted.

In the 1898 paper in which he introduced it, workmanship is the only propensity that Veblen called an instinct, and it is given a status accorded to no other – Veblen calls it "a generic feature of human nature."[6] He describes it as follows:

> All men have this quasi-aesthetic sense of economic or industrial merit, and to this sense of economic merit futility and inefficiency are distasteful … It is needless to point out in detail the close relation between this norm of economic merit and the ethical norm of conduct, on the one hand, and the aesthetic norm of taste, on the other. It is very closely related to both of these, both as regards its biological ground and as regards the scope and method of its award.[7]

The Kantian flavor of this passage is obvious and suggests that for Veblen all men perceive workmanlike efficiency as beautiful in the Kantian sense. Just as Veblen saw the teleological character of human thought as rooted in the nature of the human mind, so he apparently thought the desire for workmanlike efficiency was similarly rooted.

But when Veblen became acquainted with the Mendelian theory, he changed his view of instinct. The primary work on which he drew here was William McDougall's *An Introduction to Social Psychology*,[8] McDougall defined an instinct as follows:

> We may, then, define an instinct as an inherited or innate psycho-physical disposition which determines its possessor to perceive, and to pay attention to, objects of a certain class, to experience an emotional excitement of a particular quality upon perceiving such an object, and to act in regard to it in a particular manner, or, at least, to experience an impulse to such action.[9]

All three aspects of instincts are important. The instinct involves an innate pre-disposition to attend selectively to certain sense impressions. These impressions have meaning for the organism; hence the experience of them is cognitive and is a form of perception, however rudimentary.[10] It is this cognitive aspect particularly that sets instincts apart from tropismatic responses, which, as defined by Jacques Loeb, were purely psycho-physical responses to stimuli and involved no cognitive element.[11] The perception of the preselected impressions arouses in the organism an emotion specific to that particular instinct – an emotion that McDougall labels a "primary emotion."[12] This in turn leads the organism to act in certain ways which, although modifiable by experience, are directed to the attainment of a certain end.

> The instinctive impulses determine the ends of all activities and supply the driving power by which all mental activities are sustained; and all the complex intellectual apparatus of the most highly developed mind is but a means toward these ends, is but the instrument by which these impulses seek their satisfaction, while pleasure and pain do but serve to guide them in their choice of the means.[13]

All instincts therefore involve cognitive, affective, and conative aspects.[14] As Veblen puts it:

> Instinctive action is teleological, consciously so, and the teleological scope and aim of each instinctive propensity differs characteristically from all the rest. The several instincts are teleological categories, and are, in colloquial usage, distinguished and classed on the ground of their teleological content.[15]

The crucial point about the instinct psychology for Veblen is that it solves the problem of values. The ends of the instincts are the values that govern human thought and action. "The ends of life, then, the purposes to be achieved, are assigned by man's instinctive proclivities."[16] Hence in place of the hedonistic psychology of classical economics Veblen substitutes an alternative scheme under which all human beings are innately determined to value and seek certain things, and pleasure and pain arise as the instinctive ends are or are not attained. Furthermore, the instincts are teleological categories in the sense of Kant; they determine what experiences are attended to and they determine how experience is organized. "Men take thought, but the human spirit, that is to say, the racial endowment of instinctive proclivities, decides what they shall take thought of, and how and to what effect."[17] Characteristically, when Veblen speaks of the human "spirit," or man's "spiritual" nature, he means either the instinctive endowment or the combination of instincts and habits. It follows that human thought is teleological, since it is systematized with reference to the attainment of the instinctive ends. The conflict between the teleological and the matter-of-fact is thus built into the human mind.

But while the instincts determine the ends of life, they do not determine the means. That is the task of intelligence that must determine how the ends are to be attained. It is intelligence that chooses how we respond to stimuli, how obstacles are to be overcome, and what means are to be employed. The instinct of workmanship requires us to use the means we chose efficiently, but it does not choose the means for us. That is the task of inquiry, of search and research, and of hard thinking. It is intelligence efficiently used that leads to successful adaptations which can then be entrenched in the form of habits.[18]

What are the specific instincts? Although McDougall listed a number of instincts, as did James, Veblen focuses on three, which are more general than McDougall's and apparently involve combinations of some of the more specific ones. This does not mean that Veblen thought there were only three instincts; for example, he follows McDougall in holding that there is an instinct of pugnacity.[19] But Veblen clearly thinks that the three he proposes are the important ones. The first, and the most important, is what he called the "parental bent" and McDougall called the "parental instinct." This is not the same as the reproductive instinct, from which McDougall and Veblen explicitly distinguish it, although the two are clearly related. For McDougall the parental instinct is a desire to protect and aid others, particularly when they are in distress.[20] From it McDougall derives "wholly disinterested anger or indignation," and altruism in general; it is for him the foundation of morality and justice.[21] For Veblen, the "parental bent" is a "sentimental concern entertained by nearly all persons for the life and comfort of the community at large, and particularly for the community's future welfare."[22] Veblen took this instinct as including the conscience. Logically, this is the most fundamental of Veblen's instincts, for it sets the general end to which human endeavors are directed.

The second of Veblen's instincts is the instinct of workmanship, which may be defined as a desire for the efficient use of means.[23] It is teleological, having as a specific goal efficiency and the avoidance of waste, but since it is concerned with the use of means, it is subordinate to the parental bent which sets the end to which the means are directed. Obviously, this implies that the instinct of workmanship serves to ensure that means required for the welfare of the community at large – the end specified by the parental bent – are efficiently employed, and doing so results in feelings of gratification for the organism. As lately noted, the instinct of workmanship was the first of the instincts Veblen posited and provided the title to his most systematic exposition of his theory, but it is logically subordinate to the parental bent.

Veblen's third instinct is what he called "idle curiosity." That human beings have an instinctive curiosity was generally agreed by instinct psychologists of the time.[24] But Veblen's labeling of this instinct as "idle" can be misleading, and this impression is augmented by his account of its origin. In the 1906 paper in which he introduced the concept,[25] he argued that if the mind operates selectively on the contents of the stream of consciousness, choosing that which suits its interests and ignoring the rest, as James had claimed, then the residual content of the field of consciousness may form "another chain of response" which is "pragmatically speaking … unintended and irrelevant."[26] Because this "chain of response" is not directed to utilitarian ends, it is not teleologically organized, and so permits the apprehension of experience in non-teleological terms. It is this device through which Veblen seeks to account for our acquisition of matter-of-fact non-teleological knowledge. But curiosity is not "idle" in the sense of having no objective; rather, one needs to distinguish here between internal and external ends. Curiosity is curiosity about something; it is satisfied by knowledge about the objects that aroused it. Such knowledge Veblen takes to include its systematic formulation. At one point, he advises his readers in a footnote[27] to consult "Adam Smith on the 'idle curiosity' in *The Theory of The Moral Sentiments*,"[28] where Smith extols the "love of system" and "the beauty of order." Such ends are internal to the instinct in the sense that the instinct is satisfied when they are found. An external end is one that may be a consequence of the instinct, as for example, the discovery of the electrical character of lightning led to the invention of lightning rods, but this is not what the curiosity was originally about. The knowledge sought may be scientific, but it may also take the form of systematic theology or myth-making. This is clear in Veblen's various expositions of the concept, "The Place of Science in Modern Civilization,"[29] and the *Instinct of Workmanship*[30] but particularly chapter one of *The Higher Learning In America*.[31] Here Veblen describes the "true" university as dedicated to the development of such knowledge.

Instincts are innate; they are fixed in the founding of the race and have remained constant ever since. They determine the ends that men value; "nothing falls within the human scheme of things desirable to be done except what answers to these native proclivities of man."[32] But the means by which these ends are sought are matters of habit. We are not born knowing how to achieve our ends, we have to learn how to do so, and a way of doing something if repeated enough times becomes a habit of doing or of thought. The formation of habits is, as Dewey showed, the work of intelligence; we confront an environment in which the satisfactions of our needs must be sought, and intelligence enables us to find appropriate means of doing so. Veblen subscribed to the view of his teacher Sumner that habits are first worked out in action to secure adaptation and then rise to the level of habits of thought where they are formulated, intellectualized, and taught. Successful habits are adopted by others of the group and become the group's way of dealing with the world. As with the passage from folkways to mores in Sumner's theory, once habits become established in the group they come to be thought "right and proper"[33] and become part of the common sense of the group.[34] This process constitutes institutionalization; institutions for Veblen are habits of thought that have become so entrenched in the group that they are the approved norms of behavior. Such institutions are not biologically inheritable, but they are socially inheritable by being taught from one generation to the next, and so become a tradition. It follows from this process that, as Sumner had pointed out, institutions are always at least to some degree out of date. The passage from innovation in doing to habits of thought to institutionalized tradition takes time, during which the environment in which action takes place is constantly changing, so that by the time an institution has become established it is already on the way to becoming obsolete.[35] This theory of cultural lag was to be used by Veblen with great effect.

From the interplay of habits and instincts, there arises a further phenomenon that Veblen terms the "contamination" of instincts. Contamination takes three forms in Veblen's theory. The first is the contamination of one instinct by another. From the rather general character of the instincts it follows that there is a certain overlapping among them, and so that to some extent the same mental process will be involved in several of them. Habits developed in the service of one instinct will be carried over into the service of another, thus creating a "contamination" of one instinct by the other.[36] Superficially, this sort of contamination is an obstruction – the blocking of the free operation of the instincts by habit – but its significance can be seen in the following:

> All facts of observation are necessarily seen in the light of the observer's habits of thought, and the most intimate and inveterate of his habits of thought is the experience of his own initiative and endeavors. It is to this "apperceptive mass" that objects of apperception are finally referred, and it is in terms of this experience that their measure is finally taken.[37]

The "apperceptive mass" comprises the whole of the instincts, habits, and formulated knowledge that the mind contains and that it brings to bear on sense impressions in the process of knowing. It follows that new data are always interpreted in the light of established knowledge, and so that our knowledge is never quite abreast of the current situation. To Spencer's "whatever is, is right," Veblen answered, "Whatever is, is wrong," at least to some degree.[38]

But there are two further ways in which instinct may be contaminated. The status of emulation in Veblen's theory has always been a problem to his critics. The concept appears in his very early work in 1891 ("Some Neglected Points in the Theory of Socialism")[39] and plays a leading role in *The Theory of the Leisure Class* where Veblen's description is ambiguous. On the one hand, he presents it as the most fundamental economic motive: "with the exception of the instinct of self-preservation, the propensity for emulation is probably the strongest and most alert and persistent of the economic motives proper."[40] On the other hand, he describes it as a perversion of the instinct of workmanship:

> Whenever the circumstances or traditions of life lead to an habitual comparison of one person with another in point of efficiency, the instinct of workmanship works out in an emulative or invidious comparison of persons ... In any community where such invidious comparison of persons is habitually made, visible success becomes an end sought for its own utility as a basis of esteem. Esteem is gained and dispraise is avoided by putting one's efficiency in evidence. The result is that the instinct of workmanship works out in an emulative demonstration of force.[41]

The invidious comparison that leads to emulation ought to be a comparison of the efficiency of the particular means employed in attaining the end sought but it is misinterpreted as a comparison of the individual persons employing the means, on the assumption that such individuals are centers of processes of teleological causation. But this concept of individual persons is for Veblen largely a matter of imputation. Any man's effectiveness as an agent is the result of his instinctive endowment, which is the gift of the race, and his habits or knowledge, which are the creation of the group rather than the individual. The individual is not the prime mover that he thinks he is. Comparisons of the efficiency of the means employed to an end do not justify invidious ratings of the persons involved.[42] Thus Veblen has here a basis for holding that workmanship is more fundamental than emulation.

The most important type of "contamination" for Veblen is what he calls "anthropomorphism" or "animism." Veblen is explicit on this point.

> But the most obstructive derangement that besets workmanship is what may be called the self-contamination of the sense of workmanship itself ... The difficulty has been spoken of as anthropomorphism, or animism, – which is only a more archaic anthropomorphism. The essential trait of anthropomorphic conceptions, so far as bears on the present argument, is that conduct, more or less fully after the human fashion of conduct, is imputed to

external objects; whether these external objects are facts of observation or creatures of mythological fancy.[43]

Animism thus involves an imputation of teleological causation to what are really matters-of-fact. The instinct of workmanship, by focusing attention on the means used to attain instinctive ends, leads to a consideration of the means apart from the ends, with respect to what they are in themselves as opposed to what can be done with them, and so comes to explain their character on teleological grounds on the assumption that things have ends of their own.[44] Thus is produced an animistic habit of mind whereby causal efficacy is referred to some further ground of "intention" or "purpose" in the natural world. Here again one sees the conflict of final and efficient causes.

Veblen's emphasis on the importance of animism is also based in large part on Edward Tylor's treatment of animism and its role in primitive societies. Tylor was still a leading authority on primitive societies in 1914, and his extensive treatment of animism, which he saw as leading finally to the development of religion, underpinned much of Veblen's theory of cultural evolution, though the use Veblen made of animism was certainly not Tylor's.

Veblen retained the instinct psychology throughout his life, but his view of its status changed. When he wrote the *Instinct of Workmanship* in 1914, he remarked that instinct as a scientific concept was under attack in biology, psychology, and physiology. The term "instinct" he said, is too "lax and shifty" to serve as a technical concept in these sciences.[45] Veblen had originally adopted the instinct psychology because he thought it had solid scientific standing; William James had affirmed the existence of instincts, McDougall had made them central to his psychology, and these were only the most prominent psychologists who had adopted the notion. For Veblen, instinct played a fundamental role; it provided the unchanging goals of human activity, while habits provided the changeable institutions. And now he knew that the concept did not have the scientific standing he had thought it had. He did not abandon it; he claimed that although it might no longer be serviceable in the biological sciences, it was still useful for the study of the evolution of institutions, and continued to use it as he had before.

Race

No aspect of Veblen's work had seemed less defensible to modern critics than his writings on race. Thus of Veblen's essays on the blond race Samuels wrote,

> The final three essays, especially the last two, reflect, alas, the invidious eugenicism, yes, racism, common among social scientists of Veblen's era; except as examples of that genre, and of the conjectural natural history utilizing natural selection, they have no other permanent value.[46]

But this judgment needs to be revised; if Veblen was a "racist," his views were not those to which the term "racism" applies today. Veblen's writings on race have to be seen in the context of the social and biological theories of his time.

Veblen was a Darwinian, and along with his allegiance to Darwinian theory he inherited the problems that Darwin left. Two of these require particular note. In *The Origin of Species*, Darwin proposed a general theory of evolution, but he refrained from applying it to human beings; not until he published *The Descent of Man* in 1871 did he take that step. The reasons for Darwin's caution are quite clear; he had as evidence not one fossil remain on the basis of which he could demonstrate man's relation to the world of subhuman primates.[47] Nonetheless, the application of evolutionary theory to human beings was obvious from 1859 on, and the incompleteness of the fossil record was pressed as an objection to Darwin's theory. In defense of the theory, Darwin's defenders threw "living savage races into the fossil gap."[48] Pre-Darwinian "anthropologists" had capitalized on the rapidly growing literature provided by travelers, missionaries, colonial administrators, and others, to build up descriptions of so-called "savages" from around the world whose cultural differences from Europeans, judged by European standards, were interpreted as evidence that they were less highly "evolved" than their judges.[49] Thus cultural differences were interpreted as biological differences in order to fill out the evolutionary picture.

Veblen adopted a scheme of cultural evolution that classified societies as savage, barbarian, or civilized. This was a traditional scheme that dates from antiquity; it described stages of cultural development, not biological development.[50] He sometimes modifies the scheme to suit his needs, distinguishing for example the handicraft era of barbarism from the predatory era, or speaking of "early" or "late" barbarism, but usually he lets the terms stand unqualified. Since these terms are not new, it is impossible to say from which source he drew this typology. But certainly one source was Lewis Morgan whose elaborate stage theory (lower, middle, and upper savagery, lower, middle, and upper barbarism, and civilization) is set forth in *Ancient Society*[51] and Morgan does devote more space to the exposition of barbarism than do writers like Tylor, but Veblen's descriptions of the cultural characteristics of these stages do not match Morgan's. However, he probably did take from Morgan the notion that the lengths of the stages form a geometrical progression with savagery being by far the longest.[52] Veblen further held that the standard course of development for any society is through the "lower" stages to reach the "higher" ones, but he admits that in some cases segments of stages can be skipped, and that there is a possibility of regression from a higher to a lower stage, so "progress" is not inevitable.

This scheme underlay the "comparative method" adopted by post-Darwinian theorists. Since little or nothing was known about the real prehistoric people, existing societies were pressed into service to fill the gap. If prehistoric humans had been savages, the argument was that by studying contemporary savages, we could determine what the culture of prehistoric people must have been.[53] One is not surprised to find that Europeans and Americans considered themselves the most advanced peoples on earth.

One should note here Veblen's use of the term "culture." Veblen often refers to societies as "cultures," but his plural use of the word is not the modern one. Veblen believes in a scale of culture running from savagery to the civilization of present-day Americans and Europeans. The "stages" of "culture" mark levels of cultural development that are not equal – particularly so in technological development. Although he knew some of Boas's work, and cites it, Veblen's concept of culture is much indebted to Tylor.

The incompleteness of the fossil record was not the only problem Darwin left to his heirs. Even more crucial was the problem of inheritance. Darwin's principle of fortuitous variation held that offspring differ from their parents by minute variations, some of which are inheritable. But Darwin's explanation of heredity was in terms of what he called "pangenesis." He held that the body's cells give off minute particles that he termed "gemmules" that are collected in the sexual cells of the organism. These gemmules are created anew in each generation, and they combine with the gemmules of the sexual partner to produce a new human being.[54] But how do they combine? Darwin held, if not exactly a blending theory of inheritance, at least something very close to it.[55] So crossing a red flower with a white flower would produce a pink flower. But this theory left him open to attack. In 1867 a Scottish engineer named Fleeming Jenkin pointed out that if indeed variation was random, as Darwin held, then in a small population the chances of a given variation occurring more than once in a generation was vanishingly small. The variant would therefore mate with a partner that did not carry the variation, and on anything like a blending theory of inheritance, the variation would be diminished. Repeated matings would thus swamp the variation out of existence.[56] To this attack, Darwin had no answer. As a result, in later editions of the *Origin*, he began to retreat toward a Lamarckian position.[57]

Mendel's famous paper was published in 1865, but was ignored by scientists until 1900 when it was independently rediscovered by Erich Tschermak in Austria, Carl Correns in Germany, and Hugo de Vries in Holland.[58] As this suggests, those men, and others, had been working toward a theory like Mendel's for some time; it was this that enabled them to recognize the significance of Mendel's work. It was apparently de Vries's mutation theory, published in two volumes in 1901 and 1903, that particularly impressed Veblen, though he usually referred to the "Mendelian theory," of which he apparently thought de Vries's theory to be a formulation. The inheritance of the characteristics of organisms through separate independent units wiped out the objections of Jenkin at one stroke. Mutations for deVreis were discontinuous variations – "saltations" as he called them – without intermediaries, which took care of the cases of missing intermediate forms. New species might originate either by mutation or by hybridization, though mutation was the more common method. Although the appearance of "progressive mutations" – i.e. new characteristics – was unpredictable, de Vries believed there were "mutation periods" during which the rate of mutation was accelerated. Even though progressive mutations arose from factors internal to the organism, the "mutation periods" were induced by "external causes."[59] Thus a progressive mutation, one that had previously occurred but remained latent, would be more likely to appear during such a mutation period.[60] But what particularly impressed de Vries's contemporaries was his claim to have actually observed and experimentally induced mutations. De Vries was an established scientist who had previously demonstrated his abilities as an experimenter,[61] and his claim to have induced mutations in evening primrose was widely accepted until, beginning in 1910, it was demonstrated that he had not in fact produced mutations but complex recombinations.[62] De Vries was only one source from which Veblen drew his ideas of inheritance, but he was an important one, and at the time Veblen was writing an accepted authority on what would now be called genetics.

Mutation theory was not consistent with Darwin's account of evolution. Instead of the small random variations between generations that Darwin postulated, the mutation theory postulated significant variation due to mutation but stability of type between mutations. The contradiction was not fatal; mutations were held to occur at random like Darwinian variations, and although the process of change was different, natural selection still applied.

Mutation theory served also to encourage the proliferation of racial theories that took place in the 1890s and early 1900s. Granted the existence of the major races and the claim that they constituted different levels of evolutionary development, the same argument could be applied to the subdivisions of these races. And if indeed races were stable types over long intervals between mutations, then it became possible to argue that the different racial characteristics of peoples could explain their history, or at least large portions of it. The most famous attempt to define these sub-races was William Z. Ripley's *The Races of Europe*,[63] which claimed that Europeans were descendants of three races – the Teutonic, the Alpine, and the Mediterranean.[64] The characteristics used to discriminate these races were stature, color (obviously skin color, but among Europeans color of hair and eyes), and head form, measured by the cephalic index (width of the head, measured above the ears, divided by length of the head, forehead to back).[65] Modern Europeans Ripley regarded as hybrids of these three races, but the original regional distribution of the three was still evident, with the Teutonic (tall, blond, blue eyed, and dolichocephalic – i.e., longheaded) concentrated in Scandinavia and northern Europe,[66] the Alpines (Brachycephalic – i.e. round-headed, brunet and short) in central Europe,[67] and the Mediterraneans (dolichocephalic, brunet, and short)[68] in southern Europe. Ripley's classification became standard, although others sought to refine it. Joseph Deniker[69] held that there were six principal races and four secondary ones in Europe, though Keane[70] followed Ripley's scheme, as did Veblen.[71] The fact that different portions of Europe were predominantly settled by different races was held to be partly historical accident and partly a question of adaptation to environmental conditions. Ripley held that "the Teutonic peoples are exceedingly unelastic in power of adaptation to tropical climates,"[72] and Taylor commented, "As a rule the fair races succeed only in temperate zones, and the dark races only in tropical or sub-tropical lands."[73]

The claim that modern Europeans were descendants of these three different races led easily to claims that they had been, and their descendants were, of unequal abilities. Perhaps the most egregious example of this doctrine, at least in the US, was Madison Grant's *The Passing of the Great Race*.[74] Grant regarded the "Nordic" race as superior: "A race of soldiers, sailors, adventurers and explorers, but above all, of rulers, organizers and aristocrats in sharp contrast to the essentially peasant and democratic character of the Alpines."[75] The Mediterraneans, Grant admitted, excelled all others in art, "although in literature and in scientific research and discovery the Nordics far excel it."[76] Grant attributed the early achievements of the British colonists in North America to their being Nordics, and lamented the flood of post-1880 immigration that he held was destroying the racial purity of the United States.[77]

The popularity of such racism was closely related to political issues of the day. As the Industrial Revolution swept across Europe, it produced massive disruptions of the traditional cultures. Abetted by local factors such as the political upheavals of 1848 and the Irish potato famine, industrialization led to large-scale population movements, of which the "great immigration" to the United States from 1840 to the Great War was part. In the early years, this immigration came chiefly from northern and western Europe, especially from Ireland and Germany, but after 1880 the northern European immigration was swamped by a massive inflow from Italy and eastern Europe. Those who, like Grant, subscribed to the doctrine of "Nordic" (Teutonic) superiority were appalled, and Grant's book was only one of many contributing factors which led to the passage of the immigration restriction acts after the Great War.

It should be noted that neither Ripley nor Deniker nor the other more respectable authorities of the time used the term "Aryan" as a racial term. They took "Aryan" as referring to a language, not a people or race, and that the distribution of Aryan speech, which most believed to be of Asiatic origin, was independent of race. But the notion that an Aryan race was ancestral to Europeans that Max Müller had propounded in the 1850s and 1860s[78] was generally rejected by anthropologists of the 1890s, though it would continue to flourish at a popular level and would bloom again with Nazism.

It is against this background that Veblen's arguments on race must be seen. Veblen followed Ripley in holding modern Europeans to be descendants of three "races" – the Mediterranean, the Alpine, and what Veblen called the "dolichocephalic blonds," avoiding the use of terms such as "Teutonic," "Nordic," or "Aryan." But when Veblen wrote *The Theory of the Leisure Class* in 1898 he had yet to discover the Mendelian theory, and his theory of inheritance was a mix of Lamarckian and Darwinian elements. Present-day Europeans, Veblen held, are hybrids of these "relatively stable and persistent types," but he said, "men tend to revert or to breed true" to one or another of these types.[79] So Veblen argued:

> The man of our industrial communities tends to breed true to one or another of three main ethnic types: the dolichocephalic blonds, the bra-chycephalic brunettes, and the Mediterraneans – disregarding minor and outlying elements of the population. But within each of these main ethnic types the reversion tends to one or another of at least two main directions of variation: the peaceable or anti-predatory variant and the predatory variant.[80]

Each of these was marked by certain traits: the peaceable variant by "that instinct of race solidarity which we call conscience," truthfulness, equity, the instinct of workmanship, and also "weakness, inefficiency, lack of initiative and ingenuity," a "yielding and indolent amiability," and "a lively but inconsequential animistic sense";[81] the predatory variant is characterized by "ferocity, self-seeking, clan-nishness, and disingenuousness – a free resort to force and fraud," and particularly by emulation.[82] The dolichocephalic blond Veblen classed as belonging to the predatory variant.[83] But these "variants" and their characteristics Veblen attrib-uted to habituation: "Human nature will have to be restated in terms of habit; and in the restatement, this, in outline, appears to be the only assignable place and ground of these traits."[84] And they are inheritable: "they appear to be hereditary characteristics of the race."[85] But the rediscovery of Mendel's work offered Veblen a way to clarify and elaborate his theory of race.

Noting the contradiction between the Darwinian theory of continuous varia-tion and the Mendelian (deVriesan) theory of mutations and intermutational sta-bility, Veblen chose the latter. He accepted Ripley's theory that Europeans are descendants of three races – the Mediterranean, the Alpines, and Dolichocephalic blonds. Following Sergi, Veblen argues that the Mediterranean race entered Europe from Africa at the beginning of the neolithic, crossing by a land bridge since sunk, and destroying, displacing, or absorbing the Magdelenian peoples already there, and spread across Europe.[86] But then, Veblen argues, the last of the glaciers spread over Northern Europe, forcing the population to move south-ward, where, the land bridge to Africa having sunk, they were trapped between the ice and the sea. Glaciation produced radical changes in climate and these new conditions brought on a mutational period of the sort described by de Vries, during which one or more blond races appeared, of which the dolichocephalic blonds were the chief. Appearing as mutants in the midst of the Mediterranean population the blonds were never isolated, and crossed and recrossed with the parent stock, producing a hybrid line. The end of the glaciers again altered the climatic conditions, and the dolichocephalic blonds moved north to stay in the climate to which they were best adapted, settling in Scandinavia and the Baltic region. Citing the narrow climatic tolerance generally attributed to the blonds,

Veblen held that this area has remained ever since the center of their concentration.

Being a hybrid line, and having therefore a larger pool of "unit" characters (genes) than a pure race, the "dolichoblonds" have, Veblen holds, a wider range of adaptability in non-climatic matters than would a pure race. At the same time, he holds that under fairly uniform climatic conditions, selection has produced a stable hybrid line. Meantime, other racial stocks have constantly mixed with the dolichoblonds, so that even in the Baltic regions there are no pure blond communities.

The culture of the dolichoblonds was originally based on hunting, gathering, and fishing, but the introduction of domesticated plants led to an economy of farming, with the sea and forest as supplemental sources of food. The introduction of domestic animals followed that of plants and led to a system of mixed farming. At no point, Veblen holds, is there evidence of a pastoral (nomadic herding) culture in northern Europe, and not much evidence of it anywhere in Europe. The introduction of domesticated plants and animals Veblen attributes to the Mediterranean race. Here he follows the conclusions of the Raphael Pumpelly expedition at Anau, an eight thousand year old oasis on the plain of Turkmenistan, just east of the Caspian Sea. The expedition found evidence of domesticated barley and wheat, and cattle, sheep, and horses, integrated into a system of mixed farming that was apparently peaceable, and "racially" linked to the Mediterraneans.[87]

On Veblen's theory, the Mediterraneans, dolichocephalic blonds, and Alpines all appeared in Europe at the beginning of the neolithic era, with the dolichocephalic blonds arising as a mutant from the Mediterraneans and therefore somewhat after the Mediterranean race had become established in Europe. Since the cultural conditions were those of savagery, the fact that these races survived and prospered means, as Veblen sees it, that by native endowment they were adequately adapted to their cultural situation, and since they lived under a savage type of culture for a period of thousands of years – a period long enough for natural selection to have operated – the survivors would have been selected on the basis of that adaptation.[88] Given his view of human nature as composed of instincts and habits, this implies that the instinctive endowment of these races consists in the parental bent and the instinct of workmanship, together with idle curiosity – the instincts most serviceable for the type of savage life they led, and a variety of subsidiary instincts such as pugnacity. And this he believed to have been particularly true of the blonds who originated in this cultural situation, but nearly true of the Mediterraneans and Alpines, even though they may have carried over some traces of an earlier adaptation. Relying on the theory of the stability of races between mutations, Veblen held that this instinctive endowment still characterizes Europeans today; there has not been a sufficiently extended period under any other cultural system to have selected for a different adaptation.[89]

Today's Europeans, Veblen holds, are all hybrids of the three basic races – the Blonds, the Alpines, and the Mediterraneans. To this fact, Veblen attributes the

range of variations they exhibit and their adaptability. Being hybrids, it is difficult
to predict what characteristics any given individual will show.

> The variation must be extreme both in the number of hybrid types so con-
> structed and in the range over which the variation extends – much greater in
> both respects than the range of fluctuating (non-typical) variations obtainable
> under any circumstances in a pure-bred race.[90]

The hybrid character has served Europeans by allowing them to meet a wider
range of difficulties than a pure-bred race.

Veblen holds that the Aryan language was introduced into Europe by the
Alpines, who were generally agreed to have come from Asia. The importance of
the Aryan language for Veblen is what it tells us about the culture of those who
spoke it. Reconstructions of the allegedly primitive Aryan language show a
nomadic people with an economy based on herding animals. It was patriarchal,
militant, and predatory, with well-defined property rights, a "masterful religious
system tending strongly to monotheism,"[91] and a subjection of woman and children. The "pervasive human relation in such a culture is that of master and servant, and the social (domestic and civil) structure is an organization of graded
servitude."[92] Such a culture tends to be tribal, and on a large scale becomes "a
despotic monarchy."[93] No such culture can be shown to have existed among the
dolichoblonds – they were not pastoral or nomadic, the patriarchal system was
weak, with greater freedom for women, and grown children were independent;
although the Mediterraneans were matrilineal,[94] the blonds appear to have been
neither patrilineal nor matrilineal,[95] there was no tribal organization,[96] the religion was a "lax polytheism,"[97] the economy was mixed farming, and the way of
life was peaceable. For Europe as a whole, Veblen agues, the evidence of Aryan
institutions is weak; Europe was never fully Aryanized. The prevalence of Aryan
languages in Europe he attributes to trade relations rather than to conquest.

Veblen's theory leads to several conclusions that are important for understanding his position. First, it defines certain basic characteristics of the European
races that can be taken as constants over the course of their history since the
neolithic period. Second, it raises the question of how the European races relate
to non-European races. On Veblen's theory, these can differ, and do. Veblen
attributes the fact that the modern state of the Industrial Arts arose in Europe to
the racial characteristics of Europeans, particularly of the blonds.[98] Similarly, he
holds that the adherence of Europeans, and especially Northern Europeans, to the
doctrine of Natural Rights is partly a consequence of racial factors.[99] Third,
the existence of racial differences raises questions about the legitimacy of the
comparative method. If there are racial differences between Europeans and non-
Europeans, to what extent can it be said that the study of non-European savages
can tell us something about life under savagery in Europe? Veblen admits the
force of this objection, but he holds that "the races of men are, after all, more

alike than unalike"[100] and accepts the comparative method though admitting that "there is doubtless a wide and debatable margin of error to be allowed for in the use of all evidence of this class."[101] But he does not hesitate to say that "a specific difference in the genius of the people, is by common consent assigned, for example, in explanation of the pervasive difference in technology and workmanship between the Western cultures and the Far East."[102] Yet Veblen also holds that the Japanese are like the Europeans in being hybrids and that they exhibit the same sort of variability that he attributes to all hybrids. The remarkable industrial development of Japan in the nineteenth and twentieth centuries he attributes both to this hybrid character and to their native endowment.[103] And the fact that all races underwent an extended period of selective adaptation under savagery serves for Veblen to enforce a similar set of instinctive traits.

> In all races and peoples there should always persist an ineradicable sentimental disposition to take back to something like that scheme of savagery for which their particular type of human nature once proved its fitness during the initial phase of its life-history.[104]

Finally, it must be noted that racist arguments were common among the social scientists of Veblen's time. Speaking of the response to the "new immigration" from southern and eastern Europe, Ross writes:

> Although the confidence in America and cosmopolitan sympathies of some social scientists allowed them to face the new immigration with relative equanimity, others disdained the new immigrants, worried about "race suicide," and urged immigration restriction. Racial anxiety cut across the distinctions between positivist and historicists, left and right. Clark ignored racial issues, but his marginalist colleagues Irving Fisher and Frank Fetter, and his historicist opponents Simon Patten and John R. Commons, succumbed to them. Likewise, Albion W. Small stood above the fray while his friend Edward A. Ross and his opponent Franklin H. Giddings were leaders of the racist charge.[105]

Theory of Knowledge

When examining the work of an economist, one does not automatically ask about his theory of knowledge, but before Veblen became an economist he was a philosopher; his degree at Yale was in philosophy and his first published writing was on Kant. His training shows in his work; typically, when Veblen discusses other economists, he starts with their premises, as a philosopher would, and pursues what lies "within these premises." Moreover, Veblen is always concerned with the conceptual systems of those he discusses, and emphasizes the way in which these systems determine action. In fact, Veblen has a theory of knowledge and understanding it is essential if one is to make sense of his writings, for Veblen's whole theory of economics is a theory of knowledge.

As we saw when discussing Veblen's psychology, he takes the human mind to be composed of instincts and habits. The instincts are given in the founding of the race; the habits are acquired. Habits arise from petty acts of adjustment made to solve particular problems posed by the environment, natural and social. If these acts are successful in dealing with the problems they will be repeated, and with sufficient repetition they will become habitual ways of acting and thinking. Others facing similar problems may adopt these particular action patterns; if enough do so, it may so become part of the group's store of knowledge. If it is judged good and right as a way of dealing with problems of adaptation, it may so become an institution, for what Veblen means by an "institution" is a habit or cluster of habits which have been adopted by the group as a right and proper way of dealing with such problems. Veblen holds that all thoughts are habits, so the armory of the mind contains instinctive proclivities and habits. This theory of habit, it should be noted, is very close to that taught by William Graham Sumner, who was one of Veblen's teachers at Yale. But there may also be echoes here of Peirce's theory of inquiry with which he probably became acquainted when he knew Peirce at Johns Hopkins.

The structure of instincts and habits forms a system of belief that defines for its adherents the nature of their world and their place in it. Such a system Veblen calls a "point of view"; he defines it as follows:

> What is spoken of as a point of view is always a composite affair; some sort of rounded and balanced system of principles and standards, which are taken for granted, at least provisionally, and which serves as a base of reference and legitimation in all questions of deliberate opinion.[106]

What is real for Veblen is the situation of man as a species seeking survival in an impersonal and uncaring world. Veblen is a Darwinian, and he views the human condition in Darwinian terms – we are one species among many, seeking our survival in the long battle to survive that Darwin described. So viewed, the individual is relatively unimportant; it is the community, the group, that survives or perishes, and whose welfare must therefore be the goal of all endeavor. The parental bent and the instinct of workmanship guide us to take the actions necessary for our survival. But when the instincts are contaminated, the resulting animistic point of view will define reality quite differently; gods, spirits, invisible powers will become the ultimate reality. Their adherents will believe that they are the chosen objects of supernatural solicitude that has so ordered the world that our progress to ever greater welfare and happiness is assured. For them, the human individual becomes the center of cosmic concern, while the community is merely the aggregate of individuals. Such a view fosters individual self-assertion and self-centered acquisition; emulation becomes the ruling passion and esteem the goal. Yet even in the midst of this war of all against all the voice of the uncontaminated instincts still whispers its message.

As lately noted, the instincts define the ends of human life. For the uncontaminated instincts, what is "good" is what the parental bent says is good – for the parental bent is the "instinct of race solidarity which we call conscience, including the sense of truthfulness and equality, and the instinct of workmanship, in its naïve, non-invidious expression."[107] The goal specified by the parental bent is the welfare of the group, with a particular emphasis on its future well-being. But the parental bent can be contaminated and when that happens emulation defines the good as that which gives one individual or group an advantage over another – wealth, prowess, and power. Where the welfare of the individual supersedes the welfare of the community, the survival of the species is placed in jeopardy. Similarly when the contaminated instincts pit one group against another, the outcome can be disastrous. Patriotism is one form of this animism that can lead to war.

And what of beauty? In *The Theory of the Leisure Class*, Veblen gives an extensive discussion of beauty.

> Beauty of form seems to be a question of facility of apperception. The proposition could perhaps safely be made broader than this ... Beauty in any perceived object means that the mind readily unfolds its apperceptive activity in the directions which the object in question affords. But the directions in which activity readily unfolds or expresses itself are the directions to which long and close habituation has made the mind prone. So far as concerns the essential elements of beauty, this habituation is an habituation so close and long as to have induced not only a proclivity to the apperceptive form in question, but an adaptation of physiological structure and function as well.[108]

When he wrote *The Theory of the Leisure Class*, Veblen believed in the inheritance of acquired characteristics. The last two sentences of the above quote are an attempt to give these acquired habits a status similar to that which the instincts would soon hold in his theory. This description of beauty is I think an effort to translate Kant's theory of beauty into Veblen's late nineteenth century psychology. The basic structure of the mind is such that in the "untutored" and "unsophisticated"[109] apperception of the object, it is beautiful if the action of the mind in unfolding its activity is "facile" and unhindered. If all minds were truly unsophisticated, then men would agree on what is beautiful.[110]

But the sense of beauty can be contaminated by the "law" of conspicuous waste. This contamination involves pecuniary values, utility, and esteem. The canons of beauty must be warped by some "contrivance which will give evidence of a reputably wasteful expenditure, at the same time that it meets the demands of our critical sense of the useful and the beautiful."[111] So Veblen notes that in depictions of God there is always profuse use of gold and precious gems to give the Lord a suitable pecuniary glory. Or again, Veblen notes that the beauty of a well-kept lawn is suggestive of a pasture; he remarks that one might seek to enhance the beauty of the picture by incorporating a cow in this scene. But a cow will not do because it is associated with useful work, whereas a deer can be added since the deer has no industrial use.[112] A further example is afforded by the standards of female beauty; in communities where women are valued for their work, Veblen says "the ideal of female beauty is a robust, large-limbed woman," but where the office of the high-class wife is vicarious leisure, attention focuses on the face and "dwells on its delicacy, and on the delicacy of the hands and feet, the slender figure, and especially the slender waist."[113]

And what of truth? Veblen holds that human thought is teleological, but he also holds that nature is governed by efficient causes rather than final causes. Kant's Antinomy of the Reflective Judgment is very real for Veblen. How then can humans acquire a knowledge of nature without imputing teleology where it does not properly belong? Veblen's answer is the instinct of idle curiosity which as lately noted seeks knowledge of the world as it is. Veblen describes it as follows:

> [It is] a disinterested proclivity to gain a knowledge of things and to reduce this knowledge to a comprehensive system. The objective end is a theoretical organization, a logical articulation of things known the lines of which must not be deflected by any consideration of expediency or convenience but must run true to the canons of reality accepted at the time.[114]

Both aspects cited are important. On the one hand, idle curiosity has no utilitarian end; it is a drive to understand what is experienced for its own sake. But on the other hand, idle curiosity "must run true to the canons of reality accepted at the time" – that is, the prevailing point of view.[115] And therein lies its weakness, for in its efforts to achieve a systematic formulation of the information it has found, it may promote the development of scientific theories or the development of theological or mythological systems. While it seeks what appears to be matter-of-fact knowledge, it may unwittingly contribute to the creation of animistic systems.

This peculiar doubleness that affects the instincts has its basis in Veblen's epistemology. Thus he writes:

> Always and everywhere the acquirement of knowledge is a matter of observation guided and filled out by the imputation of qualities, relations and aptitudes to the observed phenomena. Without this putative content of active presence and potency the phenomena would lack reality. They could not be assimilated in the scheme of things human. It is only a commonplace of the logic of apperception that the substantial traits of objective facts are a figment of the brain.[116]

Veblen believes that what is given in perception is sense impressions that must be "reduced to objective fact"[117] by being brought under concepts contributed by the mind. Facts are not just given; they are constructed by a process in which the mind plays an active part. Veblen's Kantian heritage is quite clear here. But the categories involved are not Kant's. As Veblen remarks in another connection:

> All facts of observation are necessarily seen in the light of the observer's habits of thought, and the most intimate and inveterate of his habits of thought is the experience of his own initiative and endeavors. It is to this "apperception mass" that the objects of apperception are finally referred and it is in terms of this experience that their measure is finally taken. No psychological phenomenon is more familiar than this ubiquitous "personal equation" in men's apprehension of whatever facts come within their observation.[118]

The "apperception mass" comprises the total of instincts and habits that the observer brings to bear on his experience. In view of the role of the apperception mass in shaping our experience, it is not easy to escape the dead hand of the past. The categories of human thought are teleological categories, and new data is absorbed and systematized in these categories. Accordingly, it is all too easy – one might even say inevitable – that the mind will impute purposes, intentions, and final causes to objects and events experienced. To conceive the world around us as animated by intelligence and will is very nearly the natural way for human beings to interpret the world. This is why contamination is so easy. Hence the great importance of idle curiosity for Veblen. More than the other instincts, idle curiosity focuses on what is actually there. The difference is relative. Idle curiosity also has to deal with the apperceptive mass, but it rejects classifications that it finds archaic or inadequate. A Scholastic, watching the tide roll in, sees the power of God in action; Newton saw the gravitational attraction of the moon in action. Idle curiosity is our best category breaker; it provides a way by which established patterns of thought can be called in question and new paths opened.

Veblen is explicit is saying that the standards of truth and reality are internal to the point of view and can vary as the point of view varies. But he qualifies this relativism by holding that despite the variation, there are standards of validity that do not vary. What Veblen is arguing here is that beliefs are habits and are therefore changeable, but that the instincts are not changeable, and they provide these standards. Thus Veblen says:

> The test to which all expenditure must be brought in an attempt to decide the point [whether it is wasteful or not] is the question whether it serves directly to enhance human life on the whole – whether it furthers the life process taken impersonally. For this is the basis of award of the instinct of

workmanship, and that instinct is the final court of appeal in any question of economic truth or adequacy.[119]

And again:

> In order to meet with unqualified approval, any economic fact must approve itself under the test of impersonal usefulness – usefulness as seen from the point of view of the generically human. Relative or comparative advantage of one individual in comparison with another does not satisfy the economic conscience, and therefore competitive expenditure has not the approval of the conscience.[120]

Veblen holds that any given point of view can be wrong, in the sense that it may jeopardize the life process. But the instincts cannot be wrong. The instincts specify the goals for human action. The parental bent stipulates that human welfare, the furtherance of the life process, is the primary goal for mankind. To deny the parental bent is equivalent to denying that human survival is desirable. For Veblen, survival is the one imperative that the evolutionary process lays upon every species. Whether in some cosmic sense our survival is good or bad is irrelevant; for creatures such as we, it is the primary goal. Our point of view should therefore contribute to the life process. Whether it does so or not is not an easy question to answer. One can argue that it does because we have survived thus far and have prospered. But a point of view can be definitely shown to be wrong if it leads us into disaster.

Why then are there points of view with standards of the good, the true, the real, and the beautiful different from the instinctive ones? The answer is contamination. The barbarous view that conquest is good, that the gods favor the strong, that females are inferior to males, and that truth can be determined by the wager of battle all bespeak the standards of contaminated instincts. Or again, the claim that competition is good, that wealth is a sign of divine grace, that beauty is enhanced by high price, and that the white race is superior to all others are claims that characterize certain sections of the modern business culture. In Veblen's view, business is a predatory institution.

Veblen frequently contrasts matters-of-fact with matters that are "make-believe." What Veblen means by "make-believe" is those things that are due to the contamination of the instincts. Individual ownership, for example, is a product of contamination. Veblen claims that all ownership is ownership in severalty that serves as a basis for invidious comparison and emulation. Since all business [in Veblen's sense of the term] is based on ownership, the whole structure of capitalism is a make-believe creation that would be eliminated if only men would adhere to the pure instincts. But this is easier said than done. Men act in terms of what they believe is real. Men have died fighting for or against "realities" that we now regard as having been make-believe. Today's suicide bombers do really believe that they are taking a swift road to paradise. The whole point of Veblen's theory of points of view is that men act in terms of the world as they believe it to be, whether it really is the way they think it is or not.

Veblen's claim that capitalism is a make-believe creation may seem extreme, but think again. Veblen believes that there are no supernatural beings, no gods, no angels, no devil, etc. But it should take a very limited acquaintance with European history to recognize how thoroughly religious beliefs dominated the lives of people in medieval Europe. For the ordinary people, supernatural beings were as real as humans – in some ways more real. The universe, as the ordinary person saw it, was awash in the supernatural; religious rules governed conduct, defined life and death, good and bad, sin and virtue. Life was lived in the expectation of post-mortem reward or punishment. And what if, as Veblen thought, it was all make-believe. Millions of people have lived their lives so as to conform to the rules of invisible beings, whom Veblen thought did not exist. So this sort of mass delusion can happen and Veblen took capitalism to be yet another example of such lunacy.

Points of view may impair their adherents' perceptions as well as sharpen them. Veblen's case example is the Jews of Europe. In an article published in 1919, entitled "The Intellectual Preeminence of the Jews in Modern Europe,"[121] Veblen explored this question. The article was occasioned by a Zionist proposal for the establishment of a Jewish homeland in Palestine. In the proposal it was claimed that, by the establishment of such a homeland, the Jews who were scattered across Europe and the world could be at last brought together in a land of their own. Pointing to the great contributions to the intellectual life of Europe that Jews have made, the proposal argued that bringing all Jews together in a land of their own would lead to increased intellectual achievement, which would benefit all mankind.

Veblen agrees that the intellectual achievements of the Jews of Europe have been remarkable, far exceeding what might have been expected from their numerical strength. But he asks to what these remarkable intellectual achievements are due. His answer is that the Jews of the diaspora, having been forced to live as small minorities among the gentiles, have found their Jewish point of view constantly challenged, with the result that for many of them their adherence to their traditional beliefs has been undermined. But the Jews could not thereupon adopt the point of view of the gentiles. "The idols of his own tribe have crumbled in decay and no longer cumber the ground, but that release does not induce him to set up a new line of idols borrowed from an alien tribe to do the same disservice."[122] The result, Veblen says, is that with the weakening of their preconceptions, the Jews were able to see things that the preconception-bound gentiles were not. Caught between two incompatible points of view and believing wholly in neither, the Jews have been forced to become what later writers called "marginal men," and it has been this freedom from preconceptions that has enabled the Jews to make the great intellectual achievements that they have. But Veblen points out that if the Zionist proposal were accepted so that the Jews would be gathered into an all-Jewish community, the marginal status would be lost. They would, Veblen says, be re-encultured into a system of "Talmudic lore"[123] and their intellectual freedom would vanish. So Veblen concludes that the Zionist proposal to bring all the world's Jews home to Palestine would destroy the peculiar factors that have given them their intellectual preeminence.

Granted that cultures change, what is the nature of this process of change? Veblen describes it as follows:

> The growth of culture is a cumulative sequence of habituation, and the ways and means of it are the habitual response of human nature to exigencies that vary incontinently, cumulatively, but with something of a consistent sequence in the cumulative variations that so go forward – incontinently, because each new move creates a new situation which induces a further new variation in the habitual manner of response; cumulatively, because each new situation is a variation on what has gone before it and embodies as causal factors all that has been effected by what went before; consistently, because the underlying traits of human nature (propensities, aptitudes, and whatnot) by force of which the response takes place, and on the ground of which the habituation takes effect, remain substantially unchanged.[124]

The term "cumulative" is unfortunate, although I know of no better one; it suggests that the culture grows by addition only. Such is not the case. While new elements are constantly added to the culture, these additions often render older elements obsolete, so that the process of change is often one of substitution as well as addition. But the process of change is more complicated than merely one for one substitution. It is often the case that the addition of new elements to the culture disrupts established cultural systems with effects that ramify widely. The addition of penicillin to the pharmacopoeia of the West changed methods of treatment for all bacterial diseases, forcing changes in training, treatment, and outcomes. One example will make the point. Before antibiotics, one of the leading causes of death among children was mastoiditis – an inflammation of the air cells of the temporal bone and the lining of the mastoid arium. The treatment was often by a complex surgery that required the surgeons to undergo extensive special training. Antibiotics have made successful treatment of the disease possible without surgery. As a result, the highly specialized surgical techniques previously required have become obsolete and the surgeons so trained have found themselves with an obsolete technology. As this suggests, antibiotics have changed the treatment of bacterial diseases, hospital procedures, the training of medical personnel, the pharmacopoeia of the nation and so the drug industry, not to mention the treatment of diseases in animals. It has also dramatically affected the treatment of wounds, not only those suffered in war but even, as Hemingway has remarked, those suffered in bullfighting.

The intergenerational transmission of knowledge is effected by several means. On the one hand, there are formal institutions the purpose of which is to transfer knowledge from one generation to another. Schools are of course the chief such institutions, though such teaching functions are performed by a number of ancillary institutions – on the job training, apprenticeships, churches, etc. But on the other hand, much, probably most, of the transfer is accomplished informally, particularly through families and various types of adult-child interactions. TV, movies, social media, sporting events, and the press are also important conduits. For the most part, the knowledge transferred is what the older generation knows, but in the case of schools there is often an attempt to pass on an improved version of what the older generation knows – for example, in teaching science. But where significant changes are taking place in the culture, the older generation may deliberately alter what it passes on in the hope of improving their children's chances of success in the new world. After the Russian revolution of October 1917, many Russian parents deliberately changed what they taught to their children to accord with what they thought would be useful for life under the Bolshevik regime. Or consider the changes that American women who came of age during the 1960s and 1970s have made in what they have taught their daughters compared to what they themselves had been taught by their mothers. The fact that the development of human knowledge is a cumulative process does not mean that it cannot be deliberately changed. The moving body of knowledge from the past is not an avalanche that carries all before it; it is a river that can to some degree be channeled and guided.

If now one includes the effects of major innovations – the steam engine, the railroad, the telephone, the automobile, etc., the true complexity of the process is more fully revealed. The culture is in constant revision, and what is passed on to the next generation depends in part on what the passing generation believes will be to the advantage of their children.

Veblen often talks as if he were a progressionist. He is not. But it is very difficult to describe cumulative processes in English without seeming to imply some form of progress. "Evolution" itself has this character, despite the well-known fact that biological evolution is not teleological. Words like "development" and "growth" suggest progress even when the intention in their use is not to suggest progress. Veblen repeatedly warns his readers not to read evaluation into his words; these warnings are not pretenses of objectivity but often reflect the difficulty of communication. And one must bear mind that progress is in the eye of the beholder. Any cumulative process can be interpreted as progress from some perspective. But Veblen does not think cultural evolution is making things better and better; he often suggests that it may well be doing just the opposite.

Not only is cultural change cumulative according to Veblen, so are some of the subprocesses of culture, particularly technology and science. This is fairly obvious in the case of technology. Think of the development of the reaper from the machines of Hussey and McCormick to the modern combines, or the automobile from the first cars of the twentieth century to those of today. The same is true for science, as for example in the case of astronomy from Eudoxus to Hubble. The latter claim has been challenged by Thomas Kuhn,[125] but Kuhn uses a very narrow definition of progress to make his case. Any comparison of today's scientific theories with those of a century ago will suffice to show that there have been dramatic increases in the power and adequacy of our theories.

Veblen says that the process of culture change is incontinent. This is Veblen's equivalent of Darwin's random variation. And this incontinence is particularly due to technology. Taking the term "technology" as including science, it is clear that Veblen believes that science/technology is the chief, though not the only, engine of change. As Veblen repeatedly remarks, "invention is the mother of necessity." Technological innovations usually have a fairly narrowly defined purpose, but once accepted they often have consequences far beyond the originally intended. The Watt steam engine, for example, was originally developed to solve the problem of pumping water out of mines, but it has directly or indirectly transformed not only industry but transportation, migration, warfare, domestic life – indeed, it is not easy to think of any realm of human activity that was not somehow affected by that invention. Today, when discovery, invention, and innovation have become businesses themselves, these processes are more predictable than they were in Watt's time, but even now the occurrence of inventions and discoveries has a large random element. The discovery of the antibacterial uses of penicillin transformed health care, yet Alexander Fleming's discovery was unexpected; he observed something in his laboratory that many others had observed, but he recognized in what he observed something that the others had missed. It is the explosion of consequences of inventions and discoveries that makes science and technology such powerful engines of change and that enforces its incontinent character. Population growth, which is often cited as a cause of cultural change, is in significant part a consequence of scientific and technological changes, such as the increase of the food supply and the conquest of disease. But there are cultural changes that are not technology driven. The substitution of one religion for another has occurred in the past without any significant technological innovation. Yet Veblen is surely right in taking technology (in this broad sense) as the major cause of cultural change.

Ideally, cultures should be coherent systems, but they usually are not. Change is most likely to begin with the canons of knowledge and belief.

> The principles governing knowledge and belief at any given time are primary and pervasive, beyond any others, in that they underlie all human deliberation and comprise the necessary elements of all human logic. But it is also to be noted that these canons of knowledge and belief are more immediately

exposed to revision and correction by experience than the principles of law and morals.[126]

The canons of knowledge and belief concern matters-of-fact, and changes in our experience will have a direct effect on these canons. Law and morals are not so directly related to sensory experience. But they will change if the canons of knowledge and belief change in ways that contradict them. Thus the system of laws regarding witchcraft which were sufficient to lead to hangings and burnings in the medieval world crumbled away as belief in the existence of witches was undermined by advances in science.

Veblen says that modern science is marked by the change from final causes to efficient causes. While this is an improvement, Veblen sees the postulate of efficient cause as evidence of the continuing influence of anthropomorphism. He accepted Hume's argument that in an event such as the collision of two billiard balls, nothing identifiable as a cause can be observed. But he did not follow Hume to the conclusion that causation is based on an impression of reflection, nor did he follow Kant by making it an *a priori* synthetic principle. Veblen says that the popular model of efficient causation is the craftsman; efficient causes are thought of as producing their effects as the craftsman produces his goods. But Veblen holds that the causal law is a metaphysical principle.

> The means whereby this work of Nature is brought to its consummate issue are the forces of Nature working under her Laws by the method of cause and effect. The principle, or "law," of causation is a metaphysical postulate; in the sense that such a fact as causation is unproved and unprovable. No man has ever observed a case of causation, as is a commonplace with the latterday psychologists.[127]

But in the post-Darwinian world, causation has taken on a new form.

> The characteristic feature by which post-Darwinian science is contrasted with what went before is a new distribution of emphasis, whereby the process of causation, the interval of instability and transition between initial cause and definitive effect, has come to take the first place in the inquiry; instead of that consummation in which causal effect was once presumed to come to rest. This change in the point of view was, of course, not abrupt or catastrophic. But it has latterly gone so far that modern science is becoming substantially a theory of the process of consecutive change, which is taken as a sequence of cumulative change, realized to be self-continuing or self-propagating and to have no final term. Questions of a primordial beginning and a definitive outcome have fallen into abeyance within the modern science, and such questions are in a fair way to lose all claims of consideration at the hands of the scientist. Modern science is

ceasing to occupy itself with the natural laws – the codified rules of the game of causation – and is concerning itself wholly with what has taken place and what is taking place.[128]

Ever since Veblen launched his campaign to make economics an evolutionary science, he has called for it to become a science of process. He has shown why economics is not a science of process, but he has said little about what such a science would be, except that it would be "evolutionary" and therefore one can assume like biological evolution. But in this passage he comes closer to doing that than in his others. To make this clear, I will use here an example that he could not have used – a finite state Markov process. This is a conditional probability process – what happens on the nth trial of the process depends on (1) what happens on trial n-1, and (2) the transitional probabilities – the probabilities that determine what, given the outcome on trial n-1, the outcome at trial n will probably be. The transition probabilities are the key. If they are stationary – are the same for all transitions of the process – then the future of the process is probabilistically determinate; if they are not stationary, everything depends on how they change.

In the above passage, Veblen says science should be concerned with "what has happened and what is taking place" – i.e., with the state n-1 of the process and with the transition to state n. As Veblen puts it, "the process of causation, the interval of instability and transition between initial cause and definitive effect, has come to take the first place in the inquiry." The process Veblen is describing is not probabilistic – at least nothing that he says suggests that it is. But he captures part of what the above example shows to be necessary in his term "cumulative," the point of which is that at each state, the process depends on what the outcome at the prior state of the process has been. What is missing here is any transition laws – any laws determining how the process changes. But when Veblen says that the process of change is incontinent, he appears to be saying that the variation from state to state is largely unpredictable. This is of course the case for biological evolution since mutations are not predictable, but it means that the future of the process at any given point is largely indeterminate. And that is true of social change since the outcomes of the processes of discovery, invention, and innovation are largely unpredictable. New discoveries in both science and technology are often surprises to those who make them. Even long accepted theories are likely to be overthrown by new discoveries. When Vera Rubin began her study of galaxy rotation curves, no one – probably not even Rubin – expected her findings to upset established physical theories. But what she found was that the velocity of the outer stars in their galactic orbits was so great that if what held them in their orbits was the gravitational pull exerted by the visible matter of the galaxy, the galaxy should be flying apart. It was this unexpected finding that led to the theory of dark matter which has confounded physicists.

Veblen claims that this description applies to "modern science," including modern physics. The two principles of modern physics that he discusses are the prohibition against action at a distance and the conservation of energy and matter. [Post-Einstein, energy is taken to include matter.] Veblen stresses that these principles are unproven and unprovable; they are rather rules that he believes govern all physical processes. But the process of evolution is conditional; what happens at a given time is conditional upon what happened at preceding times. It is not clear how this may apply to the two physical principles, neither of which is conditional in this sense. So far as action at a distance is concerned, it is unclear just what Veblen meant. He says that actions involving light, heat, and electricity violate the prohibition, so apparently what he meant to include is mechanical action at a distance only. But the claim can be shown false by any case of mechanical action at a distance. Newtonian mechanics provided such a case in 1687. That is what so exercised nineteenth-century physicists. Veblen never discusses Newton's theory – in fact, he never mentions Newton at all, despite the fact that in Veblen's time, Newton was universally regarded as the world's greatest scientist. Although Newton's theory of gravity has now been rejected, there is currently the case of "entanglement" in quantum physics that looks very much like action at a distance. The jury is still out.

As for the conservation of energy, Veblen claims that the general acceptance of the law is due to the development of business accounting methods. He does not claim that the law originated with business accounting but only that this is what brought about its general acceptance. Presumably what delayed acceptance was the fact that the law contradicts the Biblical account of creation when God is supposed to have created everything from nothing. As the scholastics put it, *ex nihilo nihil, in nihilum nil posse reverti*, which leaves us with no explanation at all. In any case, it is difficult to see how this law fits Veblen's description; it is not conditional in the sense discussed above.

Veblen says that science is no longer interested in beginnings or endings. In the year Veblen died, Hubble discovered that all visible galaxies are receding from earth and that the further they are from us the faster they are moving away. The theory of the Big Bang followed in short order. High energy physicists have been studying the Big Bang ever since. As for endings, recent studies have shown that the expansion of the universe is accelerating. Cosmologists are busily trying to find an explanation of how that can be so. So Veblen was wrong about the interests of scientists in endings and beginnings. Predicting the future course of scientific investigations is a high-risk gamble.

Veblen believed that the reality for men was the evolutionary process, a process that governed not only biological evolution but also psychological and cultural evolution. He says repeatedly that science gives us our best approach to truth. Throughout his work, he takes matter-of-fact knowledge as preferable to any other kind, and science is the most developed form of matter-of-fact knowledge. But he also says that science is relative to the point of view of the observer.

Science consists of habits, and habits are changeable. What is not changeable is the instincts. These he tells us are fixed upon the race by selection. But what that means is that by force of the protracted selective discipline of the savage phase of culture, the human nature of civilized mankind is still that of the savage man.[129] But are those instincts well enough adapted to the conditions of life in the age of the machine to guarantee human survival? Veblen considered that an open question. The process of evolution is incontinent and unpredictable. Even if science proves to be our best guide in this endeavor, still science resets upon a metaphysical principle that may prove deficient, but how we might replace it Veblen does not say. Perhaps a better science will show us the way, but meanwhile we are like rafters on an unexplored river rushing down stream into a future we cannot see.

The Critique of Classical Economics

While Veblen struggled to develop his own theory, he also weighed the merits of the classical theory. He believed that classical economics could not deal with the problems of the industrial age. He began his critique of existing economic theories in an article entitled "Why is Economics Not an Evolutionary Science?" in 1898.[130] Modern economics, Veblen says, "is helplessly behind the times, and unable to handle its subject-matter in a way to entitle it to standing as a modern science."[131] To correct this situation requires both a specification of what an evolutionary science is, and of where economics falls short. Veblen takes these in reverse order. The classical economists, Veblen says, assume the existence, behind the economic facts, of tendencies in nature toward human progress. Veblen characterizes the work of the classical writers as follows:

> The ultimate laws and principles which they formulated were laws of the normal or the natural, according to a preconception regarding the ends to which, in the nature of things, all things tend. In effect, this preconception imputes to things a tendency to work out what the instructed common sense of the time accepts as the adequate and worthy end of human effort. It is a projection of the accepted ideal of conduct. This ideal of conduct is made to serve as a canon of truths, to the extent that the investigator contents himself with the appeal to its legitimation for premises that run back of the facts with which he is immediately dealing, for the "controlling principles" that are conceived intangibly to underlie the process discussed, and for the "tendencies" that run beyond the situation as it lies before him.[132]

Veblen believes that our savage ancestors explained the events of nature in the terms they knew best – those of will and desires. Thus for the savage there were preternatural agents who controlled the course of events. This animism has become attenuated in the course of social evolution but Veblen holds that remnants of it were still active in the eighteenth century when economics was born and lived on in classical economics. The principles and tendencies that are seen as governing the course of events are projections of supernatural guidance that reflect the benevolence of the Creator; in other words, they are animistic assumptions of an unseen hand determining outcomes. This finds expression in the belief that there is a natural or normal state of the economy which is most conducive to human welfare. This normal state of perfect equilibrium is the standard in terms of which economic phenomena are seen. All economic phenomena are classed as normal or not normal, and those that are not consistent with the normal are therefore classified as "disturbances"; they are deviations from the normal that require correction to bring the economy back to its perfect equilibrium. This is what Veblen means when he says that economics is a taxonomic discipline. "In this way, we have come into the usufruct of a cost-of-production theory of value which is pungently reminiscent of the time when Nature abhorred a vacuum."[133] But in Veblen's view the notion of a normal or of a trend in affairs guiding human society toward the ideal outcome is an animistic delusion that should be rejected out of hand. Biological evolution does not lead to some ideal end state, and neither does social evolution.[134]

The second score on which Veblen finds contemporary (1899) economic theory lacking is its view of human nature. The psychology of classical economics, and of neo-classical economics, is hedonism, and hedonism, Veblen says, will not do.

> [The man of hedonistic theory] is an isolated, definitive human datum, in stable equilibrium except for the buffets of impinging forces that displace him in one direction or another. Self-imposed in elemental space, he spins symmetrically about his own spiritual axis until the parallelogram of forces bears down upon him, whereupon he follows the line of the resultant. When the force of the impact is spent, he comes to rest, a self-contained globule of desire as before.[135]

This changeless spheroid is not the man required for evolutionary science; he is incapable of development; he is not a prime mover; he cannot function as a cause in an evolutionary process. Veblen dismissed the hedonistic psychology as archaic and called for economics to adopt a modern psychology and a concept of human nature of the sort he had found in James and Dewey.

The hedonistic man is not the man of modern psychology or anthropology. That man is an active being, a structure of habits and propensities that seeks his own satisfaction in action. If his desires are primordial, his habits are not; they are rather the cumulative outcome of all the experience of the race. Both he and his environment are the cumulative products of the past but as his stock of habits is different from those of his predecessors so his actions will be different from theirs as he confronts new situations and finds new ways to deal with them. The same is true of the group; "all economic change is a change in the economic community, – a change in the community's methods of turning material things to account."[136] The life of the community is the life of its members, each of whose actions affect the others. "There is, therefore, no neatly isolable range of cultural phenomena that can be rigorously set apart under the heading of economic institutions."[137] Economic action affects the culture as a whole, and the converse is equally true. So Veblen says, "an evolutionary economics must be a theory of the process of cultural growth as determined by the economic interests, a theory of cumulative sequence of economic institutions stated in terms of the process itself."[138]

The members of the community stand, at any given time, facing an open future. Behind them lies the whole biological evolution of the race that has made them what they are, and the culture that their ancestors have worked out by toil and strife. To guide them, there is no unseen hand; they face a material environment that is indifferent to their needs and dreams and a socio-cultural environment that is the legacy of the past. But what worked for their ancestors need not work for them; their ancestors are no more, and the answers they found were to the problems of their days, not those of their children. The massive structure of institutions that surrounds men today is composed of the entrenched social habits of their forebears; even the material apparatus of their culture is but the embodied habits of bygone times. They must act, for it is their actions that will determine the future and will create or modify the institutional heritage they will leave behind them. So the question is, what will they do? That is the question that an evolutionary theory of economics must answer.

Veblen followed up this attack on classical economic theory with three articles entitled "Preconceptions of Economic Science" in 1899.[139] He began with the comment he had made in "Why is Economics Not an Evolutionary Science?" that economics was a taxonomic science, but he holds that while the charge remains true, economics has evolved away from the taxonomic view toward a more objective and dynamic point of view. It is this transition that Veblen says he wants to explore:

> It is the aim here to present, in outline, some of the successive phases that have passed over the spiritual attitude of the adepts of the science [economics] and to point out the manner in which the transition from one point of view to the next has been made.[140]

One should note particularly Veblen's term "point of view." As noted in a previous chapter, this is a technical term for Veblen, and is close to what is now called "conceptual scheme" or "world view." Veblen takes it as including everything from the most ordinary canons of conduct to the most abstract and general principles; a point of view forms a connected whole that guides thought and action. Veblen's concern is chiefly with the premises – the most general principles of the system – but because the point of view is a unified body of thought, those premises are implicit throughout. Veblen does not say the point of view should be a logically consistent system but he does regard it as coherent.[141] It therefore makes sense to him to talk of the point of view of a particular generation as providing the common sense of a particular era and to argue that in order to understand the era we must understand its point of view.

Veblen takes the Physiocrats to be the earliest group of economists – at least in the modern sense of that term. But their economics is infused with animism. According to their point of view, God has so created nature that it will lead men to a state of well-being which is the final cause of the system. The laws of nature are not laws in the scientific sense of invariable sequences; rather they are rules for the behavior of nature. They can be violated by men but such violations do not affect their status as natural laws. Conformity to the laws of nature will lead men to greater well-being. Should men fail to act in accordance with nature's laws, the remedy is education. The laws of nature are the standard of truth; accordingly, nature is the final term of any inquiry; and inquiry is pressed until it leads to some consequence of a law of nature at which point the inquiry ceases. Whatever fits natural law is real, though not necessarily fact.

Economics deals with the physical welfare of man; it is therefore concerned with the activities that contribute to human flourishing – particularly with the production of goods that provide nutrients to man. Agricultural products therefore have value for they contribute to the well-being of the race. But the products of artisans do not have value for the artisans can only change the form of existing products, whereas nature creates them with the help of the farmer.

Clearly, the Physiocrat system is animistic. Behind nature stands the Creator who has determined nature to be what it is and to serve human welfare. The Physiocrat concept of God is deistic; he has made the system, but having done so he does not interfere with it and so economics does not deal with him; it does deal with nature because it is through nature that the divine plan is carried out. This animistic point of view is not unique to the Physiocrats; it is part of the whole natural law natural rights perspective that characterizes the eighteenth century and particularly France. Veblen does not further explore its origin, leaving that to others, but he emphasizes that the Physiocrats inherited the natural law system of belief which was the common sense of the time.[142]

Veblen then turns to the development of economics in England. Hume, he points out, was a stranger in the world of his own time. His skepticism did not fit the point of view of natural rights; yet in other respects he reflects something of the typical British point of view. Where did this British variant of the eighteenth-century point of view come from? To answer this, Veblen goes back to primitive cultures. These, he says, are universally agreed to have been animistic. Primitive men, being accustomed to explaining their own and their fellows' actions by appeal to purposes, interpret natural events in the same way, and personality and teleological action are imputed to nature. Accordingly, natural events are dealt with as the actions of persons would be but, Veblen says, the culture also contains a body of matter-of-fact knowledge relating to the activities of ordinary day-to-day life. The workman does not impute personality to his tools; he deals with them in terms of efficient cause and effect. With cultural development the sphere of the matter-of-fact has expanded, but even in the handicraft era where the workman is the central figure of the culture, causes are held to produce their effects as the craftsman produces his product and explanation still runs in teleological terms.

Men, Veblen says, are bundles of habits, and those bundles are so tightly bound that what produces change in one habit produces change in others as well. Veblen does not mention instincts here since at the time this paper was written (1899) he still believed they were acquired as habits and fixed upon the race by the inheritance of acquired characteristics. Habits are formed in action, and changes in our activities will therefore lead to changes in our habits. Cultural development rests on industrial development and industrial development leads to the expansion of the matter-of-fact realm of knowledge. Nevertheless, animism has prevailed throughout most of the history of culture. Religion, Veblen held, is animism in a relatively pure form, but even in the sciences animism has played a part. Astrology and alchemy were thought to be sciences in their day; some elements were nobler than others, some planets more influential. The social system of the time was chiefly one of status, differentiated into classes with differential wealth, honor, and power. Such a social system bred emulation. Inherited ranks and privileges differentiated the social world on the basis of imputed force and worth, regardless of the facts. Those who commanded the greatest force ruled; others obeyed. Yet despite this pervasive animism, matter-of-fact knowledge gained great influence in England by the eighteenth century.

Returning to the differences between the British and the French in the eighteenth century, Veblen notes that British Protestantism had less of the element of fealty than did French Catholicism. The governing systems were different, the British subject owed allegiance to an impersonal law, the French to a dominating king. England's geographic isolation meant that the British had less direct experience of war – British battles were fought abroad, so the general population had less experience of the discipline of military life. And, Veblen says, British industry used machines more extensively than did those of other nations. So, Veblen holds, the British had by the second half of the eighteenth century a somewhat less animistic and more matter-of-fact point of view than that which was prevalent on the Continent.

Veblen begins the second paper on the preconceptions of economic science with Adam Smith.[143] Like the Physiocrats, Smith believes in a natural order designed by God to lead to human welfare. This order, which God established at the beginning of the world, includes man; it functions by efficient causes among which human motives are included, but it is so ingeniously contrived that human welfare functions as its final cause.

By directing that industry in such a manner as its produce may be of greatest value, he [the actor] intends only his own gain; and he is in this, as in many other cases, led by an invisible hand to promote an end which was no part of his intention ... By pursuing his own interest he frequently promotes that of the society more effectively than when he really intends to promote it.[144]

The Physiocrats conceived production to be the work of nature alone; Smith views man as included in nature and therefore production is the joint product of man and nature. Smith views the "productive natural process" as the basis of economic theory. The natural price is a composite resulting from the natural wages of labor, the natural profit of capital, and the natural rent of land, each being the measure of the "productive effect of the factor to which it pertains."[145] These are the three factors of production. The "real" value of goods is the value of the labor required to create them. But the real value need not coincide with the values settled in the market by bargaining. The latter evaluation may be wide of the real or natural price since a variety of factors may affect the outcome of the exchange.

The natural price coincides with the price fixed by competition because competition means the unimpeded play of those efficient forces through which the nicely adjusted mechanism of nature works out the design to accomplish which it was contrived. The natural price is reached through the free interplay of the factors of production, and it is itself an outcome of production.[146]

Smith's animism is also evident in what Veblen calls his "normalization" of the data both in his conjectural history and his "statement of present-day phenomena in terms of what legitimately ought to be according to the God-given end of life rather than in terms of unconstrued observation."[147] His history is designed to show how the present state has come about from primitive beginnings which, Veblen says, are "altogether a figment."[148] The present-day situation constrains Smith's freedom of imagination, but he labors to make it fit what the outcome ought to be.

The role of human labor in Smith's theory may be summarized as follows. Men exert their force and skill in a mechanical process of production, and their pecuniary sagacity in a competitive process of distribution, with the view to individual gain of the material means of life. Men will behave in this fashion since it is "the necessary though very slow and gradual consequence of a certain propensity in human nature which has in view no such extensive utility – the propensity to truck, barter, and exchange one thing for another."[149] Pecuniary gain motivates the individual and productive efficiency leads to the natural end of the community's economic life. Men are much alike as Smith conceives them, which fits the order of nature of which they are part. The emphasis upon labor as the

basis of real value, Veblen says, fit the times in which Smith wrote, for the
economy of late eighteenth-century England was a handicraft economy in which
the individual workman was the central figure. Smith's theory therefore fits the
common sense of his time.[150]

Of Smith's immediate followers, Veblen considers Malthus the foremost; he
has little to say about David Ricardo. But the successors that Veblen considers
particularly important are the Utilitarians, whom he calls the "classical economists."
The preconceptions of the Utilitarians are very different from Smith's. For Smith,
the ultimate ground of economic reality is the teleological order established by
God; for the Utilitarians it is pain and pleasure, and the teleological order is the
method of its working out. If the conclusions of Smith are consonant with those
of Utilitarians, it is not because they have similar preconceptions. The central
doctrine of the Utilitarians is a theory of value. Smith dealt with value from the
point of view of production; the Utilitarians deal with production from the point
of view of value. Jeremy Bentham's work led to a substitution of utility in place
of achievement of purpose. One result of this is determinism, so that the human
agents become the pawns of environmental forces.

> In the language of economics, the theory of value may be stated in terms of
> consumable goods that afford the incentive to effort and the expenditure
> undergone in order to procure them. Between the two there subsists a
> necessary equality; but the magnitudes between which the equality subsists
> are hedonistic magnitudes.[151]

The human actor appears as uniform, passive, and unalterable; he is a transmitter
of impulses from impingement to action.

The change from Smith to Bentham is a fundamental change in point of view.
The teleological order of Smith and the Physiocrats is replaced by one of efficient
cause. The notion of production as contributing to human welfare is replaced by
the notion of production as contributing to individual pleasure. For classical
economists, production is described as the production of wealth, meaning things
having exchange value. The classical doctrine centers on pecuniary valuation, and
production, seen as pecuniary production, comes to be acquisition. The industrial
process is for the purpose of pecuniary gain, "and industrial activity is but an
intermediate term between the expenditure of discomfort undergone and the
pecuniary gain sought."[152]

Serviceability – that is, serving the interests of the community – enters, if at all,
in relation to vendibility. Society in the Utilitarian theory is the sum of individuals,
and the interests of society is the sum of individual interests. So as the individual
seeks his own gains, he is inadvertently seeking social betterment. Whatever
yields pecuniary gain is presumed to further the well-being of society, and so the
Utilitarian ends up agreeing with Smith that the "remuneration of classes or
persons engaged in industry coincides with their productive contribution to the

output of services and consumable goods."[153] A good example is furnished by the classical doctrine of wages of superintendence. What is managed here is not the processes of industry but rather the pecuniary affairs of the business; the production which is supervised is investment, the identity of production with pecuniary gain being taken for granted.

The central place given to investment reflects the changing situation of the economy which, Veblen says, has now become capitalistic. "Hedonistic economics may be taken as an interpretation of human nature in terms of the marketplace."[154] A further effect of the adoption of hedonism is the failure to discriminate between capital as investment and capital as industrial appliances. Industrial equipment helps the production of goods – hence the rate of remuneration measures productiveness. The acquisition of future capital goods increases production – hence the need for further accumulation of industrial wealth.

In the hands of the Utilitarian economists, economics thus becomes the science of wealth – of things amenable to ownership. The result is a description of an economy in which pecuniary magnitudes interact without disturbance and where the economic man pursues the greatest gain with the least sacrifice. The world of perfect competition is of course mythical but it shows what should be the case. Indeed, given the constant character of human nature, men may well be eliminated and the theory formulated as relations among capital, labor, land, supply and demand of these, profits, interest, and wages. The consequences of Utilitarianism Veblen spells out as follows:

> In hedonistic theory the substantial end of economic life is individual gain; and for this purpose production and acquisition may be taken as fairly coincident, if not identical. Moreover, society, in the utilitarian philosophy, is the algebraic sum of the individuals; and the interest of the society is the sum of the interests of the individuals; it follows by easy consequence, whether strictly true or not, that the sum of individual gains is the gain of society, and that, in serving his own interest in the way of acquisition, the individual servers the collective interest of the community. Productivity or serviceability is, therefore, to be presumed of any occupation or enterprise that looks to pecuniary gain; and so, by a roundabout path, we get back to the ancient conclusion of Adam Smith.[155]

The earnings of persons or classes employed in industry are contributions to the output of goods and services of society. One can see here the rationale by which production came to mean the acquisition of wealth, so that whatever yields a profit can be construed as productive activity. Fortunes made by fleecing the public so become contributions to society, and the acquisition of wealth becomes the standard by which individual worth is judged.

Classical economics, Veblen says, is a theory of a process of valuation but one in which the valuer can be omitted. It inherited the remnants of the natural rights theory of the eighteenth century, but reduced economics to a mechanical system in which everything is determined by strict causality. This change reflects changes going on in the society – the growing use of mechanical processes, the decline of aristocracy and priesthood, the increase of population, and the growth of science. Animism was not completely lost, but it remained in the conviction of classical economists that all things tend toward the benevolent competitive system.

> By virtue of their hedonistic preconceptions, their habituation to the ways of pecuniary culture, and their unavowed animistic faith that nature is in the right, the classical economists knew that the consummation to which, in the nature of things, all things tend, is the frictionless and beneficent competitive system. This competitive ideal, therefore, affords the normal, and conformity to its requirements affords the test of absolute economic truth.[156]

The ideal, therefore, became the standard in terms of which economic phenomena were interpreted; the systematization of observed facts became the normalization of them in which they were interpreted in terms of conforming to or deviating from the ideal. The ideal itself has little causal role with respect to economic facts; it provides a ceremonial legitimation. The result is a taxonomic science.

Veblen begins the third paper on the preconceptions of economic science with some general remarks on his subject. All systems of knowledge rest on premises or preconceptions of a metaphysical kind. These are taken for granted as parts of the common sense of the time. Those who hold these preconceptions are usually not aware of doing so; when they become aware of doing so the preconceptions are already losing their hold. Such preconceptions are subject to natural selection; they obtain so long as they fit the circumstances of life; when they no longer do so, they lose their hold to be replaced by different ones.

The preconceptions of classical economics as of the 1850s were (1) the hedonistic associational psychology, and (2) a belief in a meliorative trend in the course of events independent of the beliefs of the community members. Such, Veblen says, were the preconceptions of Mill and John Elliott Cairnes. But these metaphysical premises were already losing their grip. Mill's psychology was a more sophisticated version of hedonism than Bentham's and one that allows a greater role to the perceiver than the classical beliefs did. Individuals are now allowed different motives to guide their lives and some freedom of choice, thus undercutting the determinism of Utilitarianism, and so laissez-faire can no longer be relied upon to make all things right. The mechanics of natural liberty failed to provide solutions for the problems economics faced.

Modern psychology may still be a stimulus – response psychology, but that which intervenes between the stimulus and the response is an active organism whose constitution and interests decide what is a stimulus and what is a response.

> The causal sequence in the "reflex arc" is, no doubt, continuous; but the continuity is not, as formerly, conceived in terms of a spiritual substance transmitting a shock: it is conceived in terms of the life activity of the organism.[157]

The reference to Dewey's famous paper on the reflex arc shows what Veblen meant by modern psychology.[158] Men are now conceived as self-directing and as acting selectively on various options. Instead of pleasure determining the activity of the organism, the organism now determines what is pleasurable. Men are now seen as active beings, pursuing ends of their own choosing, teleological organisms guided by purposes.

Veblen is particularly impressed by Cairnes's work which he sees as moving economics beyond the preconceptions of the utilitarians and natural liberty. One effect of the new psychology was to break the determinism of hedonism and to modify the associationalist psychology. This in turn disrupted the doctrine of the meliorative trend that was supposed to lead to human welfare. That doctrine rested on the assumption of a teleological trend in nature governing all events including all human actions but the transformation of the human actor from a globule of desire moved by external forces to a thinking being selectively determining its own course of action freed the actor to pursue his own goals rather than nature's. The meliorative trend cannot operate in nature if the actors whose behaviors are essential parts of the trend are free to act as they choose. "When more of teleological activity came to be imputed to man, less was thereby allowed to the complex of events."[159] The human actor so became a personality capable of being a functioning agent while external nature became an impersonal complex of events. So fell two of the pillars of classical doctrine.

Veblen clearly holds Cairnes in high regard; he finds him clearer and more precise than most of his contemporaries. But Cairnes is still a man of his time; he defines economics as "the science of wealth"; and states the premises of economics as follows:

> First, the desire for physical well-being implanted in man, and for wealth as a means of obtaining it, and, as a consequence of this in conjunction with other mental attributes, the desire to obtain wealth at the least possible sacrifice; secondly, the principles of population as derived from the physiological character of man and his mental propensities; and, thirdly, the physical qualities of the natural agents, more especially land, on which human industry is exercised.[160]

These postulates Veblen says "afford the standard of normality," so the laws of the science are the laws of the normal case.[161] "The science is, therefore, a theory of the normal case, a discussion of the concrete facts of life in respect of their degree of approximation to the normal case. That is to say, it is a taxonomic science."[162] Moreover, although Cairnes wins Veblen's praise for his rejection of the doctrine of the meliorative trend, nevertheless, Veblen says, "The economists, and Cairnes among them, not only are concerned to find out what is normal and to determine what consummation answers to the normal, but they are also at pains to approve that consummation."[163]

Veblen notes that Cairnes regards economics as a "hypothetical" science. Cairnes says the premises of the theory are certain; they are either directly known by consciousness, as he believes the psychological premises are, or are adopted from other sciences. The problem is that Cairnes believes experimentation to be impossible in economics and so the sort of verification possible in the physical sciences is not possible in economics. He also believes that induction of the purely Baconian kind can never yield the intermediate laws required for economics. But he says there are "propositions which can only be established by an appeal to the intellect; the proof of all such laws ultimately resolving itself into this, that, assuming them to exist, they account for the phenomena."[164] Such laws are not rules of conduct but empirical generalizations like those of chemistry. Although the economist cannot perform experiments, he has advantages over the physical scientist in that he knows the premises of his science to be true. In developing the intermediate laws he has two weapons – the deductive method, and mental experiments. "I refer to the employment of hypothetical cases framed with a view to the purpose of economic inquiry."[165] To investigate the relation between the quantity of money in circulation in any given area of exchange transactions and its value supposes a case in which the quantity of money is increased and

> from his knowledge of the purposes for which money is used, and of the motives of human beings in the production and exchange of wealth, it will be in his power to trace the consequences which in the assumed circumstances would ensue.[166]

It is because this procedure is hypothetical that Cairnes declares economics to be a hypothetical science.

When Veblen turns to the contemporary scene, he says that the field of economics has become sufficiently diverse so that his paper can deal with only one line of development and he chooses to concentrate on the neo-classical writers who represent a continuation of the tradition he has been describing. He picks John Neville Keynes for this purpose [the father, not the son] and Alfred Marshall. For Keynes, economics is defined not by the exclusion of all phenomena not relevant to economics but rather as "concerned with any and all phenomena as seen from the point of view of the economic interest."[167] This broadening of the scope of economics Veblen endorses, though he says that Keynes does not carry out this expanded vision in practice. Marshall shared this expanded view; Veblen says he sees economics as "an inquiry into the multiform phases and ramifications of that process of valuation of the material means of life by virtue of which man is an economic agent."[168]

Despite their broadening of the scope of economics, Veblen thinks Marshall and Keynes *père*, and contemporary economists generally, are practicing a taxonomic science. He draws an interesting analogy between Marshall, whom he regards as the foremost of the neo-classical economists, and the botanist Asa Gray "who, while working in great part within the lines of 'systematic botany' and adhering to its terminology, and on the whole to its point of view, very materially furthered the advance of the science outside the scope of taxonomy."[169] Contemporary economists (c. 1900) generally accept evolution in biology, yet they have not brought the lessons of evolution into their own science. Economics is for them still the science of the normal case and is still taxonomic. In great part they (contemporary economists) formulate the normal inhibitory effect of economic exigencies rather than the cumulative modification and diversification of human activities through the economic interest, by imitation and guiding habits of life and of thought.[170] They deal with the outcomes of evolutionary processes, not with the processes themselves. Modern economists have largely abandoned the imputation of teleology to nature; it is now only human agents that are teleologically conceived. But human actions must now be conceived in terms of "habits, propensities, aptitudes, and conventions," and economic development must be conceived as a cumulative process, a process of proliferation, unfolding and growth.[171]

Veblen's attack on classical economics was devastating. Rather than contest particular doctrines, he attacked the premises of classical theory – the animistic assumptions that all things tend toward a beneficent end and the hedonistic psychology. One can see here his philosophic training at work; these are the sorts of arguments philosophers make. The criticisms were ones that his contemporaries in economics found very difficult to answer. Writing in 1928, Paul Homan looked back on the development of economic theory since the turn of the century.

> The idea of evolutionary social change was appealed to, as bearing upon the validity of statically conceived economic laws. Functional and social psychology, anthropology, history, politics, and law began to yield their tribute. Crystallizing gradually as a movement, this new approach came to center its attention upon the careful study of contemporary economic institutions and relationships, viewed as the temporary and evanescent aspects of a process of social evolution. Veblen was, of course, the outstanding and for a time almost solitary spokesman of this viewpoint. But time has recruited his legions.[172]

Notes

1   William James, *The Principles of Psychology* (New York: Henry Holt, 1910).

2   John Dewey, *Human Nature and Conduct* (Carbondale: Southern Illinois University Press, 1983).
3   Thorstein Veblen, "Why is Economics Not an Evolutionary Science?" in *The Place of Science in Modern Civilization*, intro. Warren J. Samuels (New York: Cosimo, 2007), 73–74.
4   Thorstein Veblen, "The Instinct of Workmanship and the Irksomeness of Labor," in *Essays in our Changing Order*, ed. Leon Ardzrooni (New York: The Viking Press, 1945), 78–96.
5   Veblen, "Workmanship and Irksomeness," in *Changing Order*, 88.
6   Veblen, "Workmanship and Irksomeness," in *Changing Order*, 80.
7   Veblen, "Workmanship and Irksomeness," in *Changing Order*, 81–82.
8   William McDougall, *An Introduction to Social Psychology* (Boston: John W. Luce Co., 1923), first published London 1908.
9   McDougall, *Introduction*, 30.
10 McDougall, *Introduction*, 29.
11 Thorstein Veblen, *The Instinct of Workmanship And the State of the Industrial Arts* (New York: The Viking Press, 1946), 4–5.
12 McDougall, *Introduction*, 49.
13 McDougall, *Introduction*, 45.
14 McDougall, *Introduction*, 27.
15 Veblen, *Instinct of Workmanship*, 3–4.
16 Veblen, *Instinct of Workmanship*, 5.
17 Veblen, *Instinct of Workmanship*, 6.
18 Veblen, *Instinct of Workmanship*, 7.
19 Veblen, *Instinct of Workmanship*, 32.
20 Veblen, *Instinct of Workmanship*, 26.
21 McDougall, *Introduction*, 68–84.
22 Veblen, *Instinct of Workmanship*, 27.
23 Veblen, *Instinct of Workmanship*, 31.
24 McDougall, *Introduction*, 59–61.
25 Thorstein Veblen, "The Place of Science in Modern Civilization," *The Place of Science in Modern Civilization*, intro. Warren J. Samuels (New York: Cosimo, 2007), 1–31.
26 Veblen, *Place of Science*, 6–7.
27 Thorstein Veblen, *The Higher Learning in America: A Memorandum on the Conduct of Universities by Business Men* (New York: B. W. Huebsch, 1918), 199n2.
28 Adam Smith, *The Theory of the Moral Sentiments* (London: Millar, 1759), 351.
29 Veblen, *Place of Science*, 1–31.
30 Veblen, *Instinct of Workmanship*, 82–89.
31 Veblen, *Higher Learning*, Chap. 1.
32 Veblen, *Instinct of Workmanship*, 1.
33 Veblen, *Instinct of Workmanship*, 7.
34 William Graham Sumner, *Folkways* (New York: Arno, 1979), Chaps. 1–2.
35 Thorstein Veblen, *The Theory of the Leisure Class: An Economic Study of Institutions* (New York: The Modern Library, 1934), 207.
36 Veblen, *Instinct of Workmanship*, 40–41.
37 Veblen, *Instinct of Workmanship*, 53.
38 Veblen, *Leisure Class*, 207.
39 Thorstein Veblen, "Some Neglected Points in the Theory of Socialism," *The Annals of the American Academy of Political and Social Science* 2, no. 3 (1891): 57–74.
40 Veblen, *Leisure Class*, 110.
41 Veblen, *Leisure Class*, 15–16.
42 Veblen, "Workmanship and Irksomeness," in *Changing Order*, 90–91.
43 Veblen, *Instinct of Workmanship*, 52.

44 Veblen, *Instinct of Workmanship*, 55.
45 Thorstein Veblen, "The Mutation Theory and the Blond Race," in *The Place of Science in Modern Civilization* (New York: Cosimo, 2007), 457–477.
46 Warren J. Samuels, "Introduction to the Transaction Edition," in Thorstein Veblen, *The Place of Science in Modern Civilization*, intro. Warren J. Samuels (New York: Cosimo, 2007), ix–x.
47 Loren Eiseley, *Darwin's Century* (Garden City, N.Y.: Doubleday, 1958), 256.
48 George Stocking, *Victorian Anthropology* (New York: Free Press, 1987), 148.
49 Stocking, *Victorian Anthropology*, 10ff.
50 Stocking, *Victorian Anthropology*, 10ff.
51 Lewis H. Morgan, *Ancient Society* (Chicago: Charles Kerr and Co., 1960), 37–44.
52 Morgan, *Ancient Society*, 37–38.
53 Stocking, *Victorian Anthropology*, 15.
54 Eiseley, *Darwin's Century*, 187–188.
55 Eiseley, *Darwin's Century*, 184–185.
56 Eiseley, *Darwin's Century*, 181, 185.
57 Eiseley, *Darwin's Century*, 186.
58 Eiseley, *Darwin's Century*, 193. W. E. Castle, "The Beginnings of Mendelism in America," in L. C. Dunn, *Genetics in the Twentieth Century* (New York: Macmillan, 1951), 59–76.
59 Hugo de Vries, *The Mutation Theory* (Chicago: Open Court, 1909), II, 490–496.
60 Garland Allen, "Hugo de Vries and the Reception of the Mutation Theory," *Journal of the History of Biology* 2:55-87 (1969), 62–63.
61 Allen, "Hugo de Vries," 83.
62 Allen, "Hugo de Vries," 68–69.
63 William Z. Ripley, *The Races of Europe: A Sociological Story* (London: Kegan Paul, 1900).
64 Ripley, *Races of Europe*, Chap. 6.
65 Ripley, *Races of Europe*, 37.
66 Ripley, *Races of Europe*, Chap. 9.
67 Ripley, *Races of Europe*, Chap. 11.
68 Ripley, *Races of Europe*, Chap. 10.
69 Joseph Deniker, *The Races of Man* (New York: Books for Libraries Press, 1971).
70 A. H. Keane, *Man Past and Present* (Cambridge: Cambridge University Press, 1920).
71 Thorstein Veblen, *Imperial Germany and the Industrial Revolution*, intro. Joseph Dorfman (New York: The Viking Press, 1946), 281n1.
72 Ripley, *Races of Europe*, 584.
73 Isaac Taylor, *The Origin of the Aryans* (New York: Scribner and Welford, 1890), 201.
74 Madison Grant, *The Passing of the Great Race* (New York: Scribners, 1920).
75 Grant, *Passing of the Great Race*, 228.
76 Grant, *Passing of the Great Race*, 229.
77 Grant, *Passing of the Great Race*, Part I.
78 Stocking, *Victorian Anthropology*, 59.
79 Veblen, *Leisure Class*, 213–214.
80 Veblen, *Leisure Class*, 215.
81 Veblen, *Leisure Class*, 221–224.
82 Veblen, *Leisure Class*, 225.
83 Veblen, *Leisure Class*, 217.
84 Veblen, *Leisure Class*, 221.
85 Veblen, *Leisure Class*, 222.
86 Giuseppe Sergi, *The Mediterranean Race* (New York: Scribners, 1909).
87 R. Wells Pumpelly, ed. *Explorations in Turkestan* (Washington: Carnegie Institution, 1908), 2 vols.
88 Keane, *Man Past and Present*, 16.

89   Veblen, *Instinct of Workmanship*, Chap. 3, and *Imperial Germany*, 286–294.
90   Veblen, *Instinct of Workmanship*, 22.
91   Thorstein Veblen, "The Blond Race and the Aryan Culture," in *The Place of Science in Modern Civilization* (New York: Cosimo, 2007), 486.
92   Veblen, "Aryan Culture," in *Place of Science*, 486.
93   Veblen, "Aryan Culture," in *Place of Science*, 487.
94   Veblen, "Aryan Culture," in *Place of Science*, 488.
95   Veblen, "Aryan Culture," in *Place of Science*, 488.
96   Veblen, "Aryan Culture," in *Place of Science*, 490.
97   Veblen, "Aryan Culture," in *Place of Science*, 492.
98   Veblen, *Instinct of Workmanship*, 320n3.
99   Veblen, *Instinct of Workmanship*, 298.
100 Veblen, *Instinct of Workmanship*, 115.
101 Veblen, *Instinct of Workmanship*, 115–116.
102 Veblen, *Instinct of Workmanship*, 111.
103 Thorstein Veblen, "The Opportunity of Japan," *Essays in Our Changing Order*, ed. Leon Ardzrooni (New York: The Viking Press, 1945), 248–266.
104 Veblen, *Instinct of Workmanship*, 20.
105 Dorothy Ross, *The Origins of American Social Science* (Cambridge: Cambridge University Press, 1991), 147.
106 Veblen, "The Modern Point of View and the New Order," in *The Vested Interests and the Common Man* (New York: The Viking Press, 1946), 2
107 Veblen, *Leisure Class*, 221.
108 Veblen, *Leisure Class*, 151.
109 Veblen, *Leisure Class*, 133.
110 Veblen, *Leisure Class*, 133–134.
111 Veblen, *Leisure Class*, 152.
112 Veblen, *Leisure Class*, 134.
113 Veblen, *Leisure Class*, 147.
114 Veblen, *Higher Learning*, 8.
115 Veblen, *Higher Learning*, 8.
116 Veblen, *Instinct of Workmanship*, 178–179.
117 Veblen, *Instinct of Workmanship*, 179.
118 Veblen, *Instinct of Workmanship*, 53.
119 Veblen, *Leisure Class*, 99.
120 Veblen, *Leisure Class*, 98.
121 Veblen, "The Intellectual Preeminence of the Jews in Modern Europe," in *Essays in our Changing Order*, ed. Leon Ardzrooni (New York: The Viking Press, 1945), 219–231.
122 Veblen, "Intellectual Preeminence," in *Changing Order*, 229.
123 Veblen, "Intellectual Preeminence," in *Changing Order*, 231.
124 Thorstein Veblen, "The Limitations of Marginal Utility," in *The Place of Science in Modern Civilization*, intro. Warren J. Samuels (New York: Cosimo, 2007), 241–242.
125 Thomas Kuhn, *The Structure of Scientific Revolutions* (Chicago: University of Chicago Press, 1996).
126 Veblen, *Vested Interests*, 7.
127 Veblen, *Instinct of Workmanship*, 260.
128 Thorstein Veblen, "The Evolution of the Scientific Point of View," in *The Place of Science in Modern Civilization*, intro. Warren J. Samuels (New York: Cosimo, 2007), 37–38.
129 Veblen, *Place of Science*, 26.
130 Veblen, "Economics," in *Place of Science*, 56–81.
131 Veblen, "Economics," in *Place of Science*, 56.
132 Veblen, "Economics," in *Place of Science*, 65–66.

133   Veblen, "Economics," in *Place of Science*, 67.
134   Veblen, "Economics," in *Place of Science*, 65–66.
135   Veblen, "Economics," in *Place of Science*, 73–74.
136   Veblen, "Economics," in *Place of Science*, 75.
137   Veblen, "Economics," in *Place of Science*, 77.
138   Veblen, "Economics," in *Place of Science*, 77.
139   Thorstein Veblen, "Preconceptions of Economic Science," in *The Place of Science in Modern Civilization*, intro. Warren J. Samuels (New York: Cosimo, 2007), 82–179.
140   Veblen, "Preconceptions," in *Place of Science*, 85.
141   Veblen, "Preconceptions," in *Place of Science*, 86.
142   Veblen, "Preconceptions," in *Place of Science*, 86–96.
143   Veblen, "Preconceptions," in *Place of Science*, 114.
144   Veblen, "Preconceptions," in *Place of Science*, 114–15n3.
145   Veblen, "Preconceptions," in *Place of Science*, 122.
146   Veblen, "Preconceptions," in *Place of Science*, 121.
147   Veblen, "Preconceptions," in *Place of Science*, 123.
148   Veblen, "Preconceptions," in *Place of Science*, 123.
149   Veblen, "Preconceptions," in *Place of Science*, 118n9.
150   Veblen, "Preconceptions," in *Place of Science*, 114–130.
151   Veblen, "Preconceptions," in *Place of Science*, 134.
152   Veblen, "Preconceptions," in *Place of Science*, 138.
153   Veblen, "Preconceptions," in *Place of Science*, 139.
154   Veblen, "Preconceptions," in *Place of Science*, 141.
155   Veblen, "Preconceptions," in *Place of Science*, 139.
156   Veblen, "Preconceptions," in *Place of Science*, 145–146.
157   Veblen, "Preconceptions," in *Place of Science*, 156.
158   John Dewey, "The Reflex Arc Concept in Psychology" *Psychological Review* 3 (1896): 357–370.
159   Veblen, "Preconceptions," in *Place of Science*, 157.
160   John Cairnes, *Character and Logical Method in Political Economy* (New York: Harper and Brothers, 1875), 73.
161   Veblen, "Preconceptions," in *Place of Science*, 163.
162   Veblen, "Preconceptions," in *Place of Science*, 164.
163   Veblen, "Preconceptions," in *Place of Science*, 166.
164   Cairnes, *Character and Logical Method*, 83.
165   Cairnes, *Character and Logical Method*, 90.
166   Cairnes, *Character and Logical Method*, 91.
167   Veblen, "Preconceptions," in *Place of Science*, 172.
168   Veblen, "Preconceptions," in *Place of Science*, 173.
169   Veblen, "Preconceptions," in *Place of Science*, 175.
170   Veblen, "Preconceptions," in *Place of Science*, 177.
171   Veblen, "Preconceptions," in *Place of Science*, 177–179.
172   Paul Homan, *Contemporary Economic Thought* (New York: Harper and Brothers, 1928), 444–445.

3

SOCIAL EVOLUTION

Veblen's theory of economics is part of his general theory of cultural change which is a genetic theory of the evolution of institutions. It is a stage theory, or more exactly he employs a traditional stage theory in presenting his own. He does not attempt to describe all human social evolution; there is a long period of pre-savage human development about which he is mostly silent, believing that there is too little evidence surviving to allow responsible description. He also limits his subject to Europe, or more exactly to what he calls "Christendom" – a term chosen to avoid any identification with particular countries, but inexact since he deals with Europe and the United States but ignores Christian countries such as the Philippines or Argentina. What lies outside the bounds of Christendom are other peoples whose cultures may be different from that of the people he discusses. Within Christendom, the claim is that human societies can be categorized as savage, barbarous, or civilized – a typology that goes back to antiquity, but this scheme, and modifications of it, were still common in Veblen's time. Although Veblen uses this theory, he modified it to suit his own needs. For Veblen, the stages are not static equivalence classes; they are more accurately seen as segments of a process. Within each segment, there is significant change. Veblen often indicates this by distinguishing between, for example, higher and lower barbarism or predatory and quasi-peaceable barbarism. In some cases, he seems to abandon the typology entirely; for example, it is not clear whether he considered the culture of his own time to be late barbarism or civilization. On the whole, he is most consistent in his use of "savagery," and least so with respect to "barbarism." The stages are not of equal length; they form a geometrical progression with the pre-savage stage as the longest, and each succeeding stage is shorter than its predecessor.[1]

In his general discussions of culture change, Veblen emphasized two factors – the Industrial Arts and population change. The more important of these is the Industrial Arts. There is no aspect of today's culture that is unaffected by science and technology, and that includes the amount of life we have. In the late nineteenth century, average life expectancy at birth in the United States was below 40; in 2009, it was 78.5.

The second factor Veblen cited as a cause of cultural change is population growth. In Veblen's theory, the population plays a crucial role; it is the holder and transmitter of the Industrial Arts. In any society, the size of the body of Industrial Arts is too great to be held by any one person. While some parts of the system are known to every member of the population, there are always special bodies of knowledge that are known only by a few people who are recognized as experts by the population at large. The more complex the system of the Industrial Arts, the larger the system of such specialties will be and the more intricate the relations among them. Accordingly, the size of the population sets a limit on the size and articulations of the Industrial Arts. A drastic reduction in the size of the population can have disastrous consequences for the Industrial Arts, and so for the culture as a whole. There is a danger here that Veblen remarks. Should a community suffer "a material setback within its industrial circumstances or its cultural situation more at large,"[2] it may not be able to revert to the technology it had at an earlier time because the necessary skills may no longer exist in the community. In such a case, the community may be forced to start anew "from a more rudimentary starting point than the situation might otherwise call for."[3] This, Veblen believed, is what happened in Europe in the Dark Ages.

As lately noted, the growth of population is partly dependent on changes in the Industrial Arts. One major contribution to the growth of population is the drop in infant mortality. Fewer people than formerly die at early ages, so the total number living is increased. Population increase in the United States is due chiefly to natural causation and to immigration. The former has biological causes, but its volume is also dependent on cultural factors; during the Great Depression, US birth rates declined sharply, and then recovered after the war, reaching extraordinary heights during the so-called baby boom. Since human fertility is now under control by technological means, birth rates are more responsive to cultural variation. But other factors affect population growth. Conquest, war, famine, and disease can all impact population size. The European invasion of the Americas provides what is probably history's most appalling example of what the four horsemen can do when they are loosed upon an unprepared and unsuspecting population.[4]

Savagery

The first stage Veblen treats is that of savagery, which begins in the neolithic period immediately following the formation of the three races – the dolicho-blond, the Alpine, and the Mediterranean – but with a population already hybridized. The dominant feature of savage life is the struggle for existence against nature. The population is settled in small groups or villages, and the main activity is the quest for food. Veblen thinks that at this early point, the savages have some tools and cultivate some plants. In the course of savagery, there is a remarkable development of agriculture which, Veblen believes, is borrowed from other societies; so is the animal husbandry which is acquired sometime after the plants. By the end of savagery, the economy has become one of mixed farming. But despite these advances in agriculture and technology, the quest for food and other necessities of life is all consuming and the margin of safety from starvation remains narrow until near the end of the era. The technology for dealing with inorganic nature also grows, but at a much slower pace. In such a situation, the welfare of the group is the primary concern, since it is only in groups that the population can survive at all. This is the condition in which the parental bent, idle curiosity, and the instinct of workmanship are the controlling factors in human conduct. The parental bent is the conscience that holds men to the task of community survival, while the instinct of workmanship focuses attention on the necessity of efficiency in the use of means, many of which are the products of idle curiosity.

The savage world view is animistic. Experience is assimilated through the apperception mass in the terms most familiar to the savage – those of intention and will, and preternatural agencies are invoked to account for the way the world is. Technology – the knowledge of how to get things done – requires matter-of-fact knowledge. But Veblen notes a peculiar phenomenon – advances in dealing with inorganic nature are very slow in coming in savagery but there is rapid development in dealing with organic nature. Plants and animals Veblen describes as "speechless others"; they have needs and ends of their own so that dealing with them requires an accommodation to their natural processes. Plants grow at their own pace, fruit ripens according to its own timetable; so imputing teleology to them makes a certain sense. The worker plays an auxiliary role of removing obstacles that might interfere with their natural development and providing aids to assist their growth. Inanimate objects however are much more difficult to interpret in purposive terms. These differences Veblen believes account for the fact that savages have had far more success with plants and animals than in mastering the uses of inanimate objects and materials. The difference in difficulty is clear in the rapidity with which savages acquired the two types of technology. By the end of the Neolithic, almost all the plants and animals currently raised in Europe had been acquired but the technology for inanimate objects lagged far behind. Veblen points out that at the time when American Indian cultures were interrupted by the European invasion, the Indians had "in mechanical respects, reached an advanced Neolithic phase at its best; but its achievements in the crop plants are perhaps to be rated as unsurpassed by all that has been done elsewhere in all time."[5] Veblen sees further evidence of the differential effect of animism in the mythology of savage people which is rich in details regarding plants and animals but barren when it comes to inanimate materials.[6]

The conception of plants and animals as speechless others pursuing their own ends requires that those who attend them should have a sympathetic understanding of their needs and goals. In the state of savagery, Veblen holds that such tasks are believed to be done particularly by women; pregnancy, childbirth, and childcare are viewed as giving women natural insight into the matters of conception and growth. Accordingly, Veblen holds, the care of domestic plants and animals falls naturally to women. Further, this gives to women a central role in savage society. Veblen cites evidence for the existence of matriarchal and matrilineal savage societies, and stresses the fact that female deities are found in early mythology. "The female deities have two main attributes or characteristics because of which they came to hold their high place; they are goddesses of fertility in one way or another, and they are mothers of the people."[7] The goddesses are particularly concerned with plants and animals and with agriculture generally. In all this discussion, Veblen has assumed that savage societies are peaceable so that the group is focused on the food quest and group welfare. It is not until the advent of barbarism, with its emphasis on war and slaughter, that men assume a dominant position in society. One should note here Veblen's thesis that the social structure of the heavens mirrors that of the earth.

Veblen does not believe in the existence of supernatural entities; he thinks that such creatures are the creations of human minds. They are created to account for natural phenomena otherwise unaccountable, to give security to their creators, and to proclaim and enforce standards of proper behavior. This being the case, it is obvious that the creators of the gods will endow their creations with the social structure they know best, for how else are the gods to live? If the gods then command humans to abide in such a social formation, it is only because their creators want it to be so. There is therefore an interplay between the gods and men in which men project their own ideas and ideals of order upon the gods, and can then cheerfully obey the commands of the gods that they have created to maintain that order.

The knowledge held by society is a two-clef affair. The lower clef contains the matter-of-fact knowledge obtained in the drudgery of daily life, and is held chiefly by the members of the lower classes. The upper clef contains the knowledge of the upper classes of the society, together with the creations of the thinkers, writers, and artists, if any. For savagery, the lower clef contains the body of matter-of-fact knowledge that results from experience gained in the humdrum daily tasks of savage life. Those who perform such tasks are forced to accommodate to the efficient causality of the material environment, and so come to think in matter-of-fact terms. It is here that idle curiosity plays its crucial role in allowing the accumulation of a substantial body of matter-of-fact knowledge that can be put to use by the instinct of workmanship.

> These two instinctive predispositions – the instinct of workmanship and the parental bent – will reinforce one another in conducing to an impersonally

economical use of materials and resources as well as to the full use of workmanlike capacities, and to an endless taking of pains.[8]

Bit by bit, this growing body of matter-of-fact knowledge pushes animism further and further from the work-a-day world and forces its retreat to higher levels. The contents of the upper clef Veblen describes as follows:

> [Savagery's] theoretical creations are chiefly of the nature of mythology shading off into folklore. This genial spinning of apocryphal yarns is, at best, an amiably inefficient formulation of experience and observations in something like a life-history of the phenomena observed. It has ... little value and little purpose in the way of pragmatic expediency.[9]

It has some of the functions of science, but it seeks knowledge in terms of spiritual agents and occult forces.

The materials of savage life are stone, bone, and wood. Many of the stone and some of the bone artifacts have survived; most of the wood have not. But enough of the implements of savage society have survived to allow some generalization about the culture. Veblen notes particularly the skilled workmanship of the axes made from Danish flint. In general, the assemblages of artifacts contain very little in the way of weapons, indicating that the mode of savage life was peaceable. This was not a society of great wealth that might tempt raiders; there was little acquisition beyond the bare necessities. There were no significant public buildings from this culture; shelters were apparently simple, probably of wood, and impermanent. Nor does there appear to have been much in the way of government. Wealth was insufficient to allow much in the way of class formation, and there is little evidence to suggest hierarchal organization of any kind. Even between the sexes there is little evidence of rank. The important part that women played in the agriculture and animal husbandry of the time gave them a status roughly equal to men. There is evidence among the artifacts that remain of some magical and ritualistic activity, probably associated with cattle-breeding and tillage.

The traits that characterize savages Veblen describes as follows:

> Weakness, inefficiency, lack of initiative and ingenuity, and a yielding and indolent amiability, together with a lively but inconsequential animistic sense. Along with these traits go certain others which have some value for the collective life process, in the sense that they further the facility of life in the group. These traits are truthfulness, peaceableness, good-will, and a non-emulative non-invidious interest in men and things.[10]

It should be added that there is emulation in savage society, but Veblen thinks it is limited, and chiefly sexual. The ducks always envy the swans.

Veblen particularly emphasizes the savage skill at borrowing from other cultures, which he thinks they did extensively. These items and practices appear to have been taken over and adopted easily. They seem to have survived the transfer across cultures without carrying with them the rituals, magic, and customs that were associated with them in their original cultures – a fact which made their adoption easy. The extent of the practice also shows that by late savagery there was extensive trade among savage settlements, criss-crossing Europe and extending beyond.

Veblen holds that ownership in the modern sense does not exist in savagery. Personal items of the savage "belong" to him in the sense in which his name belongs to him; they are part of a "quasi-personal fringe" bound to the savage and pervaded by his personality. Veblen notes that this is the sort of relationship that underlies sympathetic magic, whereby the savage can be injured by an attack on items from his fringe. Strands of his hair, nail parings, even images can be so used to injure the person. Such a relation is not ownership in our sense, but it is very real to the savage.

The archaeological evidence for savagery Veblen holds to be slight, but he says "less dubious evidence of its existence is to be found in psychological survivals, in the way of persistent and pervading traits of human character."[11] Veblen's problem here is that there are certain human traits – truthfulness, good-will – which he needs to account for, and the mechanisms he is willing to admit provide no other way of accounting for their presence in modern humans except as survivals from some earlier culture. The arguments rested on the claim that "ontogeny repeats phylogeny."[12] This theory of recapitulation, as it was called, was a widely held belief that the stages of maturation of the modern day child (1914) recapitulated the developmental stages of the race. The theory is found not only in the writings of Sigmund Freud and Sándor Ferenczi, but also in those of leading American psychologists. G. Stanley Hall, who was one of the leaders of American psychology, made extensive use of recapitulation theory in his writings, as did many others. Some even went so far as to claim that events that occurred in primitive societies could be inferred from the characteristics of young modern children. "It is assumed that events in the past history of the race can be reconstructed from events taking place in the early phases of the life-cycle of the [current] individual."[13] Veblen did not go that far, but he did believe that some traits of modern men were survivals from savagery.

The savage stage, Veblen holds, lasted much longer than any of its successors. That means, Veblen says, that there was time for natural selection to operate during savagery, so that human types that did not fit the mold of savagery have been eliminated. This leads Veblen to claim that all men of Christendom carry these traits of savagery, however these may have been overlaid by features derived from later cultural stages. No subsequent stage of cultural evolution has lasted long enough to have allowed the operation of natural selection, and so there are no other traits that have the same generic standing.[14]

Barbarism

By the end of savagery, the development of the Industrial Arts has reached a point at which significant surpluses of food and other items were being produced. Once such surpluses exist, they create an inducement to other communities to satisfy their needs by seizing the surpluses of a neighbor. "Given a sufficiently wealthy enemy who is sufficiently ill prepared for hostilities to afford a fighting chance of taking over this wealth by way of booty or tribute, with no obvious chance of due reprisal, and the opening of hostilities will commonly arrange itself."[15] Once this sort of raiding begins, every community must organize for defense. Even if the raiders are initially only a small part of the population, the threat they pose requires a military response from everyone. So comes war, the development of a warrior class, war-chiefs, and, for the successful, booty in the form of goods and captives. The booty captured becomes property held by those who captured it – he who captures, keeps. So comes ownership, which Veblen says is always in severalty.

> Since predation and warlike exploit are intimately associated with the facts of ownership through its early history (perhaps throughout its history), there results a marked accentuation of the self-regarding sentiments; with the economically important consequence that self-interest displaces the common good in men's ideas and aspirations. The animus entailed by predatory exploit is one of self-interest, a seeking of one's own advantage at the cost of the enemy, which frequently, in the poetically ideal case, takes such an extreme form as to prefer the enemy's loss to one's own gain. And in the emulation which the predatory life and its distinctions of wealth introduce into the community, the end of endeavor is likely to become the differential advantage of the individual as against his neighbors rather than the undifferentiated advantage of the group as a whole, in contrast with alien or hostile groups.[16]

The members of the community come to seek their own interests rather than those of the group. The parental bent is not totally suppressed.

> The sentiment of common interest, itself in good part a diffuse working-out of the parental instinct, comes at the best to converge on the glory of the flag instead of the fullness of life of the community at large, or more commonly it comes to be centered in loyalty, that is to say in subservience, to the common war-chief and his dynastic successors.[17]

As the society is transformed into a militant organization with the war-chief as monarch, so the society comes to consist of serried ranks of warrior retainers.

The course of development within barbarism is fairly straightforward. Once war and conquest are established as ways of life, the further development of feudal society proceeds apace. The Industrial Arts become fully engaged in the production of ever better weapons, armor, fortifications, transportation, and all the supplies needed for war and peace. The society is stratified with the warrior class at the top, and slaves or serfs on the bottom. Wealth is concentrated at the top of the social scale; the lot of those at the bottom of the scale is one of poverty and submission. Depending on where one stands in the social hierarchy, personal relations take the form of submission or mastery. The patriarchal family becomes institutionalized with women treated as inferiors. Animism and religion dominate intellectual life. War is a risky undertaking, and those who pursue it seek all the help they can get from preternatural sources.

In parallel with the development of war comes the development of ownership, which Veblen holds is always ownership in severalty. As lately noted, Veblen thinks this begins with booty – that is, mastery. But mastery is an unstable basis for the retention of property – what one has seized, another may take away. And one may or may not succeed in transmitting what one has accumulated to one's offspring. The development of ownership as an institution requires an organized society so that there is social support for ownership. Ownership, Veblen claims, is inseparable from emulation; it leads to invidious comparison which yields emulation. Once ownership in severalty is established as an institution, and the rights of property are secured, these two dissolve the cohesion of the group and make individual gain the goal rather than collective gain.

But why must ownership be in severalty? Veblen holds that the concept of collective ownership assumes, and is therefore later than, the concept of ownership in severalty. In his article on the beginnings of ownership[18] he wrote:

> The idea of a communal ownership is of relatively late growth and must by psychological necessity have been preceded by the idea of individual ownership. Ownership is an accredited discretionary power over an object on the ground of a conventional claim; it implies that the owner is a personal agent who takes thought for the disposal of the object owned. A personal agent is an individual, and it is only by an eventual refinement – of the nature of a legal fiction – that any group of men is conceived to exercise a corporate discretion over objects. Ownership implies an individual owner. It is only by reflection and by extending the scope of the concept which is already familiar that quasi-personal corporate discretion and control comes to be imputed to a group of persons. Corporate ownership is quasi-ownership only; and is therefore necessarily a derivative concept, and cannot have preceded the concept of individual ownership of which it is a counterfeit.[19]

Further, ownership of any kind, Veblen says, is categorically distinct from the relation of pervasion that holds between a person and the items within his quasi-personal fringe. In the latter case, the personality of the person pervades the object, but this is no part of the relation of ownership. Nor can ownership develop from pervasion. Indeed, Veblen remarks, "The two concepts are so far distinct, or even so disparate as to make it extremely improbable that the one has been developed out of the other by a process of growth."[20] The extensions of the two concepts are different. For example, one's footprint may belong to one's fringe, but it is never owned.[21] So disparate are these concepts that Veblen holds that ownership could not have developed in the savage culture but must arise from some radical change. That change he holds is the introduction of war that marks the transition to barbarism. Goods captured – booty – can only with difficulty be fitted into one's fringe – but that is particularly difficult in the case of captives. These are usually women, but they have an obvious identity which bars them from their captor's fringe; moreover, as captives, they serve the purpose of trophies very effectually; they are signs of their captor's prowess.[22] They are also workers who produce goods, and these quite naturally become the property of the owner.[23] Thus it is apparently the utility of the captives as trophies of the captor's prowess that requires ownership to be ownership in severalty from the beginning.

This argument leaves a great deal to be desired. War is a collective enterprise; there is no reason why captives taken in war should not be captives of the group. When enslaved, they could just as well be slaves of the group and their products property of the group that captures them. But as property of the group, they would be trophies of the group, not the individual, and could not therefore serve as a basis for invidious comparisons among individuals. Since it is as a basis for invidious comparison that Veblen uses ownership, he has reasons for insisting that ownership must be ownership in severalty.

Ownership in severalty is characteristic of barbarism. It is, in Veblen's view, inseparable from emulation. Ownership permits invidious comparisons among men in point of possessions, since in early barbarism possessions are signs of prowess proclaiming the owner's exploits at war. The ownership of goods comes to be a mark of honor, and as combat and slaughter become less frequent, ownership of wealth itself comes to carry the honorific. Ownership in severalty dissolves the cohesion of the community; soon class divisions arise based on occupations and ownership of wealth. Stratification also appears in the government of the society, which takes the form of monarchy where the relation of the community members to the monarch is that of servant to master. The Leisure Class is a creature of barbarism. Veblen takes feudalism to represent early barbarism at its peak.

Ownership brings with it the price system as a way of describing and measuring the possessions acquired in exchanges. The price system gives a seeming objectivity and reality to the system of make-believe reared on the basis of ownership.[24] Everything now becomes ratable in pecuniary terms. But the apparent objectivity of the accountancy of the price system also serves to encourage the Industrial Arts, seen as the source of this wealth that the price system measures. The ability to measure wealth exactly that the price system confers enables invidious comparisons among people which in turn stimulate emulation which can now develop freely among the members of the group.

Barbaric knowledge differs from savage knowledge most sharply in its upper clef. In the lower clef, matter-of-fact knowledge continues to accumulate. But for the upper clef there is worldly wisdom.

> Courtly life and the chivalric habits of that past phase of culture have left as nearly no trace in the cultural scheme of later modern times as could well be. Even the romancers who ostensibly rehearse the phenomena of chivalry unavoidably make their lords and ladies speak the language of the slums of that time ... The gallantries, the genteel inanities and devout imbecilities of medieval high life would be insufferable even to the meanest and most romantic modern intelligence.[25]

What is most surprising about Veblen's description of the barbarian world view is his failure to mention the theological creations of the scholastics. The works of Thomas Aquinas, John Duns Scotus, and the other scholastic theologians are still studied and were the greatest theological works of their time. Veblen hardly mentions them.

The stratified social order is reflected in the heavenly order, where God holds sway as an omnipotent and omniscient suzerain, and the nine choirs of angels, duly ranked, perpetually sing his praises. The war-chief assumes the role of religious leader. Animism is rampant in this culture, ranging from magic, superstition, and belief in charms and luck to highly developed monotheistic theology at the top. There is also a priesthood with assorted retainers, elaborate palaces for the divine in the form of churches and cathedrals, costly vestments, and elaborate rituals to celebrate the divine majesty. The same sorts of hierarchies characterize the church organizations as the political organizations. But despite its animism, the lower clef of the culture also contains a growing body of matter-of-fact knowledge that guides the prosaic tasks of those who are without honor.

The traits that characterize the barbarian are "ferocity, self-seeking, clannishness, and disingenuousness – a free resort to force and fraud."[26] Barbarians rank high in emulation and in servility or arrogance, depending on their position in the society, as well as cupidity, aggression, and brutality. Veblen notes that "the dolichoblond type of European man seems to owe much of his dominating influence and masterful position in the recent culture to its possessing the characteristics of predatory man in exceptional degree."[27] Veblen rather neatly used the racist claims about the blonds to put them in their place.

Veblen divides barbarism into two types. High barbarism, of the sort just described, reached its high point in Europe in the Middle Ages, but continued on in regions beyond Europe. Veblen refers particularly to those cultures of pastoral origin that have developed into "Oriental despotisms."[28] Such cultures are predatory, despotic, war-like, and superstitious, and have made no substantial contribution to modern civilization.

> What a people of these antecedents is capable of is shown by the Assyrians, Babylonians, Medes, Persians, the Hindu invaders of India, the Hyksos invaders of Egypt, and in another line by Israel and the Phoenicians, and in lesser degree by the Huns, Mongols, Tatars, Arabs and Turks.[29]

Seen in perspective and rated in any terms that have workmanlike significance:

> These stupendous dynastic fabrics are as insignificant as they are large, and none of them is worth the least of the fussy little communities that came in time to make up the Hellenic world and its petty squabbles.[30]

The other type, which Veblen calls "commercial" or "quasi-peaceable" or "handicraft" developed in Europe.[31]

Handicraft

High Barbarism proved to be an unstable system. It divided into what Veblen called the "quasi-peaceable" barbarism and a continuation of High Barbarism.

> In the full-charged predatory culture, in its earlier phases, there appear typically to be present two somewhat different economic principles (habits of thought) both of which have something of an institutional force: (a) the warrant of seizure by prowess which commonly comes to vest in the dynastic head in case a despotic state is established; and (b) the prescriptive tenure of whatever one has acquired.[32]

Where the former principle dominates, High Barbarism continues on its feudal course. Where the latter principle dominates, a quasi-peaceable form of barbarism develops, which in due course becomes the handicraft system.

Veblen locates the beginnings of the handicraft system in England in the manorial system which dominated the English countryside from the eleventh century to the end of Feudalism. The manors developed craft industries to satisfy their own needs for goods, particularly for products of the mechanic arts. As the needs of the manors grew, the crafts became more diversified and the size and scope of their craft establishments increased. In due course, Veblen says, the demands of the manors became greater than its own industry could satisfy, thus providing a market for goods produced elsewhere. This need was met by the "skilled masterless workmen" who congregated in the towns.

By tenacious assertion of the personal rights which they so arrogated to themselves, and at great cost and risk, they made good in time their claim to stand as a class apart, a class of ungraded free men among whom self-help and individual workmanlike efficiency were the accepted grounds of repute and of livelihood.[33]

These pioneer craftsman usually made their own tools, which became more specialized and elaborate as time went on. In due course, the master craftsmen acquired apprentices to whom the mysteries of the craft were passed in return for their work. As the size of such enterprises grew the craftsman employed journeymen craftsman to increase the volume and diversity of goods produced. The craftsman owned his shop and the products he made, and sold them in markets that at first were local but which expanded over time. The technical knowledge utilized by the craftsman was at first little more elaborate than the common sense of the time, but as the craft system developed, more complex and larger tools and more specialized skills were required. The craftsman was both a producer and a seller:

The new phase has this in common with the typical savage agriculture that workmanship rather than prowess again becomes the chief or primary norm of habituation, and therefore of the growth of institutions; and that there results therefore a peaceable bent in the ideals and endeavors of the community. But it is workmanship contaminated and compounded with ownership; that is to say workmanship coupled with an invidious emulation and consequently with a system of institutions embodying a range of prescriptive differential benefits.[34]

The handicraft system developed first on the continent. In due course, this led to the development of an early form of capitalism in Europe in the sixteenth and seventeenth centuries. But the political context of this development was the period of state-making, when the princes of Europe were at each other's throats. The handicraft industrial system played an important part in making these wars possible. A technology that could make tools could also make weapons and armaments. "The craftsmen spent their best endeavors and their most brilliant ingenuity on this production of arms and munitions, with the result that these items still lie over in the modern collections as the most finished productions of workmanship which the era has to show."[35] The Lords paid well for such equipment and some craftsmen became wealthy.

The handicraft industry expanded. Its products made possible an expansion of the markets and so greater profits. Such innovations as improvements in shipping enabled the princes to seize and hold wider territories, while enabling merchants to find new markets and new profits. But then as now, wars cost money, and the princes chronically ran in debt. And what they could not borrow, they took.

The princely chancelleries, being in debt as far as possible, extorted further loans from the captains [of industry] by seizure and by threats of bankruptcy; and whatever was borrowed was expeditiously used up in the destruction of property, population, industrial plant and international commerce. So, when all available resource of revenue and credit, present and prospective, had been exhausted, and all the accessible material had been consumed, the princely fisc went into bankruptcy, followed by its creditors, the captains of industry, followed by the business community at large with whose funds they had operated and by the industrial community, whose stock of goods and appliances was exhausted, whose trade connections were broken and whose working population had been debauched, scattered and reduced to poverty and subjection by the wars, revenue collectors and forced contributions.[36]

From this debacle, Europe's nascent capitalism did not recover. When capitalism next emerged, it was in England, which, until the collapse of European capitalism, had lagged behind the Continent in technological development. But the English caught up, chiefly by extensive borrowing of the technological advances that had occurred on the continent and by welcoming craftsmen fleeing the wars and taxes of Europe. What was different in the case of England was an extended period of peace during which technological and economic developments were unmolested. The geographic isolation from Europe provided by the Channel allowed England to avoid the wars that had subverted the continental capitalism, and when she did become involved, her battles were fought abroad, thus exempting the home population from the experience of war. Veblen notes that there were other countries that were similarly favored by isolation – notably, the Scandinavian countries – but they lacked both a sufficient population and the natural resources necessary for such an economic development. England had both – its natural resources, particularly coal, were copious and it had a relatively large population, so it was in England that the handicraft system was able to reach maturity and reshape the culture as it did so.

The central figure in the handicraft scheme was according to Veblen the independent craftsman-trader who owned and operated his own shop. These men were members of the lower and emerging middle classes, but their influence permeated the culture. With them, the instinct of workmanship emerged in full force, despite being contaminated with ownership. The claim that nature's God has endowed men with natural rights to life, liberty, and property seemed to such men entirely reasonable; the natural rights ideology was for them very nearly a description of their world. For these men, the labor theory of value was an obvious truth; it was only very slowly that the market succeeded in imposing exchange value. Growing population increased the demand for craft goods; in response the craft system expanded. The discipline of daily life led those who lived under the handicraft system toward a more skeptical and insubordinate point of view. Veblen commented, "It is, indeed, to be remarked as a sufficiently striking coincidence that even now the center of diffusion of the modern industry is at the same time the center of diffusion of religious Protestantism and heresy."[37] Veblen remarks that the turn to Protestantism occurred in the countries of Europe that "advanced to a high level of technological and commercial enterprise."[38] I do not know if Veblen was aware of Max Weber's *Protestant Ethic and the Spirit of Capitalism*, but he saw much of what Weber saw, although he interpreted it differently.

The knowledge of the handicraft era is a long step toward modernity. In the lower clef, matter-of-fact knowledge continues to grow, reaching the level of a sophisticated technology. In the upper clef, there are several new developments. Causal relations are given the fundamental role in the explanation of natural events, but causality itself is conceived on the model of the craftsman making his goods. In accordance with Veblen's theory that the heavens mirror the earthly society, God is transformed into a workman.

> The deity, from having been in medieval times primarily a suzerain concerned with the maintenance of his own prestige, becomes primarily a creator engaged in the workmanlike occupation of making things useful for man. His relation to man and the natural universe is no longer primarily that of a progenitor, as it is in lower barbarian culture, but rather that of a talented mechanic. The "natural laws" which the scientists of that era made so much of are no longer decrees of a preternatural legislative authority, but rather details of the workshop specifications handed down by the master-craftsman for the guidance of his handicraftsmen working out his designs.[39]

The crowning ideological achievement of the handicraft era was the Theory of Natural Rights; as Veblen points out, "The scheme of natural rights, with its principle of natural liberty and it insistence on individual self-help was well adapted to the requirements of handicraft and petty trade, whose spirit it reflects with admirable faithfulness."[40] The theory stresses individual initiative, free competition, and the rights of life, liberty, and property. In fact, property was viewed as the foundation of liberty because its ownership guaranteed economic security. The right to property as formulated by John Locke and others included the right to dispose of one's property as one chose, to buy and sell as one wished; the only limits specified were that one could not use his property to injure others in the legitimate use of their property.[41] There is, Veblen points out, a similarity between the situation of the craftsman under the handicraft system and the situation of the workman under savagery. The reassertion of the instinct of workmanship and the parental bent are hardly surprising in these circumstances.

The theory of natural rights became the basis of the political theories of the time and is embodied in the great charters of the era – the Declaration of Independence, the Constitution of the United States, and the French Declaration of the Rights of Man. It was equally important in economics; it gave the owners of property "unlimited discretion" to do with their property as they liked.[42]

The downfall of the handicraft system was a product of its success. Technology continued its relentless march, leading to improvements in transportation and communication. These developments increased the size of the market and so the demand for goods. The round-about processes of production focused attention on the tools and machines used to create the goods. As these were further developed, they lost their character as labor-saving devices and were directly designed to accomplish technical purposes. The greatest single change in the situation was the invention of the Watt steam engine. The power of steam dwarfed that of human and animal muscle and so made possible the operation of larger and heavier machinery at far greater speed. This was followed in the early nineteenth century by the creation of the machine tools that permitted precise application of steam power to working hard metals.

The costs of the new technology rose as its size and weight rose. The individual craftsmen soon found that they could not afford the new machines. The way was therefore open for men with money to become the owners of the equipment necessary for the production of the goods required by the community, with the result that the usufruct of the community's Industrial Arts passed into the hands of the owners.

The stage scheme that Veblen employed – savagery, barbarism, civilization – is a traditional one, but Veblen has no hesitation in revising barbarism, which as we have seen, he divided into two types – predatory and quasi-peaceable (or handicraft), and it is the latter that receives most of his attention. The relation between quasi-peaceable barbarism and civilization is unclear. Veblen apparently regards the present (1914) state of Western culture as still belonging to the quasi-peaceable phase of barbarism, but he also refers to it as civilized. He seems to have regarded all the nations of Christendom as civilized. Yet he also regards them as devoted to ownership and the pecuniary institutions that are characteristic signs of barbarism. Since he regards the machine industrial culture as the successor to the handicraft culture, one might suppose that it is the machine culture which makes the transition to civilization, but Veblen does not say this. Rather, it seems more likely that he found the barbarism-civilization classification inadequate. Following the Industrial Revolution, he largely ignores these categories.

The Machine

Veblen then turns to the era of the machine. He draws no sharp line between the handicraft era and the machine era. In England, improvements in technology date from at least the sixteenth century, marking a change in perspective. The machine technology developed slowly; its beginnings are clear by the early eighteenth century, but the full development, at least in Great Britain, comes in the late eighteenth century. But there are many other factors involved besides the equipment. The most important of these is the growth of matter-of-fact knowledge, not only in the sheer quantity that is known but in the movement away from anthropomorphism toward an impersonal objective view of the world. Veblen contrasts the educational requirements of the time of Elizabeth with those in the Victorian era. At the earlier time, illiteracy was no obstacle to adequate training for skilled trades. But for the Victorian era,

> it has become a commonplace that no one can now hope to compete for proficiency in the skilled occupations without such schooling as will carry him very appreciably beyond the three Rs that made up the complements of necessary learning for the common man half a century ago.[43]

In the handicraft era, the worker used his tools to produce goods; in the machine era, the machine uses the worker to produce goods. The role of the worker becomes that of an attendant on the machine. "It is the part of the workman to know the working of the mechanism with which he is associated ... This demands a degree of intelligence, and much of this work calls for a good deal of special training besides."[44]

> This specialized knowledge grows more complex year by year. The knowledge so required as a general and commonplace equipment requisite for the pursuit of these modern skilled occupations is of the general nature of applied mechanics, in which the essence of the undertaking is a ready apprehension of opaque facts, in passably exact quantitative terms.[45]

The knowledge required is basically applied mechanics; by the 1920s a knowledge of chemistry and electricity was also necessary. The work is no longer a matter of the manipulation of tools, as it was under handicraft, but of utilizing natural forces and processes to serve productive ends. For this sort of work, it is not enough to be literate; a knowledge of science is also necessary. Veblen approves the removal of children from the labor force so that they can attend schools. Common sense knowledge is no longer adequate.

But education alone will not be enough to guarantee the worker's position. "The ideal mechanical contrivance in this technological system is the automatic machine. Perfection in the machine technology is attained in the degree to which the given process can dispense with manual labor."[46] If industrial technology continues to develop along its present lines, there may come a time when the entire productive economy will be automated. Workers will no longer be required. The owners and the technical managers will run industry. What would then happen to the superfluous workers Veblen does not say.

In the age of the machine, the two clefs of knowledge virtually merge. The knowledge of the lower clef becomes an increasingly sophisticated body of technological skills, concepts, and standards, while the upper clef contains the sciences.

There are still differences between the two; Veblen insists that science is pure. Like idle curiosity on which it is based, it is driven by a desire for knowledge for its own sake without regard to its possible applications. Technology is concerned with how to get things done. But the fact that the pure knowledge of science often turns out to have very practical applications has brought the two very close together.[47]

> Modern technology makes use of the same range of concepts, thinks in the same terms, and applies the same tests of validity as modern science. In both, the terms of standardization, validity, and finality are always in terms of impersonal sequence ... Hence the easy co-partnership between the two. Science and technology play into one another's hands. The processes of nature with which science deals and which technology turns to account, the sequence of changes in the external world, animate and inanimate, run in terms of brute causation, as do the theories of science.[48]

It is easy to miss the significance of this passage. That technology is applied science is a proposition that few would deny; but this proposition gives the priority to science. For Veblen, the reverse is true; technology comes first and develops the concepts and standards of validity that subsequently appear in science. These standards and concepts are first worked out in the development of matter-of-fact knowledge that arises in making adaptations to the environment. Science can be pure because technology does the practical work.

> The reason why scientific theories can be turned to account for these practical ends is not that the ends are included in the scope of scientific inquiry. The useful purposes lie outside the scientist's interest. His inquiry is as "idle" as that of the Pueblo mythmaker. But the canons of validity under whose guidance he works are those imposed by the modern technology, through habituation to its requirements; and therefore his results are available for the technological purpose.[49]

The reason why science can be so fruitfully applied in technological and practical uses is that the basic concepts and standards of science originate in the culture and particularly in the technological and matter-of-fact knowledge of the society. In Veblen's view, the machine technology creates the cultural situation in which science has been able to bloom, so that technology and science are now "co-partners." Veblen gives technology the lead here, but the two are now inseparable. In this partnership, Veblen insists that science remains the pure search for knowledge; it is technology that creates the concepts and standards that science adopts.

But there is underlying this argument a proposition of great importance. Veblen holds that the concepts and standards of science originate in the matter-of-fact knowledge of the society. Instead of holding that concepts such as mass, field, charge, etc. are created by the scientists in the course of their work, Veblen holds that these concepts and standards originate in the community's matter-of-fact knowledge and are then taken over and used by the scientists. If this is so, it follows that science can only develop in cultures where these concepts and standards are ready at hand for the scientists. If this is true, this is an important thesis in the sociology of science, and one that contravenes much that has been written by scientists and historians about the development of science. The culture of the machine has provided the situation in which science/technology has become the dominant factor in modern civilization.

> A civilization which is dominated by this matter-of-fact insight must prevail against any cultural scheme that lacks this element. This characteristic of Western civilization comes to a head in modern science, and finds its highest material expression in the technology of the machine industry. In these things modern culture is creative and self-sufficient; and these being given, the rest of what may seem characteristic in western civilization follows by easy consequence.[50]

Accordingly, Veblen holds that science has now become the authority; whatever questions arise in the culture, the verdict of science is accepted over all others. So great is now the prestige of science that other fields of knowledge that have nothing to do with science try to pass themselves off as being scientific.

> Students of literature, for instance, are more and more prone to substitute critical analysis and linguistic speculation as the end of their endeavors, in the place of that discipline of taste and that cultivated sense of literary form and literary feeling that must always remain the chief end of literary training, as distinct from philology and the social sciences.[51]

Veblen saw the New Criticism coming!

But the effect of the machine is broader; "within the effective bounds of modern Christendom no one can wholly escape or in any sensible degree deflect the sweep of the machine routine."[52] The requirements of the machine, particularly of the railroad, have forced a new routine on the life of the community; the railroad runs on a timetable that is standard across the country, so any activities which involve the railroad must be scheduled to fit the timetable of the railroad. As a result, "Modern life goes by clockwork."[53] Workers find their day scheduled for them; they start work at a set time and finish at a set time. School children are equally scheduled; they report at a given time, march from class to class on the hour, and finish at a set time. Meetings are now scheduled as appointments. So all activities must be scheduled to fit into the timetables of others. Even religious observances are now done on a timetable. Everyone must have a clock, and the day runs on time.[54] Inventions such as the typewriter and the telephone further complicate life. The typewriter has made possible the speeding up of transactions, but at the cost, Veblen says, of doubling the volume of correspondence necessary to consummate any deal. The telephone has greatly increased the range and speed of communication, but Veblen comments that "its use involves a very appreciable nervous strain and its ubiquitous presence contributes to an unremitting nervous tension and unrest wherever it goes."[55] Any device that seems to afford one business an advantage over its rivals becomes at once a necessity for all. This regimentation of life is now current throughout the society. Commodities are standardized so that they can only be purchased in fixed quantities at fixed prices. Clothes come in standard sizes, cuts, and colors. Work schedules are as precise as train schedules. Living becomes a matter of fitting one's activities to match the routines of others, and failure to do so means that one "gets left."[56] This regimentation of life is now current throughout society.

These developments have not been greeted with universal applause. This reaction is most common, Veblen holds, among the well-to-do, but it is society-wide. There is a recrudescence of animistic beliefs in magic and make-believe, a "back to nature" movement and desire for "the simple life" and relief from the "grind" of everyday life. And there is also, Veblen notes, the increasing popularity of the "vacation."

> Growing recourse to vacations should be a passably conclusive evidence to the effect that neither the manner of life enforced by the machine system, nor the occupations of those who are in close contact with the technology and its due habits of thought, can be "natural" to the common run of civilized mankind.[57]

It has become a question whether mankind can survive the machine.

The advent of the machine has changed the industrial and business situations. Mechanization has affected chiefly the industries with large output, meaning those with large plants and equipment – far too large and costly to be owned or managed by the craftsman or his successors. Nor can they be effectively managed by their owners – a fact that has become more apparent as the scale of industry has risen. The separation between the owners and the workers has grown very wide. Workers have become essentially attendants on the machines, while the owners concentrate on pecuniary profits. As Veblen points out, ownership of the machinery that produces the goods has been taken to mean that the owners are productive, and so that the output of industry is pecuniary profit for the owners rather than the creation of serviceable goods for the community. What matters is profitability.[58] Business administration is designed to increase profits which can often be done by practices that exploit the community. Indeed, it is the aim of the owners to seize the usufruct of the Industrial Arts, leaving the community to fend for itself as may be.

The Theory of Social Evolution

Veblen's theory of social change is more complex than his critics have recognized. One must bear in mind that Veblen is a Darwinian. As he understands Darwinian theory, not only is human biology to be accounted for in evolutionary terms, but human psychology and human culture must also be the products of evolutionary change. Biologically, Veblen believes that there has been little change in human physiology since the neolithic, but there has been dramatic change in human culture. This requires, as Veblen sees it, that the evolutionary process must apply to culture, and more specifically to institutions which are, for Veblen, the key elements of culture.[59] But for Veblen, institutions are habits; they are habits that have spread through the society, have been judged right and good by the society, and have become entrenched in the members of the society. These institutions/ habits are parts of human nature. The institutions of a society are not only objective factors with which the members must deal, they are also parts of the psychic structure of the members. Social evolution must therefore account for institutions that transcend any given member but which are also parts of the human nature of the individual members. The fixed character of the instincts does not mean that human nature has not changed since the neolithic; it has changed dramatically since human habits have changed.

It follows from this position that human traits are products of social evolution. Traits such as honesty, truthfulness, ferocity, and greed must be the results of processes of habituation that are caused by changes in the environment, natural and social. Veblen needs societies whose cultures enforce the creation of these traits. The savage society, as Veblen sees it, enforces a discipline upon its members that produces an amiable set of traits, while the culture of barbaric society produces predatory traits. But some of the goals that Veblen finds men pursuing are in such flat out contradiction to the instincts that he needs to find a way to introduce alternative goals. Hence contamination. The combination of the pure instincts, contamination, and habituation gives Veblen the flexibility he needed to provide an evolutionary account of the human social evolution.

In developing his theory, Veblen took advantage of an existing theory of human development in terms of the stages of savagery, barbarism, and civilization. As lately noted, this is a traditional scheme that dates from classical antiquity but was still widely employed in Veblen's time, but he altered the scheme to fit his needs. Veblen claimed that his description of the stages, particularly that of savagery, was based on the findings of historians, anthropologists, and archaeologists, and in his most considered presentation of his theory – *The Instinct of Workmanship* – he cites some of the authorities he used. But the anthropological literature he used was far from being adequate by the standards of 1914. Veblen himself lamented the absence of ethnographic literature on savagery, and so supplemented his account with certain psychological characteristics of modern populations that he claimed were survivals from savagery.

Assuming that social evolution has occurred as Veblen describes it, what is the theory that accounts for it? In the preface to *The Instinct of Workmanship*, Veblen wrote:

> The following essay attempts an analysis of such correlation as is visible between industrial use and wont and the other institutional facts that go to make up any given phase of civilization. It is assumed that in the growth of culture, as in its current maintenance, the facts of technological use and wont are fundamental and definitive, in the sense that they underlie and condition the scope and method of civilization in other than the technological respect, but not in such a sense as to preclude or overlook the degree in which the other conventions of any given civilization in their turn react on the state of the industrial arts.[60]

Veblen is not a technological determinist; he admits that other aspects of the culture affect its development. But it is clear that for him the Industrial Arts are the dominant factor in cultural change. It should be borne in mind that the Industrial Arts as Veblen understands them include the sciences.

The origin of the savage culture is unknown; presumably it drew from the pre-savage society about which Veblen thinks we know so little that nothing much can be said. When the evolutionary process comes into view, it is clear in savagery itself and in the transitions to the later stages. Change within savagery has two major components. The first is the advance of the Industrial Arts which led to the increasing adequacy of the food quest and the growth of population. As noted above, this advance was particularly dramatic in agriculture, even though (or because) the culture of plants and animals was heavily influenced by animism. So dramatic was this achievement in agriculture that by the end of the savage era, these societies were accumulating substantial surpluses of goods. The second component is borrowing. According to Veblen, much of the success of the savage culture is due to its acquisition of domesticated plants and animals, which Veblen holds were borrowed from outside. As Veblen describes this, the new elements seem to have come largely detached from the cultural fringe they had in their original cultures and were therefore easily assimilated. Veblen attributes great importance to borrowing and devotes several pages to its discussion.[61]

How then did the transition from savagery to barbarism come about? This is the most difficult transition that Veblen has to explain. The change to barbarism involves the beginnings of warfare and the introduction of ownership, neither of which existed in savagery. As he comments:

> The temper of the people bred in the ways of the simpler plan of hand-to-mouth and common interest does not readily lend itself to such an institutional innovation, even though the self-regarding impulses of particular members of the community may set in such a direction as would give the alleged result.[62]

Veblen holds that there are three possible routes from savagery to barbarism. The first is religious. Savage societies, Veblen says, always contain shaman or sorcerers who claim to be in touch with the immaterial agents that constitute such an important part of savage animism. When savage society reaches the point where it is producing surpluses, the shaman can claim that the success of the society is due to the blessings of the preternatural agents, and that a continuation of these favors requires payments in the forms of offering, sacrifices, rituals, etc. By such means the shaman can establish a social order with the preternatural agents at the top and themselves as the servants and interpreters of these gods and so as the *de facto* rulers of the society. The society described in the early books of the Old Testament is a good example of such a barbarous society.

The second route from savagery to barbarism lies through a pastoral society. Such a society is based upon the herding of cattle or sheep. These animals are "speechless others" whose care is the chief concern of the society. But in time, these animals will exhaust any range, which means that the society must be a mobile society, constantly acquiring new ranges to replace the exhausted ones. Inevitably, this leads to war with those whose lands are desired so that the society must be a military one, constantly prepared for battle. Moreover, cattle and sheep are wealth in such a society, so it must be prepared for defense against sudden and unexpected attacks. Such a society, Veblen holds, will exhibit all the characteristics of barbarism: a military organization of society, intermittent warfare, a warrior class, a warrior-chief, a subservient population, patriarchal family, monotheistic theology, subordination of women, etc. However, Veblen holds that there is no evidence that a pastoral society has ever existed in Europe, so this route from savagery to barbarism is only of theoretical interest so far as European social evolution is concerned.[63]

The third route from savagery to barbarism is clearly the one that Veblen prefers. He holds that the existence of surpluses is sufficient to lead some savage societies to launch raids against others for the purpose of seizing their surpluses. Once raiding begins, every community must organize itself for defense. The result is a general militarization of savage society, but for defense. But whether in retaliation or in imitation, some of the savage communities, once organized for combat, adopt raiding practices themselves. By definition, raids carried out to seize the surpluses of another community result, if successful, in booty which serves as badges of honor for the captors. He who acquires the most booty acquires the highest honors. The results are (1) the conversion of booty into property; (2) the emergence of the concept of ownership in severalty; (3) the stratification of the society by honor gained in combat and by property signifying the honor of the owner; (4) rivalry of the warriors for the highest honors. Such rivalry promotes emulation and dissolves the cohesion of the community; (5) the high degree of animism of barbarian society shows in the conversion of the heavens to a monarchy ruled by a war-god in imitation of the emerging social structure of the barbaric society emerging on earth.

This explanation does not compute. Given the peaceful character of savage society and the dominance of the common interest, Veblen needs to explain how raiding begins – that is, how war comes about. In the following passage he tries:

> With the accumulation of wealth … there comes about the inducement to aggression, predation … such aggression is an easy matter in the common run of lower cultures, since relations are habitually strained between the savage and barbarian communities. There is commonly a state of estrangement between them amounting to a constructive feud, though the feud is apt to lie dormant under a *modus vivendi* so long as there is no adequate inducement to open hostilities, in the way of booty. Given a sufficiently wealthy enemy who is sufficiently ill prepared for hostilities to afford a fighting chance of taking over this wealth by way of booty or tribute, with no obvious chance of due reprisals, and the opening of hostilities will commonly arrange itself. The communities mutually concerned so pass from the more or less precarious peaceful customs and animus common to the indigent lower cultures, to a more or less habitual attitude of predatory exploit.[64]

But this evades the issue. The issue is not war between savage and barbaric communities, but war between savage communities. The problem is how peaceful communities are led to start attacking each other. Veblen assumes here that the possibility of booty is sufficient cause for war among savages. To make this plausible, Veblen says that the peace of savagery is "precarious," needing only a slight inducement to morph into war. There is nothing in his other descriptions of savagery to suggest that there is anything precarious about their peaceableness; he is compromising his usual description to make this transition to barbarism more plausible. He is here claiming that the lure of booty is sufficient motivation for aggression among his savages who are not supposed to be so motivated.

Veblen solves his problem by fudging it. He says, "Whether property provokes to predation or predation initiates ownership, the situation that results in early phases of the pecuniary culture is much the same." And he says, "The causal relation in which this situation stands to the advance in workmanship is also much the same."[65] That causal relation has two parts.

> The increase in industrial efficiency due to a sufficient advance in the industrial arts gives rise to the ownership of property and to pecuniary appreciations of men and things, occupations and products, habits, customs, usages, observances, services and goods. At the same time, since predation and warlike exploit are intimately associated with the facts of ownership through its early history (perhaps throughout its history), there results a marked accentuation of the self-regarding sentiments; with the economically important consequence that self-interest replaces the common good in men's ideals and aspirations.[66]

So it appears that surpluses cause ownership. But even Veblen does not believe that, as is clear from his claim that mastery (of booty) evolves into ownership.[67] The situation therefore appears to be that the advance of the Industrial Arts creates surpluses of goods; the existence of these surpluses is sufficient to induce one community to attack another in order to seize its goods as booty. This assumes a latent greed on the part of savages that becomes manifest once temptation offers. How this latent greed is to be accounted for Veblen does not explain.

The appearance of war and ownership opens the way for invidious comparisons among the members of the society and so generates emulation, thus destroying the cohesion of the group. The way is thus prepared for a competitive society where what is at stake is honor, i.e., prestige or esteem of the rivals, and wealth.

But there is something deeper going on here. Veblen's Darwinism requires him to show how human traits have evolved, and the theory described above is supposed to do that. But it will not have escaped the reader that the traits Veblen attributes to savages are a very benevolent lot. Not only are the goals of the savage's instincts admirable but the savage's habits are benign. Veblen's savage may be indolent and superstitious, but all in all he is a jolly good fellow. Alas, human beings also have malevolent traits, so Veblen needs to account for them. He segregates them into a different stage – barbarism – but segregation is not enough; he has to show how the bad guys evolved from the good guys. In other words, he has the problem of evil. As a Christian might formulate it: if God is good and God made the world, why is the world so evil? For Veblen this becomes, if savages are such good folk, how have they evolved into evil barbarians? The Christians solved their problem by blaming Eve, but that won't do for Veblen; he likes women too much. The result is that he ends up saying, it just happened.

But look again at this evolutionary scheme. The basic characteristics Veblen attributes to all human beings are those of savagery. And savages are good people, shiftless perhaps, but truthful, devoted to the common good, striving to enhance the life process, curious, and thoughtful. In Veblen's scheme, this is the fundamental character of human beings. By locating all the evils in the subsequent stage of barbarism, which is too short for natural selection to operate, he makes the evils less entrenched in human nature than the instincts of savagery. He can then account for them as the result of contamination of those instincts. It is therefore possible to hold that men can be freed from the grip of contamination and restored to their natural state of peace and amity. So all the evils of war, ownership, emulation, and selfishness are ephemeral, and virtue may triumph some day. Veblen is not usually thought of as a moralist, and his pose of objectivity and impartiality has led to his being seen as a skeptic. But his reaction to the Great War shows a very different man – one deeply concerned with the human life process. That is not a change from his earlier views. As his theory of social evolution shows, he always took human beings to be basically good, but the victims of delusions they themselves had created, and he never gave up hope that they might regain their sanity.

The weakness of this theory is its failure to ground what Veblen takes to be evil, and this is in part due to the inadequacy of Veblen's psychology. What is fundamental in his psychology is the instincts; everything else in the psychic structure is habit. To make his men realistic he would have to ground his malevolent characteristics in instincts. He apparently saw no way to do this within the evolutionary framework he had adopted, since those characteristics he regards as evil are those he regards as threatening the life process, i.e., as threatening human survival. The result is that man, as Veblen sees him, lacks the complexity that one would have thought the "new psychology" could provide. For example, he could have modified the parental bent to have included a strong dose of self-interest, and then held that the conditions of savage life required the subordination of all interests to that of group survival. Then as conditions improved with the creation of surpluses, self-interest could emerge in sufficient strength to incite raiding. This would have created a more realistic picture of human nature and a more plausible scheme of human evolution. So what is the role of the Industrial Arts in this transition? Veblen says, "The manner in which increasing technological mastery has led over from the savage plan of free workmanship to the barbarian system of industry under pecuniary control is perhaps a hazardous topic of speculation."[68]

But despite the hazards Veblen has a proposal. He points to the introduction of the "round about" processes of production.

> Hereby the technological basis for a pecuniary control of industry is given, in that the "round about" process of production yields an income above the subsistence of the workmen engaged in it, and the material equipment or appliances (crops, fruit-trees, live stock, mechanical contrivances) binds this round about process of industry to a more or less determinate place and routine, such as to make surveillance and control possible.[69]

The result is that the ownership of the material means of production in this situation carries with it the usufruct of the community's Industrial Arts.[70] But this proposal assumes the institution of ownership already in place; it does not explain how ownership came to be.

High Barbarism is a society organized for war, stratified on the basis of prowess, of which property is an indicator and esteem is the reward, ruled by a war-chief, with interpersonal relations of dominance or subservience, depending on one's social position, and dedicated to self-interest. It will also support a monotheistic religion with a warrior god and a hierarchically organized church, and patriarchal families. The course of the development of High Barbarism is fairly clear: intermittent war, constant struggles for wealth and honor, and acquisition of property by whatever means are available. Such a society is subject to constant turmoil from within as individuals compete for power and wealth, and from without due to war with other organized groups. The Industrial Arts grow by serving the needs of the warriors first and those of the common people last. The members of the community come to seek their own interests rather than those of the group. The parental bent is not totally suppressed.

> The sentiment of common interest, itself in good part a diffuse working-out of the parental instinct, comes at the best to converge on the glory of the flag instead of the fullness of life of the community at large, or more commonly it comes to be centered in loyalty, that is to say in subservience, to the common war-chief and his dynastic successors.[71]

Weapons, armaments, fortification, etc., absorb the workman's finest skills. But as Veblen notes, High Barbarism is not a stable social system. War and the Industrial Arts have led to a considerable amount of property in the hands of the barbarians, particularly in the hands of the upper classes. But in such a society the security and the heritability of property are both at risk.

High Barbarism, Veblen says, contained two principles regarding ownership that conflicted. On the one hand, it affirmed ownership by seizure. On the other, it affirmed ownership by prescriptive right. Where the former principle dominates, High Barbarism continues on its feudal course. Where the latter principle dominates, High Barbarism morphs into quasi-peaceable barbarism, characterized by secure prescriptive tenure and a settled nobility, which in turn becomes a commercialized industrial situation. From the standpoint of the owners, the advantage lies with the quasi-peaceable version. Tenure by seizure is risky; what is gained by war can be lost by war and inheritability is uncertain. A situation in which ownership is by prescriptive right, enforced by the community, is much safer for the owners and their heirs.

Europe chose the quasi-peaceable alternative, which means that Europe's exposure to High Barbarism was of limited duration and intensity. In due course, quasi-peaceable barbarism in Europe evolved into capitalism in the sixteenth and seventeenth centuries, but this line of development was aborted by wars. As lately noted, the handicraft system achieved its full development in England. Here again borrowing played an essential role; England borrowed the Continental technology. But equally important was the extended peace which made possible the cumulative growth of the Industrial Arts, the exploitation of the natural resources which were copious, and a sufficiently large population.

According to Veblen, the transition from High Barbarism to the quasi-peaceable form of barbarism was the result of the determination of the owners to secure their property for themselves and their heirs. It meant that the battlefield was exchanged for the marketplace. The protagonists now were craftsmen rather than warriors and the goal was no longer slaughter but wealth – that is, the acquisition of property. Ownership now became the key to success, position, prestige, and power. And ownership itself underwent a refinement with the introduction of prices. Veblen called prices an "impersonal imputation" of value, but it was one that gave precision to the value of what was owned. Invidious comparisons between individuals could now be exactly calculated, the amount of one's wealth could now be exactly measured, and pecuniary measurement could be extended to people, land, goods, occupations, and almost anything else.

Veblen claims that the craftsman was the central figure of the economy as quasi-peaceable barbarism developed into the handicraft era. The craftsman usually owned his own shop, made or bought his own equipment and tools, the raw materials upon which he worked, and the goods he made. He was also a trader who sold his goods in the local market. He might work alone, but usually he had an apprentice or two to whom he taught the mysteries of the craft in return for their work, usually for a term of seven years. If his volume was sufficient, he might also employ other craftsmen who for one reason or another did not have their own shops. But craft shops were usually small; this was an individual operation, and a craftsman's reputation depended upon his skill. It is hardly surprising that under these conditions the Instinct of Workmanship re-emerged in a strong form, but it was an instinct contaminated by ownership.

In the early days of the handicraft system, the test of a craftsman was the serviceability of the goods he made. But as time went on, the test became increasingly the prices he could command for his products. It was after all the proceeds of his sales upon which he lived and which covered the costs of his enterprise. And since his income depended upon both the quantity and the quality of his wares, he worked hard, and work became a meritorious characteristic for these men. In due course, these men became the middle class of their society, so the class structure was differentiated into upper, middle, and lower, and the craftsman became the avatar of the virtuous citizen.[72]

In the handicraft era, the craft shop became the basic industrial unit of the time. The result was an economy that consisted of many independent relatively small units which operated in a competitive system. What determined this structure was the Industrial Arts of the era. The craftsman worked chiefly with hand-held or hand-operated equipment. The only power source available beyond human or animal muscle was water power, but that required a location where nature provided a drop in the water level. Such sites were few and their possession was contested. The result was that the Industrial Arts largely determined the form of the society.

The handicraft system fell victim to its own success. As lately noted, the craftsman was both a producer and a trader. In the early days of the system, his role as producer was the more important function, and the emphasis was on his skill. But over time, the emphasis shifted, and his salesmanship began to dominate his workmanship. It was the advance of technology that brought that about. The Industrial Revolution involved the creation of machines that were at first seen as labor-saving devices. But with the invention of the Watt steam engine, a source of power became available that could drive larger and heavier machines than had been used hitherto. And in the early years of the nineteenth century, a group of English toolmakers, centered around Henry Maudsley, created the power tools that could shape hard metals with a precision previously unknown. The result was that new machines, larger and heavier than any in use before, and running at speeds that no crafts methods could match, came into use. But these new machines were far too costly for even the master craftsman to afford, with the result that a new method of funding production was required.

Firms in the earlier years of the handicraft era were usually small-scale companies operated by their owner or owners. Craft shops, as noted, were both producers and sellers, but in due course there occurred a division of labor in which the work of production developed into industry and the work of seller developed into business. Furthermore, the scale of production changed as round-about processes utilizing the new machines became increasingly important. There was nothing new about round-about processes, but, since even the master craftsmen could not afford the new machinery, the way was open for men with substantial money to buy the new machines, whether they were actually involved in their use or merely investors for profit. Groups of these men joined together and organized corporations to handle this new business. So capitalism entered the scene. Those who owned the technology of production could now regulate the use of their property, including what it produced.

> Since in the received theories the accumulated "productive goods" are conceived to be the most consequential factor in industry, and therefore in the community's material welfare and in the fortunes of individuals, it logically follows that the discretionary ownership of them has come to be accounted the most important relation in which men may stand to the production of wealth and to the community's livelihood; and the pecuniary transactions whereby this ownership is arranged, manipulated and redistributed are held to be industrially the most productive of all human activities.[73]

This doctrine of "pecuniary productivity" was a creation of the nineteenth century, and it led to such curious results as the rating of any men who acquired substantial wealth "as benefactors of the community at large and as exemplars of social virtue."[74]

The theory of natural rights was the ruling ideology of the late handicraft era. It became the foundation of political doctrines of the time, and was taken as foundational in American law; it continued in force long after the handicraft era had passed into history. But natural rights also dominated the economics of the era with the belief that God had endowed men with a natural right to property. Adam Smith was a firm believer in the theory of natural rights.

Veblen holds that the doctrine of natural liberty was formed to guarantee the craftsman's "right of purchase and sale, touching both work and its product, the right freely to hold and dispose of property."[75] But then came capitalism.

When this change had taken passably full effect the workman was already secure in his civil (natural) right to dispose of his workmanship as he thought best, but the circumstances of his employment under capitalist management made it impossible for him in fact to dispose of his work except to these employers, and very much on their terms, or to dispose of his person except where the exigencies of their business might require him. And the similarly inalienable right of ownership, which had similarly emerged from use and wont under the handicraft system, but which now in effect secured the capitalist-employer in his control of the material means of industry – this sacred right of property now barred out any move that might be designed to reinstate the workman in his effective freedom to work as he chose or dispose of his person and product as he saw fit.[76]

The system of natural liberty, designed to safeguard the rights of the craftsman of the handicraft era became, under capitalism, a system that guaranteed the powers of the owners.

It seems unnecessary to belabor the influence of science and technology on twentieth-century culture; what has already been said should be more than sufficient for that. We may turn then to Veblen's theory of the role of technology in cultural change. Veblen is not a technological determinist; his thesis is actually very modest. He regards the Industrial Arts as the most important causal factor in cultural change but not as the only one. So far as savagery, the handicraft era, and the twentieth century are concerned, Veblen has made his point. The problem for him is barbarism. Nevertheless, he believes that his theory accounts for the evolution of Western society into the technologically sophisticated and scientifically rationalized form it exhibits today (1914).

And now Veblen finds himself facing a new problem: since the basic character of human beings is that created in savagery, can his savages survive the machine? The fact that the issue is posed this way shows that for Veblen it is savagery that has set the fundamental parameters of human nature. And that nature, he believes, requires something more than cold logic and mechanical routine.

The ideal man, and the ideal of human life, even in the apprehension of those who most rejoice in the advances of science, is neither the finikin skeptic in the laboratory nor the animated slide-rule. The quest of science is relatively new. It is a cultural factor not comprised, in anything like its modern force, among the circumstances whose selective action in the far past has given to the race the human nature which it now has. The race reached this human plane with little of this searching knowledge, and throughout the greater part of its life-history on the human plane, it has been accustomed to make its higher generalizations and to formulate its larger principles of life in other terms than those of passionless matter-of-fact.[77]

The European people are best suited to the life of savagery under the guidance of the parental bent, idle curiosity, and the instinct of workmanship. Given that, it is a real question whether men so constituted can survive and flourish under a cultural regime of a very different sort, such as that being created by the discipline of the machine. Those, Veblen says, who are most increasingly exposed to the discipline of the machine often "breakdown," or "fall into premature decay."[78] So Veblen remarks, "The limits of tolerance native to the race, physically and spiritually, is short of that unmitigated materialism and unremitting mechanical routine to which the machine technology incontinently drives."[79]

The result, Veblen holds, is that a full adaptation to the requirements of the machine may not be possible. It is, he says, "Doubtful whether anything more than imperfect approximation to the logic of the machine process can be achieved, through any length of training, by the people among whom the greatest advance in that direction has already been made."[80]

What has brought this situation to a crisis point is the Great War. Veblen regarded the War as an unmitigated disaster and one that showed that the prevailing point of view was seriously wrong. There had to be a reconstruction. And he thought there could be. He noted that most peoples that have a long history have from time to time faced a situation where their survival was dependent on their revision of their institutional structure – i.e., their habits of belief. Most have chosen blindly, and some unsuccessfully – in some cases with happy outcomes and in other cases with "collapse or decay."[81] Such a choice, he says, now confronts the peoples of Christendom. How they will make it remains to be seen, but Veblen remarks:

> History records more frequent and more spectacular instances of the triumph of imbecile institutions over life and culture than of peoples who have by force of instinctive insight saved themselves out of desperately precarious institutional situations, such, for instance, as now faces the people of Christendom.[82]

Veblen's theory of social evolution is thus more than an historical and anthropological account of how we got to where we are. It is that, but it is also the story of how basically benevolent humans have sought to overcome their own demons and achieve a satisfactory culture. There is a deep irony in the fact that it is man's crowning technological achievements that now threaten his existence.

Notes

1 Lewis H. Morgan, *Ancient Society* (Chicago: Charles Kerr and Co., 1960), 37–38.
2 Thorstein Veblen, *The Instinct of Workmanship And the State of the Industrial Arts* (New York: The Viking Press, 1946), 130n1.
3 Veblen, *Instinct of Workmanship*, 131n1.

4 Charles Mann, *1491: New Revelations of the Americas Before Columbus* (New York: Knopf, 2005) and *1493: Uncovering the New World Columbus Created* (New York: Knopf, 2011).
5 Veblen, *Instinct of Workmanship*, 71.
6 Veblen, *Instinct of Workmanship*, 75.
7 Veblen, *Instinct of Workmanship*, 97.
8 Veblen, *Instinct of Workmanship*, 90.
9 Thorstein Veblen, "The Place of Science in Modern Civilization," *The Place of Science in Modern Civilization*, intro. Warren J. Samuels (New York: Cosimo, 2007), 25.
10 Thorstein Veblen, *The Theory of the Leisure Class: An Economic Study of Institutions* (New York: The Modern Library, 1934), 224.
11 Veblen, *Leisure Class*, 220.
12 A. I. Hallowell, *Culture and Experience* (Philadelphia: University of Pennsylvania Press, 1955), 14–15.
13 Hallowell, *Culture and Experience*, 19.
14 Veblen, *Instinct of Workmanship*, Chap. 3.
15 Veblen, *Instinct of Workmanship*, 156–157.
16 Veblen, *Instinct of Workmanship*, 160–161.
17 Veblen, *Instinct of Workmanship*, 161.
18 Thorstein Veblen, "The Beginnings of Ownership," in *Essays in our Changing Order*, ed. Leon Ardzrooni (New York: The Viking Press, 1945), 32–49.
19 Veblen, "Ownership" in *Changing Order*, 39–40.
20 Veblen, "Ownership" in *Changing Order*, 40–41.
21 Veblen, "Ownership" in *Changing Order*, 41.
22 Veblen, "Ownership" in *Changing Order*, 47.
23 Veblen, "Ownership" in *Changing Order*, 48.
24 Veblen, *Instinct of Workmanship*, 199–200.
25 Veblen, *Place of Science*, 22–23.
26 Veblen, *Leisure Class*, 225.
27 Veblen, *Leisure Class*, 225.
28 Veblen, *Instinct of Workmanship*, 170.
29 Veblen, *Instinct of Workmanship*, 167.
30 Veblen, *Instinct of Workmanship*, 168.
31 Veblen, *Instinct of Workmanship*, 180–184.
32 Veblen, *Instinct of Workmanship*, 202.
33 Veblen, *Instinct of Workmanship*, 276.
34 Veblen, *Instinct of Workmanship*, 204.
35 Veblen, *Instinct of Workmanship*, 270.
36 Veblen, *Instinct of Workmanship*, 273.
37 Veblen, *Instinct of Workmanship*, 267.
38 Veblen, *Instinct of Workmanship*, 266.
39 Veblen, *Place of Science*, 14–15.
40 Veblen, *Instinct of Workmanship*, 340.
41 Veblen, *Instinct of Workmanship*, 283–290.
42 Veblen, *Instinct of Workmanship*, 340–344.
43 Veblen, *Instinct of Workmanship*, 309.
44 Veblen, *Instinct of Workmanship*, 307.
45 Veblen, *Instinct of Workmanship*, 310.
46 Veblen, *Instinct of Workmanship*, 307.
47 Veblen, *Instinct of Workmanship*, 323.
48 Veblen, *Place of Science*, 17–18.
49 Veblen, *Place of Science*, 16–17.
50 Veblen, *Place of Science*, 2.

51 Veblen, *Place of Science*, 27–28.
52 Veblen, *Instinct of Workmanship*, 311.
53 Veblen, *Instinct of Workmanship*, 311.
54 Veblen, *Instinct of Workmanship*, 311–313.
55 Veblen, *Instinct of Workmanship*, 316.
56 Veblen, *Instinct of Workmanship*, 313.
57 Veblen, *Instinct of Workmanship*, 319–320.
58 Veblen, *Instinct of Workmanship*, 352.
59 Geoffrey Hodgson, *The Evolution of Institutional Economics* (London: Routledge, 2004), 134–142.
60 Veblen, *Instinct of Workmanship*, vii.
61 Veblen, *Instinct of Workmanship*, 133–137.
62 Veblen, *Instinct of Workmanship*, 155.
63 Veblen, *Instinct of Workmanship*, 231.
64 Veblen, *Instinct of Workmanship*, 156–157.
65 Veblen, *Instinct of Workmanship*, 160.
66 Veblen, *Instinct of Workmanship*, 160.
67 Veblen, *Instinct of Workmanship*, 158–163.
68 Veblen, *Instinct of Workmanship*, 149.
69 Veblen, *Instinct of Workmanship*, 150.
70 Veblen, *Instinct of Workmanship*, 151.
71 Veblen, *Instinct of Workmanship*, 161.
72 Veblen, *Instinct of Workmanship*, 184.
73 Veblen, *Instinct of Workmanship*, 208.
74 Veblen, *Instinct of Workmanship*, 217.
75 Veblen, *Instinct of Workmanship*, 289.
76 Veblen, *Instinct of Workmanship*, 290.
77 Veblen, *Place of Science*, 30–31.
78 Veblen, *Instinct of Workmanship*, 320.
79 Veblen, *Instinct of Workmanship*, 321.
80 Veblen, *Instinct of Workmanship*, 322.
81 Veblen, *Instinct of Workmanship*, 24.
82 Veblen, *Instinct of Workmanship*, 25.

4

VEBLEN'S NEW THEORY

The Theory of the Leisure Class

Veblen's theory of social evolution underlies his efforts to create a new theory of economics. Although he was formulating these ideas at least as early as 1892, his first major presentation of them came in 1899 when he published *The Theory of the Leisure Class*. One should note the word "theory" in the title. Veblen saw himself as an economic theorist, and this book is a work of economic theory. It is, in fact, a model of what he thought a Darwinian theory should be. Accordingly, he turned first to a genetic account of the Leisure Class. As described above, Veblen holds that the earliest stage of culture of which we know anything is savagery; human beings existed before that, but we know little about them beyond the fact that they did exist. Veblen does not consider them sufficiently developed to merit being classed as cultured; that honor is given to savagery. The savage state of humanity is characterized by poverty and peace. The food quest absorbs the energies of the people, and given the primitive character of their tools, it took all of their time.

But savage society was not static. The dynamic factor in this situation was technology. As tools improved the food supply became more adequate and population expanded. In due course, the point was reached where the technology was sufficient to create surpluses. The existence of surpluses made them a target for raids and seizure. It also allowed some part of the community to live without participating in the food quest or other useful labor. Emulation now found a fertile field. Veblen gives a very careful explanation of the origin of emulation:

> As a matter of selective necessity, man is an agent. He is, in his own appre-
> hension, a center of unfolding impulsive activity – "teleological" activity. He

is an agent seeking in every act the accomplishment of some concrete, objective, impersonal end. By force of his being such an agent he is possessed of a taste for effective work, and a distaste for futile effort. He has a sense of the merit of serviceability or efficiency and of the demerit of futility, waste or incapacity. This aptitude or propensity may be called the instinct of workmanship. Wherever the circumstances or traditions of life lead to an habitual comparison of one person with another in point of efficiency, the instinct of workmanship works out in an emulative or invidious comparison of persons.[1]

Note that Veblen holds emulation to be a perversion of the instinct of workmanship. It is therefore not as primordial as the instinct of workmanship.

Once raiding begins, every community must prepare for combat. Superior tool-making technology is also superior weapon-making technology. Whether defensive or offensive, warfare makes its appearance, and with it barbarism begins. Prowess in combat now becomes the most honorable of achievements. As Veblen had argued in his earlier articles, the concept of property emerged to embrace booty taken as trophies in war. With ownership came the institution of marriage by capture and the beginnings of the patriarchal family. There emerged a division of labor between those who fought and those who did the useful work of food preparation and household drudgery. Honor attached to the warriors, dishonor to the drudges – chiefly women, children, and the old. In this situation, in the transition from savagery to barbarism, the Leisure Class emerged.

In the predatory stage of barbarism, property served as a sign of the prowess of the warrior. When population expands and life becomes more sedentary, opportunities for the demonstration of prowess in combat diminish, and the acquisition of property becomes a sign of prowess in its own right. Military prowess still commands high honor, but for most the scene of combat becomes the marketplace rather than the battlefield.

Classical economics holds that the acquisition of property is for the purpose of consumption. But Veblen says that this does not fit the facts. Property is sought and accumulated far beyond any conceivable use for consumption. True, for the very poor for whom subsistence is an issue, property may be sought only for consumption, but that explanation will not work once the standard of living rises above the subsistence level.

The motive that lies at the root of ownership is emulation; and the same motive of emulation continues active in the further development of the institution to which it has given rise and in the development of all those features of the social structure which this institution of ownership touches. The possession of wealth confers honor; it is an invidious distinction. Nothing equally cogent can be said for the consumption of goods, nor for any other conceivable incentive to acquisition, and especially not for any incentive to the accumulation of wealth.[2]

Under these circumstances, one's social standing depends on one's property.

Its possession in some amount becomes necessary in order to any reputable standing in the community. It becomes indispensable to acquire and accumulate property in order to retain one's good name. Not only does one's social repute require property, but so does one's self-esteem, "since the usual basis of self-respect is the respect accorded by one's neighbors."[3]

This is a major theoretical point for Veblen. The motive behind the acquisitive behavior of people in Western society is not just the desire for wealth; it is the desire for esteem, including self-esteem. Veblen had argued this point in his earlier articles, particularly in "Some Neglected Points in the Theory of Socialism";[4] now he attempts to prove his case. Accordingly, he proposes to substitute esteem for wealth as that the maximization of which is the objective of economic behavior. This change, if made, would be a fundamental alteration of classical economics. To make his case, Veblen needs to show what difference the substitution would make, and to present evidence for why his theory is better than the classical alternative.

Suppose one accepts Veblen's proposal: what follows? What behavior would one expect from the upper class on the classical theory? If they are money motivated, then it should be the accumulation of money that characterizes them. But if Veblen's proposal is accepted, the upper class will behave differently. They will still seek wealth, for wealth itself is honorific, but they will want above all to be esteemed by others. For that to happen, the wealth must be displayed so that others not only can see it but cannot avoid seeing. That is, it must be conspicuously displayed. And given the difference in honor accorded to occupations as Veblen has described them, they will seek to avoid all forms of dishonorable work – useful work which is thought to be "ceremonially unclean."[5] Hence the upper class becomes a Leisure Class.

But there is a problem: to live a life of leisure is one thing, to be esteemed for living a life of leisure is another. To be esteemed by others, one's leisure must be put in evidence. How is this to be done? One way is to acquire characteristics the acquisition of which are well known to require extended time and effort but which are of no practical use. Such for instance is knowledge of the

dead languages and the occult sciences; of correct spelling; of syntax and prosody; of the various forms of domestic music and other household arts; of the latest proprieties of dress, furniture and equipage; of games, sports, and fancy-bred animals, such as dogs and race-horses.[6]

A particularly valuable acquisition for this purpose is manners. This is a class of behaviors that admit of endless refinement and is a very effective sign of misspent time.

> A knowledge of good form is *prima fascie* evidence that that portion of the well-bred person's life which is not spent under the observation of the spectator has been worthily spent in acquiring accomplishments that are of no lucrative effect.[7]

Or one can resort to vicarious leisure. Most commonly, those who serve this purpose are one's wife and children, whose abstention from useful work was in Veblen's time almost mandatory in the middle and upper classes. It was less common to find others enjoying leisure at one's expense, but aged parents and wastrel relatives were not uncommon.

A further way of demonstrating one's freedom from toil is the employment of servants. One is clearly not indulging in useful activity if one has hired someone else to do the work. Depending on the sort of investment one wishes to make, there are various types of servants for any number of tasks, and of course the more employees one has, the less one will be thought to do the work oneself. A further refinement is achieved by employing personal servants – those whose function it is to wait upon the person of the master or mistress, such as valets and maids. If one can afford servants to care for one's wardrobe, style one's hair, or cut one's toenails, one is surely opulent. Or one can devote oneself to what may be called "the Leisure Class occupations" – war, governance, sports, and devout observances. These employments share the virtues of being honorific, paying little or nothing (in Veblen's time, sports generally did not pay), and requiring much effort spent in futile endeavors.

It is clear that Veblen's Leisure Class man works very hard at doing nothing. Veblen does not take "leisure" to mean idleness; he takes it to signal abstention from useful work. The members of the Leisure Class are in fact very busy. If they are not involved in one or more of the employments lately noted, they will be involved in "calls, drives, clubs, sewing circles, sports, charity organizations, and other like social functions."[8] So long as the activity is conspicuous, useless, time-consuming, and unremunerative, it qualifies as leisure under the Veblen system of classification.

With the growth of population and the increasing mobility of individuals, conspicuous consumption emerges as a method of displaying one's status that is superior to conspicuous leisure. Both fall under the rubric of conspicuous waste; it is just a question of which is more effective. When the spectator whose envy one wants to capture has only a fleeting exposure to one's presence, displays that are instantly recognizable become essential. This is particularly true in the urban setting, where casual contact is the rule. It is here that conspicuous consumption comes to the fore, for it takes only a glance to recognize someone's dress or house or conveyance as signifying high status. But the requirements of conspicuous consumption are severe.

For conspicuous consumption to fulfill its mission, it is essential that the Leisure Class member "consumed freely and of the best, in food, drink, narcotics, shelter, services, ornaments, apparel, weapons and accoutrements, amusements, amulets, and idols or divinities."[9] But this requires that one become a connoisseur of such things, and that requires a protracted training – hence leisure.[10] The Leisure Class man consumes copiously in a variety of ways. One such is the consumption of alcohol. Drunkenness has at times been regarded as becoming conduct for the Leisure Class man, though never for his wife. Another is to make his household a theater for the exhibition of furnishings of the most elegant sort. And of course the building in which he lives can demonstrate his pecuniary strength by its size, building materials, design, grounds, etc. His employment of servants of various sorts demonstrates his ability to pay, and the practice of putting them in liveries goes even further to advertise his wealth. And of course his wife and family must consume vicariously for him. And then there is the question of where and how to display one's choice articles. Feasts, balls, and similar entertainments are preferable because of the numbers attending, especially if one's rivals in the war for esteem are among them and can be made witnesses to one's triumph. Such Leisure Class people qualify as being of "gentle" blood – a quality which, unlike its medieval ancestor, has become the result of protracted contact with money. The lower strata of the Leisure Class contains those of less opulence, whether of gentle birth or not, and those who devote themselves to the service of their superiors.

> Modern society is stratified with the Leisure Class at the top. The result is that the members of each stratum accept as their ideal of decency the scheme of life in vogue in the next higher stratum, and bend their energies to live up to that ideal. On pain of forfeiting their good name and their self-respect in case of failure, they must conform to the accepted code, at least in appearance.[11]

The Leisure Class, as the highest class of the society, is the model for all the classes below it. In the middle class, it is not possible for the head of the household to avoid remunerative work. But

> it is by no means an uncommon spectacle to find a man applying himself to work with the utmost assiduity, in order that his wife may in due form render for him that degree of vicarious leisure which the common sense of the time demands.[12]

Middle-class wives have become a leisure subclass who loyally uphold the standards of the classes above them and impose their proprieties on their households. Even among the poor, where the iron grip of poverty requires a desperate focus on gainful employment, the wives continue to indulge in what conspicuous consumption they can. There is, Veblen says, "No class and no country that has yielded so abjectly before the pressure of physical want as to deny themselves all gratification of this higher or spiritual need."[13]

The instinct of workmanship is opposed to all forms of waste, and since this instinct is innate in all men, the flagrant examples of conspicuous waste arouse a certain amount of guilt in those who perform such actions. The result is a resort to make-believe.

> Many and intricate polite observances and social duties of a ceremonial nature are developed; many organizations are founded, with some specious object of amelioration embodied in their official style and titles; there is much coming and going, and a deal of talk, to the end that the talkers may not have occasion to reflect on what is the effectual economic value of their traffic.[14]

Such make-believe activities may lower the stress from the underlying contradiction, but they do not eliminate it even when they succeed in making it invisible to those who carry out this pantomime.

Granted that the behavior of conspicuous leisure and conspicuous consumption – i.e., conspicuous waste, and the behavior of seeking to appear to belong to the class above one's own, do follow as consequences of Veblen's thesis that what is maximized in economic activity is esteem, do they not follow also from the classical view that what is maximized is wealth? Veblen would probably agree that leisure and consumption may be consequences of the accumulation of wealth, but he would deny that classical theory can account for the conspicuous manner in which they are displayed. What is evident in these displays is their emulative character. One's riches are but dead objects until they are vivified by emulation. That is what breathes life into them and gives one the warm feeling of having outshone one's competitors. Similarly, the frenzied drive to appear to belong to a class higher than one's own is obviously behavior based on emulation. Mere desire to accumulate wealth would not lead to such behavior; conspicuous leisure and conspicuous consumption involve large expenditures of wealth – expenditures that are by definition not aimed at producing revenues for the spender. Indeed, such behavior may deplete one's assets and in extreme cases can even lead to bankruptcy. These are not behaviors that one would expect from a man whose goal in life is the acquisition of the largest possible fortune.

In any society or class, Veblen holds, there will be a certain standard of living that characterizes the members and which defines for them a "standard of decency in the amount and grade of goods consumed."[15] This standard is flexible: it has no upper bound; when increased resources become available it is easily raised. The minimum is set by the requirements of bare subsistence, below which it cannot go. There will also be a standard of expenditure considered appropriate for that class.

The standard of expenditure which commonly guides our efforts is not the average, ordinary expenditure already achieved; it is an ideal of consumption that lies just beyond our reach, or to reach which requires some strain. The motive is emulation – the stimulus of an invidious comparison which prompts us to outdo those with whom we are in the habit of classing ourselves. ...The accepted standard of expenditure in the community or in the class to which a person belongs largely determines what his standard of living will be.[16]

It does this by setting a standard of what is right and good, and by motivating its adherents to strive to achieve it "under pain of disesteem and ostracism." Accordingly, the standard of living will normally be as high as the available resources will allow.[17]

Each class of the society strives to attain the standard of living of the class next above itself. This gives the Leisure Class a special role. As the top class of the society, it sets the standard to which all other classes of the society strive to conform. How close the lower classes come to matching the standard is largely a question of resources, but they come as close as they can. Where resources are insufficient, it is common for people to skimp on the items of expenditure that are not publicly observable in order to concentrate on those that are, thus preserving the appearance of reputability if not the substance.[18] The declining birth rate (and in Veblen's time it was declining) Veblen also attributes to the requirements of conspicuous consumption. To raise a child in the manner required for "reputable maintenance" requires substantial expenditure over a protracted period, and Veblen says that this "is probably the most effectual of the Malthusian prudential checks."[19]

The standard of living is a habit, and the difficulty of departing from it is the difficulty of breaking a habit. But the tenacity of the hold of this habit is at least partly determined by a person's inherited aptitudes and will vary among people. In some cases, such as for example the habit of alcoholic consumption, the habit is quickly learned and is often nearly impossible to break. The aptitude or propensity on which such habits as the standard of living depends is emulation.

The aptitudes or propensities to which a habit of this kind is to be referred as its ground are those aptitudes whose exercise are comprised in emulation; and the propensity for emulation – for invidious comparison – is of ancient growth and is a pervading trait of human nature ... With the exception of the instinct of self-preservation, the propensity for emulation is probably the strongest and the most alert and persistent of the economic motives proper.[20]

It is the force of emulation that drives the desperate effort at social climbing and makes it so difficult to reduce one's standard of living.

Note here the status Veblen assigns to emulation. Earlier he defined it as a result of the contamination of the instinct of workmanship. Here he comes close to making it co-eval with that instinct. At this point (1899), Veblen had not worked out just how workmanship and emulation were related. On the theory that acquired characteristics are inheritable, which Veblen then held, it is not easy to see why emulation is not as fundamental as workmanship, yet for Veblen's theory to work he needs workmanship to be the more basic.

As an example of the working of the economic principles he has discussed, Veblen cites the case of scholars. By virtue of the presumed superiority and scarcity of the gifts and attainments that characterize them, they tend to be assigned to a higher class than their pecuniary assets can justify. The result is that "there is no class of the community that spends a larger portion of its substance on conspicuous waste than [they]."[21] Having fewer resources than the usual members of the Leisure Class, scholars must spend a larger percentage of their assets to meet the required standard of living.

Veblen then turns to the pecuniary canons of taste.

> Under the selective surveillance of the law of conspicuous waste there grows up a code of accredited canons of consumption, the effect of which is to hold the consumer up to a standard of expensiveness and wastefulness in his consumption of goods and in his employment of time and effort.[22]

Such canons can affect the consumer's sense of duty, sense of beauty, sense of usefulness, and the "scientific sense of truth."[23] Religious practices provide Veblen with an easy case of dutiful expenditure. Church buildings and furnishings and priestly vestments are obvious examples of wasteful expenditure. At the same time, priestly decorum and behavior are required to exhibit abstinence from useful work and avoidance of pleasure and levity. As servant of a master, the priest must serve only him. The master himself is depicted as living in opulence and power with innumerable retainers whose time is wholly spent in praising him. But Veblen stops his treatment of devout observances here with the promise he will return to them in a later chapter.

As lately noted, Veblen believes that all men share an innate sense of beauty that is evident in their "unsophisticated" judgments of beauty. But this sense can be contaminated, yielding such results as pecuniary beauty. As examples of this, Veblen cites the domestic animals – the cat, the dog, and the fast-horse. But of the animals he discusses, the cat is the least suitable since cats are often kept for utilitarian reasons. The dog however is a fine example.

> He is the filthiest of the domestic animals in his person and the nastiest in his habits. For this he makes up in a servile, fawning attitude toward his master, and a readiness to inflict damage and discomfort on all else. The dog, then, commends himself to our favor by affording play to our

propensity for mastery, and as he is also an item of expense and commonly serves no industrial purpose, he holds a well-assured place in men's regard as a thing of good repute.[24]

Veblen goes on to note the "canine monstrosities" which dog breeders have produced in the belief that they are enhancing the animals' beauty.

"The case of the fast-horse," Veblen says, "is much like that of the dog." He has no industrial use; his utility is suitability for emulative purposes; "it gratifies the owner's sense of aggression and dominance to have his own horse outstrip his neighbor's."[25] But Veblen remarks that the horse is a beautiful animal. The same contaminated pecuniary standards of beauty are applied to the judgments of beauty in persons, which Veblen demonstrated with respect to the standards of female beauty, as lately discussed.

Veblen then turns to the way in which cost enters into the rating of goods. People, he says, fall into "the habit of disapproving cheap things as being intrinsically dishonorable or unworthy because they are cheap."[26] Hence, Veblen says, the sayings "cheap and nasty" and "a cheap coat makes a cheap man."[27] Many prefer the hand-made even when the machine-made is the more serviceable. "Goods, in order to sell, must have some appreciable amount of labor spent in giving them the marks of decent expensiveness."[28] So, Veblen says, all the goods that now go to market must have some honorific marks.

Veblen remarks that the adaptation of design to the end of conspicuous waste, and the substitution of pecuniary beauty for aesthetic beauty, has been especially effective in the development of architecture.[29] He finds no public or private buildings that can claim anything more than "relative inoffensiveness." He then turns to the question of why hand-made objects are preferred to machine-made objects, despite the greater utility of the latter. As he puts it, "hand labor is a more wasteful method of production; hence the goods turned out by this method are more serviceable for the purpose of pecuniary respectability."[30] The marks of hand labor therefore become honorific. Hence, Veblen says, has arisen the "exaltation of the defective" of which Ruskin and Morris were advocates. Veblen uses the example of the Kelmscott Press to reduce the passion for the handmade to absurdities.[31]

Here and elsewhere Veblen is at pains to emphasize that consumers who are guided by the canons of conspicuous leisure, conspicuous consumption, and conspicuous waste do not perceive themselves as being so guided; rather, they seek things and activities that seem good and reputable by the standards of their community. But by whose standards, then, are these things classified as evidence of conspicuous leisure, conspicuous consumption, and conspicuous waste?

Veblen's answer is the standards provided by the instincts. As we have already discussed, it is the parental bent and the instinct of workmanship that provide these standards. The parental bent is the conscience,[32] and the instinct of work-manship is the "court of final appeal" on issues of waste.[33] Veblen is claiming that the instincts provide the standards in terms of which questions of truth and worth must be answered.

Having presented his theory of emulative economics, Veblen then turns "by way of illustration" to show in some detail how the economic principles so far set forth apply to everyday life. For this purpose, he chooses dress – particularly women's dress. Veblen has dealt with this subject before, most notably in his 1894 article "The Economic Theory of Women's Dress," and is careful not to make this simply a repetition of that article.[34]

In the early paper, Veblen carefully distinguished dress from clothing, and argues that a woman's dress serves as an index to the pecuniary strength of the "unit" she represents – for modern women, the household. Veblen laid down three principles that govern women's dress: (1) expensiveness – it must be con-spicuously more costly than the requirements of mere clothing would necessitate; (2) novelty – her dress must give evidence of having been worn only once or at most a very few times; and (3) ineptitude – it must make it obvious that the wearer is incapable of performing any useful work. In the chapter of the book, Veblen reaffirms the governing role of these principles, but he concentrates on the requirement of novelty. Dress is clearly and obviously associated with the person of the wearer. It is always in view whenever the person is in view. As a walking billboard to display one's goods it is unsurpassed. Fashions affect the dress of both men and women, but they do so differently. Women's dress, Veblen says, is designed to show that the wearer is incapable of useful work. Devices such as the "French heel" (high heel) and the corset make any sort of useful effort impossible for the wearer. Men's dress on the contrary does not show incapacity for work or other effortful activities. Men are expected to work or to be other-wise engaged in activities involving motion and effort, and incapacitating dress is not appropriate for them.

The central issue Veblen raises here is, why do fashions change so quickly? Particularly in the case of women's dress, the changes are rapid – a given style often falls from grace in a single season. Why? This is a question often asked, but Veblen thinks never satisfactorily answered. His first point is that novelty does not always characterize women's dress. There are and have been societies where fashions are stable. The Greeks and the Romans, he says, did not submit to yearly changes of dress styles; similarly for "oriental" nations such as Japan. In Europe, there are local styles of dress considered traditional that have been stable over a long time. But Veblen notes that it is in the more developed countries of Christendom that the flux of fashions is most in evidence. He explains this in terms of two principles. First, the principle of conspicuous waste requires clothes be wasteful, and the more so the better. But at the same time, dress is an object of aesthetic appraisal, and the truly wasteful dress is apt to be hideous. The second principle is set forth as follows:

The process of developing an aesthetic nausea takes more or less time; the length of time required in any given case being inversely as the degree of intrinsic odiousness of the style in question. The time relation between odiousness and instability in fashion affords ground for the inference that the more rapidly the styles succeed and displace one another, the more offensive they are to sound taste. The presumption, therefore, is that the farther the community, especially the wealthy classes of the community, developed in wealth and mobility, and in the range of their human contact, the more imperatively will the law of conspicuous waste assert itself in matters of dress, the more will the sense of beauty tend to fall into abeyance or be overborne by the canons of pecuniary respectability, the more rapidly will fashion shift and change, and the more grotesque and intolerable will be the varying styles that successively come into vogue.[35]

Thus, a repulsive style may become the fashion owing to its wastefulness, cumbersomeness, and novelty but after a time the sense of beauty will reassert itself, and the style so enthusiastically embraced in the spring becomes revolting by the fall.

The excesses of fashion are sufficient to show that the wearer is both disabled and discomfited. This being the case for female dress, it follows that the wearer is not bearing this cross for herself alone, but she acts as the vicarious agent of her master. She can so bring honor upon the household she represents, and particularly upon the head of the household, the enhancement of whose status is after all the objective of this performance.[36]

In more recent times, Veblen says, there has been some mitigation of women's burden. The use of the corset has declined, although it is still worn among some groups. Further, as the Leisure Class has enlarged, the preferred audience for the demonstration of the master's opulence has become increasingly other members of the Leisure Class. These are people capable of recognizing more subtle signs of expense – the quality of the fabric or the skill and cost of the design. It is no longer necessary to appear as a moronic clotheshorse when a more effective impression can be made by wearing a Vera Wang creation.

In Chapter 8, Veblen begins his treatment of the role of the Leisure Class in social evolution. The life of man in society, he says, is a struggle for existence, and is a process of selective adaptation. Humans must adapt to the natural and social environments in which they live. That environment is constantly changing, so constant readjustment is required of humans as the price of survival. Such adaptations, once established, become institutions, and natural selection applies to institutions as well as individual human beings. Institutions that are not well adapted to their environment will be eliminated and replaced by others that are better fits. Human individuals must adapt not only to their natural environment but also to the institutions that constitute the social environment in which they live. This evolutionary process is cumulative, for any adaptation, once achieved, becomes at once part of the social or natural environment to which further adaptation must be made. The process of social evolution is therefore very complex and predictions of its future course are nearly impossible, since the environment to which one is adapting is changed by one's adaptation. The development of institutions, Veblen says, is the development of society. On the psychological side, institutions are the "prevalent spiritual attitude or a prevalent theory of life."[37]

Human institutions represent adaptations made by society to the environmental conditions that prevailed at some point in the past; they come to us as part of our social inheritance. Since the environment is constantly changing, the institutions we inherit are always somewhat out of date and require new adaptations.

> The evolution of society is substantially a process of mental adaptation on the part of the individuals under the stress of circumstances which will no longer tolerate habits of thought formed under and conforming to a different set of circumstances in the past.[38]

It is, Veblen says, repeating the Spencerian formula, an "adjustment of inner relations to outer relations," but this adjustment is never definitively established, since the "outer relations" are subject to constant change as a consequence of the progressive change going on in the "inner relations."[39] That is to say, humans react upon external stimuli, and by their reactions change the external stimuli.

The economic institutions of society are the "habitual methods of carrying on the life process of the community in contact with the material environment in which it lives."[40] But with the increase of population and of knowledge and skill, the economic institutions that were optimal under an earlier set of circumstances will no longer be so under a later set of circumstances. The alterations that are made in the economic institutions to adapt to the new circumstances will affect the different classes of society differently depending upon their exposure to these economic pressures, and will affect the individuals of the classes in the form of pecuniary exigencies. The resulting changes in economic institutions require changes in the society's "scheme of life" – changes as to what is good and right as well as in what forms of action are effective. Faced with the necessity of such changes, men often revert to the certainties of an earlier time, and such a reversion under current conditions will be to the barbarian scheme of adaptations. Veblen thinks this particularly likely in the case of the dolichoblonds, whose affinity for predatory ways has already been noted.[41]

Having sketched his general theory, Veblen then turns to the effects of the Leisure Class on the social structure. Of the classes of society, the Leisure Class is the most sheltered from the environmental pressures forcing change in the economic institutions. Accordingly, it is the class that responds to those pressures most slowly. "The office of the leisure class in social evolution is to retard the movement and to conserve what is obsolescent."[42] Veblen remarks that this proposition is "a commonplace of popular opinion." This conservatism, Veblen notes, is not the result of unworthy motives, as is often claimed, but is a consequence of the process of social evolution. "The members of the wealthy class do not yield to the demand for innovation as readily as other men because they are not constrained to do so."[43] The association of conservatism with the Leisure Class is sufficiently marked that it has become honorific, and this has led to the spread of conservatism into the classes below the Leisure Class. Hence,

> by virtue of its high position as the avatar of good form, the wealthier class has come to exert a retarding influence on social development far in excess of that which the simple numerical strength of the class would assign it.[44]

The retarding influence of the Leisure Class affects society in other ways. Veblen stresses the interconnectedness of society – the relations among its components that cause any change in one component to ramify through the whole system and force other changes. The aversion to any considerable change exhibited by the members of society is therefore partly due to the "bother of making the readjustments which any given change will necessitate."[45] That "bother" will involve a significant amount of nervous energy, and for the lower classes such an expenditure is made more difficult by the necessity of assiduous application to earning a livelihood. It is one effect of the Leisure Class's role as exemplar of good form that what energy the poor may have left after a day's work will be expended in conspicuous consumption, thus wasting the energy that might have gone to innovation. And the amount of "excess energy" left to the poor will in any case be slight since by engrossing society's wealth the Leisure Class leaves the lower class in poverty and privation.

> The institution of a leisure class hinders cultural development immediately (1) by the inertia proper to the class itself, (2) through its prescriptive example of conspicuous waste and of conservatism, and (3) indirectly through that system of unequal distribution of wealth and sustenance on which the institution itself rests.[46]

The characteristic attitude of the Leisure Class toward change is summed up in the maxim "whatever is is right," whereas Veblen holds that "whatever is is wrong" since the prevailing scheme of life is adapted to an economic situation of the past rather than to one that we currently confront.

The economic institutions of society may be divided into the pecuniary and the industrial. The relation of the Leisure Class to the industrial institutions of society is a pecuniary relation based on ownership. "Their office is of a parasitic character, and their interest is to divert what substance they may to their own use, and to retain whatever is under their hand."[47] The immediate effects of the pecuniary interest are obvious in society. They include the protection of property, enforcement of contracts, limited liability, trusts, pools, and similar devices aimed at exploitation. But the long run effects are even more important. By reducing exploitation to routine, they eliminate the need for the Captain of Industry and substitute in his place what Veblen calls the "soulless joint stock corporation."[48]

Having dealt with the effects of the Leisure Class on social structure, Veblen turns to its effects on individuals. The "point of view" (world view) of a society affects individuals partly by education and enforced adaptation, and partly by selection, eliminating or repressing those who do not fit. Pecuniary emulation (conspicuous waste) and industrial abstention have by these means become canons of life. These canons operate selectively to change not only institutions but human nature itself. We have reviewed above Veblen's theory of race, and his belief that present-day Europeans are hybrids of the three races – the dolichoblond, the Alpine, and the Mediterranean. This division, however, is cross cut by a division between the peaceable and the predatory. The former, Veblen holds, "is nearer to the generic type" which is that which prevailed in savagery – the earliest form of "associated life" known. The latter is a survival of barbarism, and particularly of the quasi-peaceable stage of barbarism. It is the latter type that is currently dominant. However, Veblen holds that the predatory is less stable than the peaceable, due he believes to the greater time spent in savagery than in barbarism. Of the three races, the dolichoblonds are the most predatory, with the Alpine second, and the Mediterraneans less so.

Departures from the current types of human nature are "most frequently of the nature of reversions."[49] Veblen therefore devotes some attention to the characteristics of the historical types. He admits that there is a serious lack of evidence concerning the savage stage, but he finds the best evidence in the survivals of certain psychological factors. Among these he cites a sense of group solidarity involving "sympathy with others and a revulsion against waste."

> Among the archaic traits that are to be regarded as survivals from the peaceable cultural phase, are that instinct of race solidarity which we call conscience, including the sense of truthfulness and equity, and the instinct of workmanship, in its naïve, non-invidious expression.[50]

Here again we have the identification of conscience with the parental bent – the instinct of race solidarity. Also taken as traits of savage men are "truthfulness, peaceableness, good-will, and a non-emulative non-invidious interest in men and things."[51]

Veblen faces a problem here. In line with his evolutionary point of view, he needs a genetic explanation for the presence of these benign traits in human nature. He does it by attributing the origin of these traits to savagery where the character of savage life and the long duration of savagery are used to account for both the presence of these traits and their indelible imprint on human nature.

Given his stage theory of social evolution and his view of inheritance, he has no other way of explaining their presence. These traits, he believes, could not have been formed under barbarism; they have survived in human nature despite the long period of barbarism; therefore they must date from an earlier era and be more deeply rooted in human nature than the barbaric traits. Hence they are products of savagery where the much longer period allowed for a deeper inculcation. The traits that characterize predatory man, Veblen says, are "ferocity, self-seeking, clannishness and disingenuousness – a free resort to force and fraud."[52] These traits Veblen holds are particularly associated with the dolichoblonds. "The dolichoblond type of European man seems to owe much of its dominating influence and its masterful position in the recent culture to its possessing the characteristics of predatory man in exceptional degree."[53]

Veblen accepted some of the claims for the masterful character of the dolichoblonds, but he clearly thought them reprehensible – he describes the blonds as "disturbers of the peace."

Current society, Veblen believed, belongs to the quasi-peaceable phase of barbarism – the phase in which pecuniary predation has replaced physical combat as the dominant mode of achievement. But Veblen argues that the more recent changes in the industrial system of society require different sorts of characteristics than those of the predatory man. What are now required are traits similar to those of savage men.

> The collective interest is best served by honesty, diligence, peacefulness, goodwill, an absence of self-seeking, and an habitual recognition and apprehension of causal sequence, without admixture of animistic belief and without a sense of dependence on any preternatural intervention in the course of events.[54]

But these are not the traits that best suit barbarism.

> Under the regime of emulation the members of a modern industrial community are rivals, each of whom will best attain his individual and immediate advantage if, through an exceptional exemption from scruple, he is able serenely to overreach and injure his fellows when the chance offers.[55]

The present society is divided along lines of employment: the pecuniary employments fit the predatory type of man while the industrial employments fit the savage type. Each of these types of employment exerts a discipline upon the employees; industrial employments instill the industrially useful traits, while the predatory employments instill the predatory traits. Of the two, the predatory currently enjoys the highest repute and commands the greatest rewards. But Veblen notes that as the pecuniary system develops, more and more of its workers find themselves doing routine work where the predatory traits have diminished scope and utility.

Leisure Class employments belong to the predatory type. Veblen notes that the Leisure Class is largely sheltered from the economic exigencies that compel change; hence, the chance for the preservation of archaic traits is greatest among the members of the Leisure Class. Further, Veblen notes that the Leisure Class recruits from among those engaged in pecuniary employments and particularly from the most successful in their work. These people are exceptional examples of pecuniary achievement and tend to reinforce the predatory characteristics of the Leisure Class.

Given the way Veblen has characterized the two types – the pecuniary and the industrial, one might expect that each type would dominate a particular set of classes – the pecuniary the upper classes and of course the Leisure Class, the industrial the lower classes. But Veblen holds that this is not entirely so. The reason he says is that the Leisure Class holds a prescriptive role in society so that the other classes adopt its scheme of life and try to follow its canons. Further, all classes are engaged in the pecuniary struggle; industrial workers work for wages, pay rent, and consume goods bought in the market. Hence the pecuniary canons have come to apply throughout our society. The unequal distribution of wealth leaves the poor lacking in time and energy to rebel against the standards of the Leisure Class. But Veblen adds a peculiar twist to this; he claims that the pecuniary man is very similar to the lower class delinquent.

> The ideal pecuniary man is like the ideal delinquent in his unscrupulous conversion of goods and persons to his own ends, and in a callous disregard of the feelings and wishes of others and of the remoter effects of his actions, but he is unlike him in possessing a keener sense of status, and in working more consistently and far-sightedly to a remoter end.[56]

In closing his argument at the end of Chapter 9, Veblen remarks that little research has been done on the survival of archaic traits in modern populations. This leaves a gap in Veblen's theory, since much of what he has argued assumes survivals from earlier cultural stages. Accordingly, he says that what he can offer is a "discursive review of such everyday facts as lie ready to hand."[57] He undertakes to do this in the five remaining chapters of the book, remarking that "it seems necessary to the completeness of the argument."[58] But the subjects chosen for discussion in these chapters illustrate more than survivals; they are also examples of the application of his economic theory to matters not usually considered by economists.

The first of these five chapters he entitles "Modern Survivals of Prowess." The most obvious of these is warfare, the martial spirit, and the honor accorded to war. This, Veblen says, is particularly notable among the upper classes of Europe and the United States. "The enthusiasm for war, and the predatory temper of which it is an index, prevail in the largest measure among the upper classes, especially among the hereditary leisure class."[59] The common people do not share this passion for combat, and can only be induced to military action by exceptional circumstances. This class division in militancy, Veblen notes, may be due to "the inheritance of acquired traits,"[60] in which Veblen believed at the time this was written. But it may also reflect the "ethnic derivation."

A further example of class differences in prowess is furnished by the duel. In civilized countries, the duel is found almost exclusively among members of the hereditary Leisure Class. The only notable exceptions to this are military officers and lower-class delinquents. The German student duels Veblen calls a "bizarre survival of bellicose chivalry,"[61] but he also notes that among boys there is a period during adolescence when fighting appears to be natural. This, he thinks, is a normal part of maturation and reflects the recapitulation in the individual of the stages of development of the race.[62] Recapitulation theory was a widely held doctrine in Veblen's time, though it is rejected today.

A more common evidence of the survival of predatory traits is to be found in sports. "The ground of an addiction to sports is an archaic spiritual constitution – the possession of the predatory emulative propensity in a relatively high potency."[63] Sports vary from those which involve physical combat through those which emphasize skill to those marked by cunning and chicanery, but they usually involve substantial elements of make-believe and "a good share of rant and swagger."[64] As Veblen notes, the vocabulary of sports is largely drawn from the vocabulary of warfare.

It is a peculiarity of sports that those who indulge in them often find it neces- sary to justify doing so by assigning other than predatory motives to their indul- gence. Thus love of nature is used to justify hunting, fishing, and similar outdoor sports – a peculiar justification, Veblen remarks, since the sport consists in destroying some of the chief attractions of nature. Similarly, sports such as football are justified by the claim that they contribute to "physical culture" and "manly spirit." To this Veblen replies "it has been said, not inaptly, that the relation of football to physical culture is much the same as that of the bull-fight to agriculture."[65] What sports actually encourage is the spirit of emulation and competition which is indeed a fundamental trait of our current version of quasi- peaceable predation. But Veblen says although there is widespread public approval of sports, there is also "a pervading sense that this ground of sentiment wants legitimation."[66]

What Veblen thinks underlies this uneasiness is the instinct of workmanship "which is an instinct more fundamental, of more ancient prescription, than the propensity to predatory emulation."[67] This notion that the hold of emulation on present culture is waning is a recurrent theme in Veblen's writing.

But what this review of the evidence makes clear, Veblen thinks, is that the Leisure Class fosters the predatory traits both military and sportsmanlike. Veblen thinks the addiction to sports is not shared by the lower classes except for the lower class delinquents. These predatory traits, he says, are "of no use for the purposes of the collective life."[68]

In the next chapter, Veblen turns to the belief in luck. This belief, in some form or other, he says is very widespread in modern society, reflecting its ancient origin and long career. Veblen holds that it is present in savagery as a component of an animistic view of the world that attributes teleological actions to objects and events. This involves a belief in a preternatural agency that determines the course of happenings. But it receives further refinement in barbarism where it crystallizes into the form of an anthropomorphic power underlying nature. It is of course to the benefit of men if they can influence this power, especially with respect to activities such as war and sports where the risks of loss are high and the outcomes uncertain. Veblen claims that when people bet, they do so in the belief that by doing so they can influence the chances of victory for their favorites. The same idea underlies the "wager of battle" which is based on the assumption that justice must prevail.

The belief in luck, that is to say, in a preternatural power determining the course of events, has economic consequences. In the handicraft era, and even today with respect to the farmer, "The workman is himself the prime mover chiefly depended upon, and the natural forces engaged are in large part apprehended as inscrutable and fortuitous agencies, whose working lies beyond the workman's control or discretion."[69]

In such circumstances, animistic projections of preternatural agencies have a plausibility and even utility. But in the case of modern industry, where production is done by machines and the relations of importance are those of efficient causality, such animism can produce nothing but trouble and confusion.

The presence of animism serves as an index of the presence of predatory traits. The belief in preternatural powers leads to efforts to influence them, which cast men in the role of supplicants for the aid of an unseen master and so encourages servile behavior. Predatory traits encourage ideas of status.

> In their finest development, the predatory temperament, the sense of status, and the anthropomorphic cult all together belong to the barbarian culture; and something of a mutual causal relation subsists between these phenomena as they come into sight in communities on that cultural level.[70]

"Status" of course is "a formal expression of such an invidious comparison duly gauged and graded according to a sanctioned schedule."[71] Veblen develops the relations among these factors as follows:

> On the one hand, the system of status and the predatory habit of life are an expression of the instinct of workmanship as it takes form under a custom of invidious comparison; on the other hand, the anthropomorphic cult and the habit of devout observances are an expression of men's animistic sense of a propensity in material things, elaborated under the guidance of substantially the same general habit of invidious comparison.[72]

So we come to devout observances.

The preternatural agents lately described become the animistic spirits inhabiting the material objects of the world. It is hardly surprising to find Veblen holding that those who are involved in sports also tend to be religious. For example, he claims that college athletes are more religious than other students – a claim advanced by the colleges themselves to show the benefits of their programs. Affiliation with anthropomorphic cults carries with it the predatory notion of service to an invisible master, and so promotes such habits. Devout observances are usually for the purpose of propitiating or pleasing a divine agent, and these put the one seeking favor in the position of a servant addressing his master. Veblen regards such behavior as evidence of "arrested spiritual development."

The most obvious economic consequences of devout observances are in the direct consumption of goods and services. "The consumption of ceremonial paraphernalia required by any cult, in the way of shrines, temples, churches, vestments, sacrifices, sacraments, holiday attire etc., serves no immediate material end."[73]

All of it, Veblen says, should be considered conspicuous waste. The observances for which these things are used enforce habits of thought antithetical to those required by modern industry. The priestly Leisure Class presents an example of conspicuous leisure and conspicuous waste. Its members are barred from participation in gainful work, their leisure being a vicarious leisure in service to the master, and their behavior decorous as befits the servants of such a divinity.

Veblen believes that in the modern world the predatory traits, religion among them, are losing their hold. While religiosity remains strong in the Leisure Class and the indigent lower class, whose mode of life leaves them without energy to rebel, he thinks it is failing in the artisan class. The middle class, however, presents a problem. Religion remains strong for the middle class, but among the women rather than the men. Veblen's explanation for this fact is that middle-class women form what is actually a secondary Leisure Class. Sheltered from economic exigencies by their exclusion from useful work, and largely confined to the domestic world by the doctrine of separate spheres, middle-class women live in an environment of the patriarchal family. Accordingly, predatory traits have survived in this group, including the bent toward devout observances. The upper class, which is the true Leisure Class, of course conserves predatory traits, but Veblen notes that unlike Europe, America has no hereditary Leisure Class. The nearest approach to that he finds in the South where the upper class exhibits more predatory traits than its northern counterpart. The South is famous for its duels, brawls, feuds, drunkenness, horse racing, cockfighting, and gambling, male sexual incontinence, and sense of honor.[74] It is also the most backward section industrially, which leaves its predatory survivals undisturbed.

In summary, Veblen says that the devout attitude marks a type of man more consonant with the predatory mode of life than with the industrial.

It is an expression of the archaic, habitual sense of personal status – the relation of mastery and subservience – and it therefore fits into the industrial scheme of the predatory and quasi-peaceable cultures, but does not fit into the industrial scheme of the present. ...In this as in other relations, the institution of a leisure class acts to conserve, and even to rehabilitate, that archaic type of human nature and those elements of the archaic culture which the industrial evolution of society in its later stages acts to eliminate.[75]

In his description of the Leisure Class, Veblen has stressed the fact that it is a survival of the predatory era. He has also stressed the sheltered character of the Leisure Class; it is less exposed to the economic exigencies than the industrial workers. Although the Leisure Class is much involved in the pecuniary culture, its sheltered character means that it is open to survivals not only from barbarism but from savagery as well. This is particularly true of the Leisure Class women who as lately noted are relatively free from all economic stress. The result is that in recent years traits have appeared in some members of the Leisure Class that are survivals of the savage era antedating barbarism, and this is particularly true with respect to Leisure Class women. This has shown itself in a variety of movements and organizations endorsing reforms of various sorts.

The fact itself that distinction or a decent good-fame is sought by this method is evidence of the prevalent sense of the legitimacy, and of the presumptive effectual presence, of a non-emulative, non-invidious intent as a constituent factor in the habits of thought of modern communities.[76]

The result is a contradiction within the Leisure Class; some who have received the savage heritage in large measure engage in non-emulative reforms while the bulk of the Leisure Class remains wedded to its predatory ways.

The reemergence of savage traits Veblen thinks is particularly marked among Leisure Class women. As it shows itself in the "New Woman" movement this is a demand for a radical change in the lives of Leisure Class women. For them, the "woman's sphere" has become a suffocating prison; they demand "emancipation and work" rather than enforced leisure. "It is among the women of the well-to-do classes, in the communities which are the furthest advanced in industrial development, that this sense of a grievance to be redressed is most alive and finds most frequent expression."[77] The gilded cage is still a cage.

Thus Veblen sees the reemergence of the savage in the very heart of the predatory culture. When the habits superinduced by the emulative

method of life have ceased to enjoy the sanction of existing economic exigencies, a process of disintegration sets in whereby the habits of thought of a more recent growth and of less generic character to some extent yield the ground before the more ancient and more pervading spiritual characteristics of the race.[78]

Veblen does believe that men's generic traits will out and that the reign of emulation will end.

Veblen then turns to the effects of the Leisure Class on higher education. Historically, Veblen notes, higher education derives from religious education intended to teach ways of serving and manipulating the gods. To achieve this, rituals were developed, involving magic and elaborate paraphernalia. The association of higher education with religion still persists. Veblen notes that the majority of US colleges are affiliated with churches (this was true in Veblen's time) and their curricula emphasize the acquisition of archaic knowledge. Ritual and paraphernalia still characterized higher education; the cap and gown are ubiquitous in American colleges as are ceremonies and processions.

Veblen notes that this emphasis on ceremony has been particularly strong in late nineteenth-century America. He attributes this to the influence of the Civil War. Habituation to war entails a body of predatory habits of thought that he believes are characteristic of the post-bellum era but that he believes are now fading away.

Higher education is very conservative, preferring the humanities and classics to science, and only slowly admitting new ideas into its curriculum. This conservatism shows in many ways. For example, the higher education of women is still rare; what is considered appropriate for women is training with domestic applications and the acquisition of "accomplishments" that are wholly useless. A further mark of the influence of the Leisure Class on higher education is the emphasis on sports that characterizes the colleges. And Veblen notes that in recent years Captains of Industry have begun to replace ministers as college presidents, presumably because of their superior skills in fundraising and advertising. Although the role of the sciences in higher education is increasing, they are still subordinate to the humanities. And the most advanced education offered is in fields such as law and governance rather than science.

For Veblen, real knowledge is scientific knowledge – "the field of learning in which the cognitive or intellectual interest is dominant – the sciences properly so-called."[79] Veblen notes that science is "knowledge for its own sake, the exercise of the faculty of comprehension without ulterior purpose."[80] Given the leisure and educational attainments of the Leisure Class, one might expect that such a pursuit would be congenial to the members of this class. But this is not the case. "The habits of thought which characterize the life of the class run on the personal relations of dominance, and on the derivative, invidious concepts of honor, worth, merit, character, and the like."[81]

Veblen also notes the importance of what he calls the "Maecenas relation" – i.e., the subsidization of higher education by wealthy members of the Leisure Class.[82] It was a matter of common knowledge that in the late nineteenth century American colleges and universities were receiving large monetary gifts from the wealthy and that many such institutions were founded with endowments from businessmen who had made fortunes – Veblen was teaching at the University of Chicago which had been founded by John D. Rockefeller. Veblen likens this to the system of patronage:

> The scholar under patronage performs the duties of the learned life vicariously for his patron, to whom a certain repute inures after the manner of the good repute imputed to a master for whom any form of vicarious leisure is performed.[83]

But the archaic system of patronage was not a good match for the relation of late nineteenth-century colleges to their benefactors.

Veblen holds a curious view of the history of science. He says that science really begins with the Industrial Revolution and has been the creation of the lower classes, not of the college-educated. He attributes this to the discipline in matter-of-fact thinking that is provided by direct contact with the material environment, and particularly by the machine. He admits that some members of other classes have made important contributions to science, but he claims this is true only for those whose parents came from the working class. This is what ought to be the case under Veblen's theory but it happens not to be the case.

Veblen holds that higher education in the United States is largely hostile to science, despite the fact that college curricula of the time were steadily increasing their scientific content. But he finds hope in lower education – particularly in the kindergarten movement.

> The peculiarly non-invidious trend of the kindergarten discipline, and the similar character of the kindergarten influence in primary education beyond the limits of the kindergarten proper, should be taken in connection with what has already been said of the peculiar spiritual attitude of leisure-class womankind under the circumstances of the modern economic situation.[84]

It is these women who Veblen believes are the driving force behind the kindergarten movement. In the long run, Veblen says, the kindergarten movement and the "New Woman" movement may even undermine the Leisure Class itself.

Veblen regards the time spent on the study of the classics and in learning the dead languages as time wasted – points he makes on a page on which he ostentatiously inserts a three-line quotation in Latin.[85] This opprobrium he expands to other features of humanistic education. The emphasis on classic English and on correct spelling is misguided.

> English orthography satisfies all the requirements of the canons of reputability under the law of conspicuous waste. It is archaic, cumbrous, and ineffective;

its acquisition consumes much time and effort; failure to acquire it is easy of detection. Therefore it is the first and readiest test of reputability in learning and conformity to its ritual is indispensable to a blameless scholastic life.[86]

Thus spake Professor Veblen!

In *The Theory of the Leisure Class*, Veblen presented a theory of a particular social institution – the Leisure Class – as a model of the sort of evolutionary theory that he believed economics should develop. This theory offers an account of the origin and development of the Leisure Class, of the behavior of its members, of its role in social evolution and its effect on individuals and institutions. Within this account, Veblen proposed a radical change in the traditional economics, arguing that the driving force behind economic behavior is not just the accumulation of wealth but the attainment of esteem or prestige, and he demonstrated how this revised theory applies to a wide variety of human behaviors, ranging from women's dress to religious observances, sports, military activities, luck, and higher education. Veblen's theory accounts for more than the behavior of individuals. The role of the Leisure Class as the standard for emulation of the other classes is explained by Veblen's theory but not by the classical theory of wealth maximization. There is no way that wealth maximization can account for many of the phenomena with which Veblen deals. Yet most of his readers missed the point; they thought his carefully worked out treatise was just a satire on the Leisure Class.

The Theory of the Leisure Class was a step, and a big one, toward the reconstruction of economic theory that Veblen wanted to achieve. But the goal was not fully realized here. He still had problems in the theory that required resolution, such as the relation between emulation and the instincts. But he was also feeling his way toward new categories for economic analysis. The division between industry and business is introduced late in the book, and plays a subordinate role in this work; Veblen relates industrial occupations to savagery and pecuniary occupations to barbarism, and the division in occupations serves to account for savage and barbarian traits in modern society. Nevertheless, the elements of his new theory are already here, as was soon to become apparent. Further, Veblen has shown that if one takes the basic motive of business activity to be emulation and the goal that of maximizing esteem, the scope of economics expands to include very nearly the whole of the social sciences. If his readers did not understanding what he was doing, that is not because he was obscure, but because what he was proposing was so radical that they could not grasp it.

Industrial and Pecuniary Employments

In 1900, Veblen followed up the beginnings of the new theory of economics that he had made in *The Theory of the Leisure Class* with an article entitled "Industrial and Pecuniary Employments."[87] His intentions were made very clear in the opening two paragraphs where he says that the claim of the early economists that the three factors of production were land, labor, and capital "has proven inadequate for certain purposes of theory which were not contemplated by the men who elaborated it."[88] The early economic writers believed that the order of nature was established by God to serve the goal of human welfare. Their focus was, therefore, on what served the needs of the "society" and so on the production of goods that would satisfy the requirements of society. Smith and his followers focused on production. Their analysis led them to conclude that the three factors of production were land, labor, and capital; a conclusion still accepted by most economists. But if land, labor, and capital are the factors of production, it seemed reasonable to these men that the proceeds of production should be distributed among these three. This accorded with their view that the order of nature was a perfectly designed and efficient system, and since men are part of the order of nature, so the economic system should be a balanced system in which nothing is wasted. This conviction was embodied in what Veblen calls the "Law of Equivalence."

> So it is, by implication, assumed that the product which results from any given industrial process or operation is, in some sense and in some unspecified respect, the equivalent of the expenditure of forces, or of the effort, or whatnot, that has gone into the process out of which the product emerges.[89]

Not only does this Law of Equivalence describe what happens, but since it is a consequence of the order of nature, it describes what ought to be. The three factors being responsible for production, the Law of Equivalence required that the proceeds of production be distributed among them. Purely pecuniary activities were then treated as incidental to production, and pecuniary acquisition became a sub-head under production.

But in the course of the nineteenth century, a new element emerged in the form of the undertaker (entrepreneur), and as the importance of the undertaker increased, it became necessary to find a category under which he could be placed. "The undertaker gets an income; therefore he must produce goods. But human activity directed to the production of goods is labor; therefore the undertaker is a particular kind of laborer."[90] The remuneration of the undertaker is defined as "wages of superintendence." But increasingly as time goes on what the undertaker superintends is the financial side of the enterprise.

The undertaker, however, is not the only problem. As the division of labor progresses, those who carry out the technological processes of production are increasingly isolated from the financial activities of the enterprise, while those like the undertaker who specialize in such financial matters become isolated from the technological processes of production. There thus emerges a division between industry and business. Business is concerned with ownership, with prices, and with exchange; industry is concerned with the making of goods that are service-able to the society. Not only are the goals of business and industry different, but the employments are different. Industrial employments involve the use of machines for the making of goods; to deal effectively with machines, the workers must learn to think in terms of efficient causes and matters-of-fact. The tasks of business are to manage the financial affairs of the enterprise and to obtain the highest price possible for the goods of industry which they sell. These are very different employments.

Business does of course affect industry because the ownership of the industrial equipment enables the owners to manipulate industry to serve their ends. The objective of business is to maximize the amount of goods owned; the objective of industry is to produce material goods to meet the needs of the community. Workers, Veblen says, are "occupied with the production of goods; the business men, on the other hand, are occupied with the acquisition of them."[91] Veblen notes the importance of the large-scale consolidations among business that were attracting so much attention at this time (1900). These are claimed to result in increased efficiency which, it is said, benefits the community. Such consolidations are the work of businessmen, but the possibility of such consolidations depends on the state of the industry's technology, since technological compatibility is a precondition of such a consolidation. But the fact that such a consolidation is technologically possible does not mean that it will occur. That depends upon the relations among the businessmen involved. There are many cases in which a con-solidation that is technologically possible never occurs, because the businessmen involved cannot reach agreement. What the cost of these foregone consolidations may be to the community it is impossible to say.

The distinction between business and industry runs deep and shows that the traditional doctrine of the three factors of production required revision.

> Wealth turned to account in the way of investment or business management may or may not, in consequence, be turned to account, materially, for industrial effect. Wealth, values, so employed for pecuniary ends is capital in the business sense of the word. Wealth, material means of industry, physically employed for industrial ends is capital in the industrial sense. Theory, there-fore, would require that care be taken to distinguish between capital as a pecuniary category, and capital as an industrial category, if the term capital is retained to cover the two concepts.[92]

The gains obtained from pecuniary capital stand in no specifiable relation to the serviceability of the results from the use of industrial capital. The objective of those in pecuniary employments is to maximize the return realized from the sale of the goods produced by industry – hence with the vendibility of these goods. But vendibility is only partially determined by serviceability to the community. Furthermore, the two forms of capital do not coincide with respect to the concrete things comprised under each. ...Pecuniary capital is a matter of market values, while industrial capital is, in the last analysis, a matter of mechanical efficiency, or rather of mechanical effect not reducible to a common measure or a collective magnitude.[93]

Market values, being a psychological matter, can vary widely, as is shown in times of panic, whereas, "industrial capital, being a matter of industrial contrivances and adaptation, cannot similarly vary through a revision of valuations."[94] It is also a matter of common note that pecuniary capital cannot be summed to yield an aggregate sum since in addition to material things it includes intangibles such as "good will, fashions, customs, prestige, effrontery, personal credit."[95] The distinction between business and industry applies also to employments. Industrial employments, Veblen says,

> begin and end outside the market. Their proximate end and effect is the shaping and guiding of material things and processes. Broadly, they may be said to be primarily occupied with the phenomena of material serviceability, rather than those of exchange value.[96]

But "pecuniary employments have to do with wealth in point of ownership, with market values, with transactions of exchange, purchases and sale, bargaining for the purpose of pecuniary gain."[97] Clearly, these have little in common.

By this point in the article Veblen has established the difference between business and industry, between pecuniary capital and industrial capital, and between pecuniary and industrial employments. He is now ready to deal with two fundamental questions regarding cultural change: how do institutions affect individuals? and how do individuals affect institutions? He poses the problem as follows.

> What the Marxists have named the "Materialistic Conception of History" is assented to with less and less qualification by those who make the growth of culture their subject of inquiry. The materialistic conception says that institutions are shaped by economic conditions; but as it left the hands of the Marxists and as it still functions in the hands of many who knew not Marx, it has very little to say regarding the efficient force, the channels, or the methods by which the economic is conceived to have its effect upon institutions. What answer the early Marxist gave to this question ... was to the effect that the causal connection lies through a selfish, calculating class interest. But, while class interest may count for much in the outcome, this answer is plainly not a competent one, since, for one thing, institutions by no means change with the alacrity which the sole efficiency of a reasoned class interest would require.[98]

Veblen's answer comes directly from his theory of knowledge. Institutions as Veblen conceived them are entrenched social habits. Veblen holds that habits are formed from adaptations that resolve problems posed to humans by their environment, natural or social. When a new problem arises, if some individual finds a satisfactory technique for dealing with it, his repeated use of this technique will form a habit in that individual. Other individuals, similarly situated, dealing with the same or similar problems, may copy the habit of the first individual, and so the habit spreads through the group. If it proves successful it will be approved by the community as good and right, and so becomes entrenched as an institution. To alter a habit, then, either a more efficient method of solving the problem must be found, or the environment must alter so that the established institution no longer meets the original need. What habits are formed, therefore, depends upon the solutions of problems posed for the individual by his environment. And for the worker, it is the environment to which his occupation exposes him that will determine what habits he forms, for the environment that most affects him is that which he encounters in the eight to twelve hours (the work day in 1900) that he spends working each day at his occupation. For workers, at least those employed in the large-scale industries, their work environment is composed of machines, whereas for managers it is the pecuniary affairs of the business. "It is the periods of close attention and hard work that seem to count for most in the formation of habits of thought."[99] So institutions determine the habits of their employees by determining the environment in which they work and the nature of the work they do. And individuals change institutions when the habits of the employees change in new and unforeseen ways. Thus Veblen holds that the employments that men hold exert a discipline on them that determines their beliefs and actions – i.e., their habits – and that men can change institutions when an accepted habit proves inadequate. Veblen is not so naive as to believe that industrial workers are beyond the reach of the pecuniary discipline; they buy in markets, they work for wages, and they pay rent. But he believed that the discipline of their occupations would dominate everything else.

But Veblen recognized that more than argument is required to make his case convincing. "An *a priori* argument as to what cultural effects should naturally follow from such a difference in discipline between occupations, past and present, would probably not be convincing, as *a priori* arguments from half-authenticated premises commonly are not."[100] Veblen therefore presents examples of institutional changes that he claims are due to the discipline of modern work. The first example is the alleged improvidence of workers in modern factories.

> It is, e.g., a commonplace of current vulgar discussion of existing economic questions, that the classes engaged in the modern mechanical or factory industries are improvident and apparently incompetent to take care of the pecuniary details of their own life.[101]

Veblen argues that the experience of working with machines leads to an erosion of beliefs in conventions such as ownership that are not grounded in objective matter-of-fact considerations. A second example that Veblen cites is the growing popularity of socialism which has, he claims, acquired increasing strength among urban workers, particularly among those of the highly mechanized industries. Other American reform movements, such as the Populists, who were very much in people's thoughts in the 1890s, wanted the redistribution of ownership. But the socialists want the abolition of ownership. Veblen notes that other factors, particularly ethnic ones, are involved in the growth of socialism, but he believes that the discipline of the machine is the major factor. There are, Veblen says, other examples, such as the decline of religious belief among industrial workers, but he does not pursue them here.

Veblen's belief that institutions change employees by the discipline of their work and that individuals change institutions by habit formation provided him with tools for the explanation of culture change. But it also required that he be able to cite cases exemplifying these processes of change. The use of socialism for this purpose was an obvious one in the light of the growth of the socialist movement in the United States, the increasing intensity of labor strife in the country, and the rising tide of votes for the Socialist Party in the years leading up to the Great War. But other cultural changes that he could reasonably attribute to the discipline of the machine proved hard to find, and were less enduring when he did find them. But these developments were in the future; in 1900 Veblen thought he was on solid ground.

Veblen's Theory of Industry

In an article on industrial and pecuniary employments already discussed Veblen had claimed that the term "capital" must be differently defined when applied to industry than when applied to business. In two articles , "On the Nature of Capital I" and "On the Nature of Capital II"[102] that he published in 1908, Veblen undertook to do this; the first article deals with industrial capital and the second with business capital. By "industrial capital" Veblen means the Industrial Arts – the knowledge of science and technology held by the community. The Industrial Arts embrace that part of the world view that deals with how things are done; it is the knowledge of what is useful for human life, of how it is to be made useful, and what its uses are. In other words, it is the scientific and technological knowledge of the community. The body of such knowledge is far greater than any one individual can hold; even in the simplest of cultures, the industrial arts are so large and complex a system that it is beyond the ability of any one person to grasp. There are some portions of the Industrial Arts that everyone in the society knows, but there is also a division of intellectual labor according to which more specialized parts of the system are held by different groups within the society. These specialties may take many forms – sorcerers, witchdoctors, lawyers, etc., but they all rest on the base of the knowledge common to all members. The Industrial Arts are a community product, created and transmitted by the community. They are the community's primary intangible asset.

What is often called "capital" is the goods used in the process of production – the so-called "capital goods." But the capital goods – tools, machines, whatever – are among the products of the Industrial Arts. It is the knowledge that is crucial, not the products. For a savage society such as the "Digger Indians" of California, the loss of their entire stock of capital goods would be relatively inconsequential so long as their knowledge of their Industrial Arts remains since they could easily replace the goods, but the loss of their industrial knowledge would be catastrophic.[103] Veblen made the same point in discussing the effects of the Great War on Germany that might destroy her capital equipment.[104] So long as the German people retained their industrial knowledge, the capital goods could be rapidly replaced.

Discoveries and inventions are the work of individuals, and they become the property of the community by diffusion and assimilation within the community. If an invention offers a more effective way to achieve some goal of the community, it will render the old way obsolete and take its place. Always inventions build on the foundation of knowledge already held by the community; the contribution of an individual as an inventor is actually slight compared to what is contributed by the community's Industrial Arts. Individual achievements are of little effect unless they are adopted by the community and added to the existing stock of knowledge. The cumulative growth of the Industrial Arts "lies in the feasibility of accumulating knowledge gained by individual experience and initiative, and therefore it lies in the feasibility of one individual's learning from the experience of another."[105] The Industrial Arts are Veblen's prime example of a process of cumulative development; "the history of its growth and uses is the history of the development of material civilization."[106]

The Industrial Arts are a community product. It is the community that creates them, holds them, and transmits them to the next generation. A solitary individual isolated from the community's stock of knowledge would be helpless in dealing with his environment and would be dead within the week. Only the community as a whole can hold the Industrial Arts and only the community can transmit the Industrial Arts from generation to generation. Accordingly, Veblen's equivalent to the traditional factor of labor is the community at large. The Industrial Arts are the capital of the industrial system, the crucial intangible asset of the community, and it is the community that puts the Industrial Arts to work. The extent of this community is not limited by national boundaries, for scientific and technological knowledge is transnational. It includes all civilized people, for the Industrial Arts are the technological aspect of civilization.

That upon which industrial capital is deployed is the material environment, but what constitutes the relevant material environment for industrial purposes depends upon the state of the Industrial Arts. Iron was of no value until human beings learned how to smelt it; petroleum was of no value until humans learned how to refine it; penicillin was of no value until its ability to kill bacteria was discovered. It is the state of the Industrial Arts that determines which elements of the material environment can be put to serviceable use and how. What constitutes the economically relevant material environment is therefore constantly changing as the Industrial Arts develop. Obviously, the material environment, so understood, is for Veblen the industrial analog of the traditional factor of land.

There is a fourth factor of production that was attracting much attention in Veblen's time – the entrepreneur. If the entrepreneur is understood to be the person who combines the other factors of production so as to achieve a successful output, then his analog in Veblen's economics is the technological expert; Veblen calls such men "engineers." Industrial production is a physical process; it requires an expert knowledge of science and technology to combine the physical processes involved in the production of goods so as to achieve a satisfactory product, particularly in modern industry where the physical processes of production are complex; only someone having a considerable technical expertise can perform this function adequately. The engineers are, Veblen says, the "General Staff" of the production process, and their importance can only increase as the Industrial Arts become more sophisticated.[107]

From Veblen's point of view, business is a corruption of industry; the entire business system is an imputation of make-believe processes and entities onto the industrial system. This becomes obvious if one views the industrial system without business – that is, as a purely physical process. Abstracting from all monetary considerations, it is a system for transforming raw materials into finished goods and distributing these goods to consumers. Seen in these purely physical terms, the whole system is an integrated series of physical processes. In calling it the "machine process" Veblen is speaking metaphorically, but the metaphor is apt. Not only are materials transformed and transported by machines but all the component processes of the system exhibit an interdependence similar to that of the parts of a machine. Thus in the automobile industry, not only does the product undergo a series of changes wrought by machines as it moves along the assembly line of the factory, but all the separate inputs to the process, the steel, copper, chrome, glass, etc., must be introduced in precisely the right amounts at precisely the right times. This sort of precise articulation among the various constituent processes gives to the whole manufacturing process the character of a single mechanical process.

As Veblen points out, this description applies chiefly to a limited number of industries, namely:

> Transport and communications; the production and use of coal, oil, electricity, and water power; the production of steel and other metals; of wood pulp, lumber, cement and other building materials; of textiles and rubber; as

also grain-milling and much of the grain growing, together with meatpacking and a good share of stock-raising industry.[108]

Even in these industries the integration was less than complete in Veblen's time. But these were basic industries, and others either depended upon them or were sufficiently minor that they could be ignored. Moreover, Veblen thought the metaphor of the machine would become increasingly applicable not only in these industries but in others as well as technological progress continued.

What Veblen emphasized in describing industry is the manufacture of goods, which was in fact the dominant activity of the American economy of his time. But the same sort of analysis applies to services. The precise articulation of the machine process has introduced a comprehensive standardization in the economy, with work of all kinds rigorously timed, scheduled, and standardized, with standard units of weight and measure, timetables for trains and all transportation, scheduled appointments and meetings, each service performed in its proper place at the right time for the right period. Only so can services be priced; being immaterial, it must be possible to package them by time consumed in order to fix their prices. Such is the dance of modern life.

Veblen's analysis of industrial distribution follows the same line as his theory of production, though he devotes little space to its discussion. From an industrial point of view, the problem of distribution is the problem of physically transporting material goods from the point of production to the consumer.[109] The problems here are those of sorting, transportation and storage, and the physical moving and placing of objects. As to the allotment of goods among individual consumers, Veblen is remarkably silent; there is no formula such as "to each according to his needs." But in one of his reports to the government, he does outline a possible distribution system based on the system of mail order distribution employed by Sears and Montgomery Ward. The system would be operated by the Post Office Parcel Post division. Consumers would shop by catalogues; their orders would then go to the central distribution agency, would be filled, and the ordered goods would then be sent to the consumer by parcel post. No money would be involved.

What Veblen means by "industry" is the economy viewed as a purely physical process of producing and distributing serviceable goods and services. This industrial system does not include prices or other monetary considerations; it does not involve private ownership, wages, profits, stocks, or bonds. It is the industrial system without business, a purely material system of production and distribution. Workers will continue to do their jobs; goods will be delivered to consumers; services will continue to be rendered; all without the use of money. Veblen assumes that all the many functions required by production and distribution will continue without interruption; industry will hum along at full blast providing all that consumers want.

To a modern reader, conditioned as we all are by our current economic system, Veblen's description of industry seems bizarre and utopian. But in so far as the problems of economics are those of making and distributing physical goods and services, Veblen's account is entirely sensible. The reason the modern critic would find it utopian is because it flies in the face of our current theory of economic value. We at once ask, why would people work? What would motivate the entrepreneur? Who would own the plants and equipment? etc. These questions seem obvious and reasonable to us. But Veblen's answer is that they seem reasonable to us because we subscribe to the value scheme of classical economics. If instead we adopt Veblen's value scheme, defined by the instincts, the picture is very different. According to the instinct of workmanship, people enjoy work; they do not have to be bribed into doing it. Since the parental bent motivates people to serve the material interests of the community at large, industry will be run so as to produce all that the community needs, and the distribution system will ensure that goods reach consumers without benefit of prices. And given the mass production capability of the machine process, industry can produce more than enough goods to satisfy the material needs of the community. None of this requires the intervention of business; ownership does not create material goods and is not necessary for their consumption; wages are not necessary to induce people to work when they want to do so anyway. Why then is the actual economy so obviously a business economy? Veblen's answer is that the whole notion of business is a mistake, a delusion arising from the contamination of the instincts, and one that would vanish if only we could rid our world of our animistic habituations and see it as a mechanical system of cause and effect that it is.

But, it is said, labor is irksome; no one would expend such energy without a reward; to which Veblen would reply, look at the energy expended in sports (which in Veblen's time were largely amateur). People do not find play to be irksome; in fact, they often expend far more energy in sports than in work. Furthermore, Veblen remarks, if labor really were irksome, man would be an anomaly in nature; he would be the only species with the disinclination to the form of activity upon which his survival depends. People have been taught that labor is irksome and so they believe it. And the conditions under which they work are often such as to make it irksome. But conditions can be changed. They work much harder on a tennis court or ball field than they ever do in a factory and they enjoy doing it.[110] Veblen has a point.

What Veblen wants to establish is that the economic functions necessary for society – the production and distribution of serviceable goods and services – can be adequately performed without the use of ownership or pecuniary evaluations. If this is so, then he can argue that the whole business system – ownership, prices, the market, etc. – is irrelevant to the processes of industry. And not only is business irrelevant, it is a parasite feeding on industry, whereby a few greedy and unscrupulous men are able to appropriate the output of industry for themselves, compel the community's members to labor for the enrichment of the owners, and dominate the society. The key relation by which this perversion of industry is accomplished is the ownership in severalty of the productive goods. So Veblen's point is that if ownership in severalty were to be abolished, the liberated industrial system could fulfill the economic needs of society far better than the current business system, wage slavery would end, and a society of masterless men could establish a truly democratic order.

Notes

1   Thorstein Veblen, *The Theory of the Leisure Class: An Economic Study of Institutions* (New York: The Modern Library, 1934), 15–16.
2   Veblen, *Leisure Class*, 25–26.
3   Veblen, *Leisure Class*, 29, 30.
4   Thorstein Veblen, "Some Neglected Points in the Theory of Socialism," in *The Place of Science in Modern Civilization*, intro. Warren J. Samuels (New York: Cosimo, 2007), 387–408.
5   Veblen, *Leisure Class*, 342.
6   Veblen, *Leisure Class*, 45.
7   Veblen, *Leisure Class*, 49.
8   Veblen, *Leisure Class*, 65.
9   Veblen, *Leisure Class*, 73.
10   Veblen, *Leisure Class*, 74–75.
11   Veblen, *Leisure Class*, 84.
12   Veblen, *Leisure Class*, 81.
13   Veblen, *Leisure Class*, 85.
14   Veblen, *Leisure Class*, 96.
15   Veblen, *Leisure Class*, 102.
16   Veblen, *Leisure Class*, 103, 111.
17   Veblen, *Leisure Class*, 111–112.
18   Veblen, *Leisure Class*, 112.
19   Veblen, *Leisure Class*, 113.
20   Veblen, *Leisure Class*, 109–110.
21   Veblen, *Leisure Class*, 114.
22   Veblen, *Leisure Class*, 116.
23   Veblen, *Leisure Class*, 116.
24   Veblen, *Leisure Class*, 141.
25   Veblen, *Leisure Class*, 143.
26   Veblen, *Leisure Class*, 155.
27   Veblen, *Leisure Class*, 169.
28   Veblen, *Leisure Class*, 158.
29   Veblen, *Leisure Class*, 154.
30   Veblen, *Leisure Class*, 159.
31   Veblen, *Leisure Class*, 162–165.
32   Veblen, *Leisure Class*, 221.
33   Veblen, *Leisure Class*, 99.
34   Veblen, *Leisure Class*, 179–182.
35   Veblen, *Leisure Class*, 178.
36   Veblen, *Leisure Class*, 181.
37   Veblen, *Leisure Class*, 190.
38   Veblen, *Leisure Class*, 192.

39 Veblen, *Leisure Class*, 192.
40 Veblen, *Leisure Class*, 193.
41 Veblen, *Leisure Class*, 197.
42 Veblen, *Leisure Class*, 198.
43 Veblen, *Leisure Class*, 199.
44 Veblen, *Leisure Class*, 200.
45 Veblen, *Leisure Class*, 203.
46 Veblen, *Leisure Class*, 205.
47 Veblen, *Leisure Class*, 209.
48 Veblen, *Leisure Class*, 211.
49 Veblen, *Leisure Class*, 219.
50 Veblen, *Leisure Class*, 221.
51 Veblen, *Leisure Class*, 224.
52 Veblen, *Leisure Class*, 225.
53 Veblen, *Leisure Class*, 225.
54 Veblen, *Leisure Class*, 227.
55 Veblen, *Leisure Class*, 228–229.
56 Veblen, *Leisure Class*, 237–238.
57 Veblen, *Leisure Class*, 244.
58 Veblen, *Leisure Class*, 245.
59 Veblen, *Leisure Class*, 247.
60 Veblen, *Leisure Class*, 248.
61 Veblen, *Leisure Class*, 250.
62 Veblen, *Leisure Class*, 253–254.
63 Veblen, *Leisure Class*, 255.
64 Veblen, *Leisure Class*, 256.
65 Veblen, *Leisure Class*, 261.
66 Veblen, *Leisure Class*, 268.
67 Veblen, *Leisure Class*, 270.
68 Veblen, *Leisure Class*, 275.
69 Veblen, *Leisure Class*, 284.
70 Veblen, *Leisure Class*, 290.
71 Veblen, *Leisure Class*, 291.
72 Veblen, *Leisure Class*, 292.
73 Veblen, *Leisure Class*, 307.
74 Veblen, *Leisure Class*, 326.
75 Veblen, *Leisure Class*, 331.
76 Veblen, *Leisure Class*, 341.
77 Veblen, *Leisure Class*, 357.
78 Veblen, *Leisure Class*, 360.
79 Veblen, *Leisure Class*, 383.
80 Veblen, *Leisure Class*, 383.
81 Veblen, *Leisure Class*, 384.
82 Veblen, *Leisure Class*, 382.
83 Veblen, *Leisure Class*, 382.
84 Veblen, *Leisure Class*, 389.
85 Veblen, *Leisure Class*, 395.
86 Veblen, *Leisure Class*, 399.
87 Thorstein Veblen, "Industrial and Pecuniary Employments," in *The Place of Science in Modern Civilization*, intro. Warren J. Samuels (New York: Cosimo, 2007), 279–323.
88 Veblen, "Employments," in *Place of Science*, 279.
89 Veblen, "Employments," in *Place of Science*, 281.

90   Veblen, "Employments," in *Place of Science*, 289n4.
91   Veblen, "Employments," in *Place of Science*, 299.
92   Veblen, "Employments," in *Place of Science*, 308.
93   Veblen, "Employments," in *Place of Science*, 310.
94   Veblen, "Employments," in *Place of Science*, 311.
95   Veblen, "Employments," in *Place of Science*, 311.
96   Veblen, "Employments," in *Place of Science*, 294.
97   Veblen, "Employments," in *Place of Science*, 307.
98   Veblen, "Employments," in *Place of Science*, 313–314.
99   Veblen, "Employments," in *Place of Science*, 317.
100 Veblen, "Employments," in *Place of Science*, 317.
101 Veblen, "Employments," in *Place of Science*, 318.
102 Thorstein Veblen, "On the Nature of Capital I" and "On the Nature of Capital II," in *The Place of Science in Modern Civilization*, intro. Warren J. Samuels (New York: Cosimo, 2007), 324–386.
103 Thorstein Veblen, "Professor Clark's Economics," in *The Place of Science in Modern Civilization*, intro. Warren J. Samuels (New York: Cosimo, 2007), 185.
104 Veblen, *Imperial Germany*, 272.
105 Veblen, "Nature of Capital," in *Place of Science*, 328.
106 Veblen, "Nature of Capital," in *Place of Science*, 328.
107 Veblen, *The Engineers and the Price System* (New York: B.W. Huebsch, 1921), 135.
108 Veblen, *Engineers*, 56.
109 Veblen, "Employments," in *Place of Science*, 297.
110 Veblen, "Workmanship and Irksomeness," in *Changing Order*, 78–96.

5

THE CRITIQUE CONTINUED

Biographical Note

By 1906, Veblen's welcome at the University of Chicago had run out, apparently as a result of what may delicately be called his "marital problems." Given the circumstances under which he left Chicago, finding a new academic job could have been difficult, but he was lucky in finding a place at Stanford where he was appointed associate professor – the highest academic rank he ever held. Ellen joined him in Palo Alto, but not for long, and the pattern of separation and reconciliation continued.[1]

By this time, Veblen had acquired a coterie of former students who cannot be said to have been his disciples, for he had no disciples, but whose work was greatly influenced by the time they spent with him and who were devoted to him personally. He had also acquired the respect of a number of leading economists who, although they did not share his perspective, were impressed by his work.

It was generally believed that Veblen was a socialist, but of just what sort no one knew. He was very reticent about stating his political or economic views, preferring to let his writings speak for him. Although he was no doubt sympathetic with many of the reform movements of his time – it was called the "Progressive Era" for a reason – he was not a joiner, preferring the position of a detached observer. In his writings he maintained the stance of disinterested objectivity that he considered proper for a scientific investigator. Veblen saw himself as an economic theorist and he continued his critique of economic theories with his reviews of Fisher, Clark, marginal utility, and his lectures on Marx.

Marginal Utility

In 1909, Veblen published an article entitled "The Limitations of Marginal Utility."[2] We have noted above the victory of marginal utility theory in the period from 1880 to 1900; by 1909, it had become well established in the United States. But Veblen regarded the theory as misguided and he attempted to undercut its popularity. Marginal utility theory, he says, is a theory of value, and therefore belongs to the field of distribution. There have been attempts to extend it to production, the most impressive of which Veblen attributes to Clark, but he says that none of them have succeeded. Further, Veblen says, it is a purely static theory and is not applicable to questions of growth or evolution. But the theory is more limited than even this suggests, for it is a teleological theory; the determinants of action are the anticipations of future rewards. Final causes are not transformable into efficient causes; the two modes of description are incommensurable. Accordingly, marginal utility theory has nothing to say about economic change which is a matter of efficient causes. The domain left to the theory is thus a very narrow one. But it is narrower yet. Marginal utility theory assumes a perfectly rational actor influenced solely by his expectations of future pains and pleasures. It is therefore a theory with a very restricted field of application.

The theory of marginal utility is unobjectionable within its own field. But what does its tiny field embrace? Comparing the problems of institutional change to those with which marginal utility deals, Veblen comments:

> The former bear on the continuity and mutations of that scheme of conduct whereby mankind deals with its material means of life; the latter, if it is conceived in hedonistic terms, concerns a disconnected episode in the sensuous experience of an individual member of such a community.[3]

But Veblen comments that economic explanations cannot be given solely in terms of individuals "because it cannot be drawn in terms of the underlying traits of human nature simply, since the response that goes to make up human conduct takes place under institutional norms and only under stimuli that have an institutional bearing."[4] Individuals are embedded in a culture in which their wants and hates are conditioned by cultural actors. What the individual wants is a function of an institutional variable that is omitted from the calculations of the hedonistic calculus.

The postulates of the theory, Veblen says, are, first, a certain institutional situation taken as a fixed and unchangeable characteristic of the economic world, and second, the hedonistic calculus. The institutional situation consists chiefly of the natural rights of ownership, with all the related doctrines of property, all taken as immutable features of the world. The hedonistic calculus is assumed in as unqualified a form as it was by the economists of the early nineteenth century. The theory is deductively derived from these premises which are assumed *a priori* rather than based on observation. It is therefore clear that marginal utility theory is an offshoot of British classical economics, more narrowly focused and sharply defined.

Marginal utility theory leaves out of account all questions of change, of growth and development. But Veblen says these are just the questions that economists need to be focusing on. To assume that our current institutions of property are eternal is to ignore all questions of how this institutional structure came to be, and even more importantly all questions of what form it may take in the future. This is to project the institutional status at a particular time through all times, and therefore to abandon any inquiry into economic dynamics.

Veblen then turns to a description of the current business system, emphasizing the pecuniary character of modern business. Businessmen think and act in terms of pecuniary concepts such as price, not in terms of the sensuous gratifications of consumption.

> The hedonistically presumed final purchase of consumable goods is habitually not contemplated in the pursuit of business enterprise. Business men habitually aspire to accumulate wealth in excess of the limits of practicable consumption, and the wealth so accumulated is not intended to be converted by final transaction of purchase into consumable goods or sensations of consumption.[5]

Marginal utility theory does not therefore fit the facts of business life. Nor are business phenomena translatable into hedonistic terms – for example, "loans, discounts, and capitalization."[6] Moreover, Veblen points out that in modern culture, pecuniary concepts such as price are applied to matters that lie well beyond the scope of business.

> Indeed, so great and pervading a force has this habit of pecuniary accountancy become that it extends, often as a matter of course, to many facts which properly have no pecuniary bearing and no pecuniary magnitude, as, e.g., works of the arts, science, scholarship and religion ... and this in spite of the fact that, on reflection, most men of normal intelligence will freely admit that these matters lie outside the scope of pecuniary valuation.[7]

Thus Veblen views marginal utility theory as incapable of dealing with the phenomena of current business and so narrowly focused on individual decisions making as to be virtually useless.

Fisher

Irving Fisher was born in 1867 – a decade after the cohort of Veblen, Clark, and Ely. He attended Yale, where he became a student of William Graham Sumner, to whom he dedicated his book on capital and income. He graduated in 1888, studied in Berlin and Paris, and in 1891 became Yale's first PhD in economics.

His subsequent career was spent at Yale. Fisher was a conservative economist; he was also a gifted mathematician, and a pioneer in several types of economics, particularly monetarism, for his contributions to which he has won the praises of Milton Freedman.

Veblen's review of Irving Fisher's *The Nature of Capital and Income*[8] was published in 1906.[9] The review is among the most scathing Veblen ever wrote, despite the fact that Fisher was already among the country's leading economists. But Fisher's book illustrated precisely those aspects of the marginal utility school that Veblen found most objectionable. Veblen describes Fisher's book as an essay in taxonomy and definition rather than as an attempt to extend theory to explain new phenomena. Fisher laid great stress on the development of precise definitions which he saw as a way of resolving the ongoing debate over the nature of capital; in this sense the book is more an effort at conceptual clarification than an explanation of new data.[10] Fisher defined capital in terms of wealth which he defined as "signifying material objects owned by human beings" and includes persons, for one owns oneself.[11] Fisher wants a definition of capital that will be permanent. Veblen replies that as the concept of capital actually functions in business, it constantly changes as the character of business changes. If Fisher had derived his concept of capital from observations of actual business practices he would have known that, but instead he drew his concept from Bentham and his followers, with the result that it is irrelevant to actual business. Fisher's goal, Veblen says, is a taxonomic theory, but Veblen replies, "Taxonomy for taxonomy's sake, definition and classification for the sake of definition and classification, meets no need of modern science."[12]

> If we include the body as a transforming instrument, while we must credit with their respective services all those outside agencies … we must also at the same time debit the body with these same items. In this case the only surviving credit items after these equal debits and credits are canceled are the resulting final satisfactions in the human mind.[13]

This is what Fisher calls the "final income." This remarkable bit of creative accounting draws from Veblen the following comment.

> The absolute merits of the hedonistic conception of economic theory need not be argued here. It was a far-reaching conception, and its length of life has made it a grand conception. But great as may be the due of courtesy to that conception for the long season of placid content which economic theory has spent beneath its spreading chestnut tree, yet the fact is not to be overlooked that its scheme of accountancy is not that of the modern business community. The logic of economic life in a modern community runs in terms of pecuniary, not of hedonistic, magnitudes.[14]

Veblen's basic charge against Fisher is that capital and income as he defines them are those required by the hedonistic theory and not those used in the real world of business. Fisher wants precise definitions that never require change; Veblen notes that as used by businessmen these concepts constantly change and that fact requires explanation. Although Fisher makes a point of giving examples from business life, Veblen says he has failed to observe how businessmen actually use these concepts, which in modern business are pecuniary concepts, not hedonistic ones. In fact, the goal of Fisher's book seems to be to show how capital and income can be defined in the hedonistic terms of the marginal utility school. The book therefore exemplifies the faults Veblen found with classical economics and with the attempts to rationalize it in terms of marginal utility.

In 1909, Veblen wrote a review of Fisher's *The Rate of Interest*[15] in which he further elaborated his criticisms of Fisher's theory.[16] As Fisher's theory of interest rests upon his theory of capital and income, many of the criticisms Veblen made of the earlier book apply here. Fisher's theory is an agio (premium) theory similar to that of Eugen Böhm von Bawerk, to whose work Fisher pays homage.[17] He defines the rate of interest as "the excess above unity of the rate of exchange between the values of future and present goods taken in relation to the time interval between the two sets of goods."[18] In other words, present income is preferred to future income. "All time preference resolves itself into the preference for early income over late income. Moreover, the preference for present income over future income resolves itself into the preference for present *final* income over future *final* income."[19] Thus, remembering Fisher's definition of "final income" in the earlier book, the incomes compared here are hedonistic magnitudes. It is income that is fundamental for Fisher; the rate of interest is essentially the price required to exchange a future income for a present one.[20]

Veblen finds this whole approach objectionable. Besides confusing interest with price, it ignores the role of interest in business. Interest in anything like its present sense is a creation of the modern business system and is a pecuniary institution, not a hedonistic one. As such, it is a creature of the current institutional situation and cannot be otherwise understood. "The phenomenon of modern business, including the rate of interest, can no more be handled in non-pecuniary terms than human physiology can be handled in terms of the amphioxus."[21] (The amphioxus, also called the lancelet, is a marine invertebrate that is an important link in the evolution leading to vertebrates.) One hesitates to impose a sporting simile on Veblen, but his point is that explaining interest in terms of psychic income is like explaining the kickoff in football in terms of knee flexion. Even if the marginal utility theory were true, which Veblen denies, explaining interest rates in terms of "the supply and demand of present and future incomes"[22] ignores the role interest actually plays in business, as Veblen had described it in Chapter 5 of *The Theory of Business Enterprise*. Furthermore, Veblen argues that some of the cases Fisher cites as "verifications" of his theory actually tell against it.

Clark

In 1908, Veblen published an article on "Professor Clark's Economics."[23] John Bates Clark had been Veblen's teacher at Carleton College; by 1900 he was recognized as the foremost economist in the United States. Veblen is properly respectful. "Mr. Clark's position among this generation of economists is a notable and commanding one. ...In more than one respect Mr. Clark's position among economists recalls the great figures in the science a hundred years ago."[24] Veblen notes the affection with which Clark's students regard their old teacher, but he also says that his role as critic requires that he deal with Clark's work objectively and impersonally.

Clark is a true heir of classical economics, Veblen says. Although he is a marginalist – having developed the marginal utility theory on his own independently of the Austrian economists – his work belongs in the classical tradition. His psychology is hedonism as unqualified as that of James Mill and his work centers on ownership, price, and acquisition. It is his theory of distribution that is the centerpiece of Clark's work. Although it was the publication of Clark's *Essentials of Economic Theory*[25] that occasioned this article, it is his theory of distribution to which Veblen gives the greatest emphasis.

Clark distinguishes two states of the economy: the static and the dynamic. It is the static state that Clark regards as the "natural" or normal one. In such a state, the economic system is in perfect equilibrium; it is a state of perfect competition in which all the variables defining the system stand in normal relations. It is also a state that is never realized in the real world; rather, it is one to which the actual economy always "strives" to return. As Clark puts it, "We think, then, of society as striving toward an endless series of ideal shapes, never reaching any one of them and never holding for any length of time any one actual shape."[26] Dynamics, in contrast, deals with the deviations from the static state. These deviations are due to external factors; in the static state the economy has no tendency to change. But Veblen notes that Clark's static state is not really static. As the economy moves through time and suffers repeated disruptions due to external causes, the system seeks to regain equilibriums though the values of the variables may differ from one equilibrium state to another. It is the relation among the variables that defines the equilibrium, not the specific values.

Like other classical economists, Clark makes extensive use of what he calls "primitive" economic conditions to illustrate his points – solitary hunters, wholly self-sufficient men who satisfy all their own needs by their own labors. Veblen points out that this conjectural history has no basis in fact; Clark really uses it to focus attention on certain economic processes that he wants to isolate for discussion. Veblen notes that in these cases, the "capital" of Clark's self-sufficient primitives always consists of physical objects. But, Veblen says, if one takes as an example the "Digger Indians" of California, whose cultural level is that of Clark's primitives, the loss of their entire stock of capital goods would have little importance, since they could easily replace them. What would be of real consequence would be the loss of their technological knowledge, which is their real capital, since without that knowledge they could not cope with their environment. Actual savages, Veblen holds, were and are never solitary; they live in groups. It is the group that carries the technological knowledge and that survives or does not survive, not the individual.

These historical remarks open the way for Veblen's discussion of Clark's concept of capital. Clark distinguishes "capital" from "capital goods." The latter are the physical objects employed in production – tools, machines, whatever. The former consists of a fund of such capital goods. The fund is permanent, the capital goods that compose the fund are perishable. When a tool or machine is worn out and is replaced by another, the fund as such continues on. Capital goods are tangible physical objects; the fund is not – it is an abstract entity the members of which are the capital goods. Veblen objects to this way of conceptualizing capital. As the term "capital" is used in current business, Veblen says, it is a pecuniary concept, not a physical one. The problems with Clark's concept become clear when he speaks of the mobility of capital. Shifting capital from one line of endeavor, A, to another, B, means to Clark that instead of replacing a capital good of type A with another of type A, what replaces it is a physical object of type B. As Veblen points out, what is really involved here is a change of investment. Similarly, Clark speaks of the "destruction" of capital, but Veblen says he does not mean the destruction of physical goods or the fund but a loss of pecuniary values. Clark cannot deal with intangible assets, but it is intangible assets that dominate business activities today, and so Clark's theory is inadequate as a theory of modern business. And what is most peculiar about this situation is that Clark's "fund" is itself an intangible object; the capital goods that compose the fund are tangible, but the fund itself is not.

Clark deals with labor in a manner similar to that which he uses for capital. Just as capital is a permanent fund the members of which are particular capital goods, so Clark defines "social labor" to be an abstract entity composed of individual laborers. "Men come and go but work continues forever."[27] There are, then, two permanent entities combined in the industry of the world. The one is capital, or the wealth that continues forever by casting off and renewing material bodies – capital goods. The other is labor which continues in a similar way. It is represented today by one set of men, and tomorrow by another. Both of these permanent agents of production have an unlimited power of transmutation: they are changing their embodiment every year and every day.[28]

Clark divided economics into statics and dynamics. The static state is the ideal; it is the "natural" or normal state of the economy. The dynamic states are of five sorts: population growth, increases of capital, changes of method, changes in organization, and changes in consumer wants.[29] These are disturbances, unwelcome disruptions of the normal static state.

Nowhere is there a sustained inquiry into the dynamic character of the changes that have brought the present (deplorable) situation to pass, nor into the nature and trend of the forces at work in the development that is going forward in this situation. None of this is covered by Mr. Clark's use of the word "dynamic."[30]

Once the static state is reached, the business of economic theory is done. For economic theory of this kind, that is all there is to any economic situation. "The hedonistic magnitudes vary from one situation to another, but, except for variations in the arithmetic details in the hedonistic balance, all situations are, in point of economic theory, substantially alike."[31]

Clark has no theory of economic dynamics as such, no theory of how or why these disruptions occur; he has only recommendations of how to correct them. What this yields, Veblen says, is a taxonomy – the classification of economic phenomena. Clark's economic system as Veblen sees it, is a taxonomic system, not an evolutionary science.

Veblen then turns to the examination of Clark's "law of nature": the law of "natural" distribution says that, in the static state, any productive agent "naturally" gets what it produces.[32] This law, Veblen notes, is the heart of Clark's system. Clark is fundamentally a Christian economist; the acceptability of the present economic system depends for him upon its justice. This is made very clear at the beginning of the *Distribution of Wealth* where he writes:

> The indictment that hangs over society is that of "exploiting" labor. "Workmen," it is said, "are regularly robbed of what they produce. This is done within the forms of law, and by the natural working of competition." If this charge were proved, every right-minded man should become a socialist, and his zeal in transforming the industrial system would then measure and express his sense of justice.[33]

That capitalism exploited labor was a charge most famously made by Marx. It is Clark's goal to prove that every worker gets all he produces. Clark takes it for granted that if he can prove this, he has proven the justice of the system. The underlying idea is apparently Locke's notion that a man has a natural right to whatever he has made by his own labor. Clark intends to show that when the economy is in its "natural" state it gives "to each producer the amount of wealth that he specifically brings into existence."

Throughout his books, Clark talks in the standard language of economics – goods, production, distribution, etc. But to achieve the generality he wants, he requires a common denominator into which he can translate his terms. This common denominator is for Clark "utility" (and "disutility"). So far as the individual worker is concerned, the basic argument is then fairly simple, from the employer's point of view. An employer hires labor to produce a particular sort of goods. Assuming that all other factors remain unchanged, according to the law of diminishing returns, the amount of product created by each new unit of labor will decrease as the number of units increases. Following the marginal utility doctrine, the employer will add units of labor until the cost of the last unit (wages) becomes equal to the value of the product it creates. This marginal point fixes what wages labor gets and what product is produced per unit. It is then true that each unit of labor gets in its wages the full value of the product it creates. There is no exploitation. Translating these terms into utilities, the utility that the marginal unit of labor receives through its wages equals the utility of the product created by that unit of labor.[34] Veblen replies:

> A product is such by virtue of and to the amount of the utility which it has for a consumer. The utility of the goods is measured, as value, by the sacrifice (disutility) which the consumer is willing to undergo in order to get the utility which the consumption of the good yields him. The unit and measure of productive labor is in the last analysis also a unit of disutility; but it is a disutility to the productive laborer, not to the consumer. The balance which establishes itself under competitive conditions is a compound balance, being a balance between the utility of the goods to the consumer and the disutility (cost) which he is willing to undergo for it, on the one hand, and, on the other hand, a balance between the disutility of the unit of labor and the utility for which the laborer is willing to undergo this disutility. It is evident, and admitted, that there can be no balance, and no commensurability, between the laborer's disutility (pain) in producing the goods and the consumer's utility (pleasure) in consuming them, in as much as these two hedonistic phenomena lie each within the consciousness of a distinct person.[35]

Clark agrees. "When the enjoying falls to one party and the suffering to another there is no offsetting in the case. There is, therefore, no equivalent established between the disutility of such work and the utility of the product."[36]

But Clark's argument takes a different course. He says that his statement of his law of distribution

> will be complete enough to reveal all the general and essential facts of distribution when we know how we may measure labor, capital and their products. But we need, evidently, a universally usable measure of values … It is clear that we must have some unit that will give us absolute sums.[37]

The necessary comparisons can be made if we can find an objective measure of capital, labor, and consumer's wealth.[38]

> If each man could measure the usefulness of an article by the effort that it costs him to get it, and if he could attain a fixed unit of effort, he could state

the utilities of a number of different articles in a sum total. Similarly, if all society acts in reality as one man, it makes such measurements of all commodities, and the trouble arising from the fact that there are many measurers disappears. A market secures this result, for society acts as unit – like an individual buyer.[39]

How does society evaluate goods? Clark says, "Society, in short, sets value upon a thing by ascertaining how much work is necessary to replace it or to get an equivalent for it.[40] Otherwise put, the pain (disutility) of a loss of an article is measured by the amount of work necessary to replace it or find an equivalent. Clark then claims that although pleasures are various, pain (disutility) is homogeneous. Pains (disutilities) may vary in amount but not in quality.[41] In particular, Clark holds that the disutility of work increases with the number of consecutive hours of work, so the maximum disutility of work is in the last hour worked, and he assumes that the last hour's disutility is uniformly distributed over the final hour. He then defines the "efficiency of labor" as follows, "Efficiency of a worker is, in reality, power to draw out labor on the part of society. It is capacity to offer that for which society will work in return."[42] So,

> If A, by working for a year, can induce society to work two minutes, and if B, in the same way, can induce it to work three minutes, the former is only two thirds as efficient as the latter. The labor of each one of a thousand men working in as many different trades may be measured, and the amounts given by the different measurements may be added, compared and averaged.[43]

The trick is the conversion of the efficiency of labor into intervals of time that can be measured by cardinal numbers and so manipulated. "Three things," Clark says, "can be measured in terms of this ultimate standard of value, namely, consumers' wealth, capital and labor."[44] And Clark holds that this is sufficient to prove his law. Veblen was not impressed.

> The equitable balance between work and pay contemplated by the "natural" law is a balance between wages and "efficiency," as above defined; that is to say, between the wages of labor and the capacity of labor to get wages. So far, the whole matter might evidently have been left as [Frédéric] Bastiat left it. It amounts to saying that the laborer gets what he is willing to accept and the consumers give what they are willing to pay.[45]

To refute Clark's claims for his law of just remuneration, Veblen invokes the consumer's surplus. Assuming that the exchange is between the producer of the goods offered and a consumer who pays in return.

The law works out through the mediation of price. Price is determined competitively, by marginal producers or sellers and marginal consumers or purchasers: the latter alone on the one side get the precise price-equivalent of the disutility incurred by them, and the latter alone on the other side pay the full price-equivalent of the utilities derived by them from the goods purchased. Hence the competitive price – covering competitive wages and interest – does not reflect the consensus of all parties concerned as to the "effective utility" of the goods, on the one hand, or as to their effective (disutility) cost, on the other hand. It reflects instead, if anything of this kind, the valuations which the marginal unfortunates on each side concede under the stress of competition; and it leaves on each side of the bargain relation an uncovered "surplus" which marks the (variable) interval by which price fails to cover "effective utility."[46]

The wages of labor (i.e., the utility of the goods received by the laborer) is not equal to the disutility undergone by him, except in the sense that he is competitively willing to accept it; nor are these wages equal to the utility got by the consumer of the goods, except in the sense that he is competitively willing to pay them. This point is covered by the current diagrammatic arguments of marginal-utility theory as to the determination of competitive prices.[47]

It follows, Veblen says, that no man "is paid an amount that equals the amount of the total product he personally creates."[48]

Veblen then turns to the issue of monopoly. If a business raises its prices, it will, under competitive conditions, decrease the volume of its sales. But if there is a point at which the returns from setting prices at a higher level are greater than from the lower price level, despite the smaller volume of sales, then it will pay the company to set its prices at that point. This is of course the secret of monopoly. Putting this in utility terms, it is clear from the standard marginal diagrams that by reducing the number of items sold, the utility of the last item that is sold will be increased. Monopoly may therefore increase the utility of its products, to the benefit of consumers. This result leads Veblen to remark:

> The monopolist is only pushing the principle of all business enterprise (free competition) to its logical conclusion; and, in point of hedonistic theory, such monopolistic gains are to be accounted the "natural" remuneration of the monopolist for his "productive" service to the community in enhancing their enjoyment per-unit of consumable goods to such a point as to swell their net aggregate enjoyment to a maximum.[49]

What this shows, Veblen holds, is that monopoly is a natural outcome of competitive business as Clark describes it – it is a result that contradicts Clark's attack on monopoly.

The later portion of Clark's *Essentials* is devoted to current economic problems and the means of their solution. Veblen remarks that Clark's proposals for dealing with these problems have no relation to the economic theory presented in the earlier part of the book.[50] For example, Clark recognizes that in the current economy, monopolies are chiefly generated through holding companies. But Veblen argues that the essential factor is the ability of the monopolist to gain control of companies through stock manipulation, and particularly through stocks covering intangible assets. But Clark's theory of capital does not admit the existence of intangible assets and so offers no basis for dealing with this problem. Clark's economics is a hedonistic economics, and like most hedonistic economics is chiefly a theory of distribution. Consumption is taken for granted as a matter of insatiable appetites, and production deals with the gains to be acquired by production, and so with distributive acquisition. It is an essential claim of hedonistic theories, Clark's included, that "the acquisitive activities of mankind afford a net balance of pleasure."[51] This claim, Veblen says, is never proven; it represents a continuation of eighteenth-century optimism, and is one that is not supported by Clark's theory.

According to Clark's theory, men acquire utilities at the cost of producing them. At the margin, the utility produced by the last unit of labor is equal to the disutility of the effort expended in that labor. The effective utility of the whole is given by the product of the effectual utility of the marginal unit times the total number of units produced. This equals the total effective disutility of the pains of acquisition.[52] There is then no net balance of utilities. Worse yet, the equation "pain-cost = pleasure-gain" ignores the fact that the pleasure-gain is largely pleasure expected in the future from the article produced. Notoriously, comparison of present pleasures with future pleasures requires that the future pleasures be discounted, since their realization is contingent. Hence the equation ought to be "pain-cost > pleasure-gain"; the production of utilities is, mathematically speaking, "a function of the pig-headed optimism of mankind."[53] Surely, a theory that leads to such conclusions is far from satisfactory.

Veblen finds much of Clark's theory an elaborate reformulation of classical doctrine; at one point, he remarks, "It is not easy to see that some hundreds of pages of apparatus should be required to find one's way back to these time-worn commonplaces of Manchester [i.e., the theory of laissez-faire]."[54] But Veblen's basic objection to Clark's theory (and others like it) is their preconception that there is "one right and beautiful definitive scheme of economic life to 'which the whole creation tends.'"[55] Any deviation from the path of this goal must be corrected forthwith; "the future, such as it ought to be – the only normally possible, natural future scheme of life,"[56] guides the development of the economy to its preordained goal.

By 1906, Veblen had become a widely recognized figure and had won the respect of a number of the leading economists of the nation. In 1906, Frank Taussig, Harvard's professor of economics, invited Veblen to give a series of lectures on Marx. The four lectures Veblen gave dealt with Marx's economic theory and with the fate of Marxist theory in the years since Marx's death. Veblen had hopes that he might receive an appointment at Harvard, but this did not occur, despite Taussig's good will. But these lectures have considerable interest on their own. Veblen was generally believed to be a socialist, but just what kind of socialist no one was sure. These lectures show that he was not a Marxist socialist.

Marx

If Clark represented the best that classical economics had to offer, the best alternative to the classical theory was offered by Marx. In 1906, Veblen gave four lectures on Marx and his followers at Harvard. Although Marx drew heavily on Hegel and the British classical economists, Veblen pays tribute to the originality of Marx's work; there is nothing like it before Marx. Since the publication of *Das Kapital* in 1867, Marxist theory has become the dominant form of socialism everywhere, and it is socialism as Marx conceived it that is the focus of current discussion. Marx was both a propagandist and an economic theorist and the two aspects are often confused, but not by Marx; his economic theory can stand alone, apart from any propagandistic use made of it.

Marx was a product of the Hegelian left of writers such as Ludwig Feuerbach, and his materialistic conception of history comes from that source. But it is a peculiar form of materialism. This is not a materialism that denies the existence or importance of thought; rather it is a materialism in the sense that what men think is a reflex of material economic conditions. It is a theory of change, or development, but of a teleological development directed to the "complete realization of life in all its fullness."[57] Unlike Hegel, for whom history is the unfolding of the life of the world spirit, for Marx the process is driven by the class struggle; it is thus a self-acting process, but one that takes place in human consciousness. The class struggle determines the social order, and the form of the class struggle is determined by the prevailing modes of production and exchange. And Veblen remarks, "It is a sublimated materialism, sublimated by the dominating presence of the conscious human spirit; but it is conditioned by the material facts of the production of the means of life."[58] What drives the class struggle is the interests of the classes involved, conceived in hedonistic terms.

Marx's theory of production is based on the labor theory of value. Marx takes the principle that value equals labor cost to be self-evident; no proof for it is offered, for none is thought necessary. In the Hegelian theory, "the only substantial reality is the unfolding life of the spirit."[59] As Marx translates this doctrine into his materialism, "the reality is translated into terms of the unfolding [material] life of man in society."[60] The goods produced by industry embody this life process since they embody the "metaphysical substance of life – labor power."[61]

The true value of the goods is given by the labor power they contain, so any two products that embody the same amount of labor power are equal in value, but not necessarily in exchange value.

> The labor power expended in production being itself a product and having a substantial value corresponding to its own labor-cost, the value of the labor power expended and the value of the product created by its expenditure need not be the same.[62]

Under capitalism, wages measure the value of the labor power expended in producing a product, while the value of the product in exchange is determined by competitive bidding. The difference between these two is the surplus value that is appropriated by the capitalist.

> Under the capitalistic system, wages being the value (price) of the labor power consumed in industry, it follows that the surplus product of their labor cannot go to the laborer, but becomes the profits of capital and the source of its accumulation and increase.[63]

The surplus is added to the owner's capital and steadily accumulates. As this happens, more funds are invested in "constant capital" (equipment and materials). Labor-saving devices proliferate, so less labor is required even though output increases. The labor no longer needed accumulates in an increasing number of unemployed workers. The capitalist uses this army of the unemployed to force down wages, which Marx held would fall below subsistence level – as he believed was happening in England of his time. At the same time, the workers (employed and unemployed) are decreasingly able to buy the goods produced by industry, with the result that the markets will be glutted and the economy will fall into depression. Eventually, Marx believed, the condition of the workers would become so desperate and the reserve army so large that class consciousness would bond the poor into a revolutionary force, and the capitalist system is overthrown. What comes after then, Veblen notes, Marx does not say, except that private property will be abolished.

Such, Veblen holds, is the theory of Marx. But today (1906) it is losing followers, and is being radically modified by several major developments. The vogue of Hegel is over, having collapsed by 1875, and the dialectic has become an embarrassment. Marx saw the class struggle as proceeding by a logical argument to a destined end. In the Darwinian age, no such theory can stand; the question is what direction the process of efficient causes will take. History shows that human behavior is more apt to be governed by sentiment than by logic. Marx held that the material means of production governs life. On Darwinian grounds, this is questionable, since multiple factors affect life. Marx held that the proletariat would become progressively more distressed. But on Darwinian grounds, even if that were so, the result is as likely to be apathy and submission as revolt. Marx believed in a life force, but modern science knows of no such thing. Marx talked of exploitation, but Darwinian theory says nothing of any such right of labor to its full product. Thus the basic principles of Marxist theory are being called into question.

Further, Marxists have become a political party, and as such have been forced to accommodate to the changing political situation. In Germany, the labor movement has become powerful, and although there is no place for such a business accommodation between labor and capital in Marxist theory, the Marxists have had to reinterpret their theory to fit the facts. Similarly, the agricultural population has been notably cool to Marxism. Accordingly, the theory has been modified. Perhaps agriculture does not need to pass through a capitalist phase on the way to socialism. Worse yet, the condition of the workers has not deteriorated as Marx predicted but has improved. So it is now argued that a healthy proletariat will be a more effective revolutionary force than a malnourished one. And although Marx was opposed to national aggrandizement and military adventures, the situation in Germany has changed and patriotism has become essential for any group that would command a hearing. Thus Veblen believed in 1906 that Marxism was on its way to assimilation into the current mainstream of political life. He did not foresee that eleven years later the ten days that shook the world would give Marxism a new lease on life.

Notes

1 Joseph Dorfman, *Thorstein Veblen and His America* (Clifton, New Jersey: Augustus M. Kelley, 1972), 270–271.
2 Thorstein Veblen, "The Limitations of Marginal Utility," in *The Place of Science in Modern Civilization*, intro. Warren J. Samuels (New York: Cosimo, 2007), 231–251.
3 Veblen, "Marginal Utility," in *Place of Science*, 240.
4 Veblen, "Marginal Utility," in *Place of Science*, 242.
5 Veblen, "Marginal Utility," in *Place of Science*, 249.
6 Veblen, "Marginal Utility," in *Place of Science*, 247.
7 Veblen, "Marginal Utility," in *Place of Science*, 245–246.
8 Irving Fisher, *The Nature of Capital and Income* (New York: Macmillan, 1906).
9 Thorstein Veblen, "Fisher's Capital and Income," in *Essays in our Changing Order*, ed. Leon Ardzrooni (New York: The Viking Press, 1945), 148–172.
10 Fisher, *Capital*, 53–57.
11 Veblen, "Fisher's Capital," in *Changing Order*, 153.
12 Veblen, "Fisher's Capital," in *Changing Order*, 149.
13 Fisher, *Capital*, 167.
14 Veblen, "Fisher's Capital," in *Changing Order*, 160.
15 Irving Fisher, *The Rate of Interest* (New York: Macmillan, 1907).
16 Thorstein Veblen, "Fisher's Rate of Interest," in *Essays in our Changing Order*, ed. Leon Ardzrooni (New York: The Viking Press, 1945), 137–147.
17 Fisher, *Interest*, Chap. 4.
18 Fisher, *Interest*, 340.
19 Fisher, *Interest*, 89.

20 Veblen, "Fisher's Interest," *Changing Order*, 144.
21 *Encyclopædia Britannica Online*, s.v. "amphioxus," accessed October 03, 2016, www. britannica.com/animal/amphioxus.
22 Fisher, *Interest*, 131.
23 Thorstein Veblen, "Professor Clark's Economics," in *The Place of Science in Modern Civilization*, intro. Warren J. Samuels (New York: Cosimo, 2007), 180–230.
24 Veblen, "Clark," in *Place of Science*, 180–181.
25 John Bates Clark, *Essentials of Economic Theory* (New York: Macmillan, 1915).
26 Clark, *Essentials*, 253–254.
27 John Bates Clark, *The Distribution of Wealth* (New York: Augustus Kelly, 1965), 158.
28 Clark, *Distribution*, 158–159.
29 Clark, *Essentials*, 203–206.
30 Veblen, "Clark," in *Place of Science*, 188.
31 Veblen, "Clark," in *Place of Science*, 193.
32 Clark, *Distribution*, 201.
33 Clark, *Distribution*, 4.
34 Clark, *Distribution*, 201.
35 Veblen, "Clark," in *Place of Science*, 203–204.
36 Clark, *Distribution*, 390.
37 Clark, *Distribution*, 374.
38 Clark, *Distribution*, 395.
39 Clark, *Distribution*, 380.
40 Clark, *Distribution*, 379.
41 Clark, *Distribution*, 392–393.
42 Clark, *Distribution*, 394.
43 Clark, *Distribution*, 395.
44 Clark, *Distribution*, 395.
45 Veblen, "Clark," in *Place of Science*, 205.
46 Veblen, "Clark," in *Place of Science*, 208–209.
47 Veblen, "Clark," in *Place of Science*, 204–205.
48 Veblen, "Clark," in *Place of Science*, 209.
49 Veblen, "Clark," in *Place of Science*, 216–217.
50 Veblen, "Clark," in *Place of Science*, 218.
51 Veblen, "Clark," in *Place of Science*, 222.
52 Veblen, "Clark," in *Place of Science*, 223.
53 Veblen, "Clark," in *Place of Science*, 229.
54 Veblen, "Clark," in *Place of Science*, 206.
55 Veblen, "Clark," in *Place of Science*, 230.
56 Veblen, "Clark," in *Place of Science*, 230.
57 Thorstein Veblen, "The Socialist Economics of Karl Marx," in *The Place of Science in Modern Civilization*, intro. Warren J. Samuels (New York: Cosimo, 2007), 430.
58 Veblen, "Marx," in *Place of Science*, 415.
59 Veblen, "Marx," in *Place of Science*, 420.
60 Veblen, "Marx," in *Place of Science*, 420.
61 Veblen, "Marx," in *Place of Science*, 420.
62 Veblen, "Marx," in *Place of Science*, 423.
63 Veblen, "Marx," in *Place of Science*, 424.

6

VEBLEN'S THEORY OF BUSINESS

In 1904, Veblen wrote "A theory of the modern economic situation must be primarily a theory of business traffic, with its motives, aims, methods, and effects."[1] In *The Theory of Business Enterprise*, published that year, he sought to present such a theory. Business, Veblen held, is founded on the principle of ownership, which takes its present form from the writings of Locke.

> Though the earth and all inferior creatures be common to all men, yet every man hath a property in his own person: this nobody hath any right to but himself. The labour of his body and the work of his hands we may say are properly his. Whatsoever, then, he removes out of the state that nature hath provided and left it in, he hath mixed his labour with, and joined to it something that is his own, and thereby makes it his property.[2]

The right to property that Locke described was a Natural Right, according to the Theory of Natural Rights that dominated late eighteenth-century thought in England and America. These rights, it was held, were an endowment given to men by God and were inalienable. This theory became the basis of the political theory of the time. It was this theory that Jefferson invoked to explain and justify the American Revolution and that was enshrined in the Declaration of Independence. It is the theory underlying the Constitution of the United States, the French Declaration of the Rights of Man, and other charters of the era. American law was based on the theory of Natural Rights and has kept it alive and well throughout the nineteenth century and the early twentieth century. But its role in economics was no less important than its role in politics; Adam Smith was one of its proponents. It remained the American theory of property, even though there were other theories in play, such as that which Veblen invoked regarding the ownership of natural resources.

From this doctrine, the men of the eighteenth century drew the conclusion that every man has a Natural Right to the ownership of his own productions. And this right they took as including not only the right of possession but also of buying and selling, giving and receiving, and of doing with his property what he pleased. Thus, contracts, freely made, are protected by this natural right. Further, Veblen says, workmen have

> a natural right to turn their workmanship to account for a valuable consideration in working up material owned by another, without becoming owners of the resulting products, which gives rise to the wage relation. ... [But] ownership of natural resources – lands, forests, mineral deposits, water-power, harbor rights, franchises, etc. – rests not on a natural right of workmanship but on the ancient feudalistic ground of privilege and prescriptive tenure, vested interests, which runs back to the right of seizure by force and collusion.[3]

Business consists in the transference of owned and valued items from one person to another. The valued items may be property in the sense just described, or resources, rights, services, claims – anything people want, the sale of which is not prohibited by law. There are always some items the sale of which the law forbids: for example, persons. But laws change; at one time not so long ago people were bought and sold in the United States. There are also items that are sold despite legal prohibitions – narcotics for example. Such sales are not recognized in law, and the items sold can be confiscated upon detection. Owned items need not be material; they can be immaterial, intangible, and invisible, but they have a real existence created by the law. Nor need the owners be tangible – a corporation is not a tangible entity, but it can own property, buy and sell property, give and receive property.

The model of early business that Veblen cited the most was that of the handicraft era. The central figure of the handicraft system was the craftsman who was both producer and trader. The state of the Industrial Arts made possible the production of a wide variety of serviceable consumer goods, but the processes involved in production involved chiefly hand operated tools. The emphasis was upon the manipulative skill of the craftsman rather than his equipment. Accordingly, the productive unit was the craft shop, a small individually owned and operated enterprise. Similarly, the trading activities of the craftsman were geared to the local market. The transportation technology of the day made access to a wider market difficult, so the demand for craft products was met by his own output and that of his few competitors. Thus the technology of the time led to a large number of independent craft shops specializing in particular products according to the talents of the craftsman. For this society, the doctrine of Natural Rights and independent ownership was made to order.

> The principle of equal opportunity was, no doubt, met only in a very rough and dubious fashion; but so favorable became the conditions in this respect that men came to persuade themselves in the course of the eighteenth century that a substantially equitable allotment of opportunities would result from the abrogation of all prerogatives other than the ownership of goods.[4]

What changed this situation was the Industrial Revolution. It began in industries like textiles with the invention of wooden machines that could spin yarn and weave cloth more rapidly that humans could. This early machinery was powered by water, which meant that the early factories were limited to places where nature provided a drop in the water level – such as falls and rapids. Such sites were available in limited numbers, chiefly in the United States along the fall line. The products so made were then shipped by water to cities and towns for sale. Obviously, what was needed was a source of power not limited by geography.

The steam engine solved the problem. The early engines, such as the Newcomen engine, were too inefficient to support industrial use, but the Watt engine overcame these difficulties while providing a source of power that far exceeded what human or animal muscle could do. But the Watt engine had certain limits. First, Watt would only use steam at low pressure because of the danger of boiler explosions, and second the problem of how to apply the increased power with precision required solution. The first was solved by men who cared more about power than about safety and built high pressure engines despite the explosions, and the second by a group of men gathered around Henry Maudsley's machine shop. These men invented power tools that could harness steam for fine precision work even in metals such as iron and steel.

The costs of the new industrial equipment were beyond the resources of even master craftsmen. As a result, investment for profit became the way in which industry was financed in the era of the machine. This is the point, Veblen says, at which the economic system became capitalistic. Men who had money, and wanted more, now controlled the economic system, not as workers, or managers, but as investors. The law accommodated this situation by endowing the investors with limited liability for the uses to which their invested wealth was put; they could have the profits from their investments but had no responsibility beyond that. Veblen referred to them as "absentee owners."

As a result of the new machines, the output of industry increased dramatically, but so did the population, partly from natural increase and partly from the massive immigration that began in the United States in about 1840. As the population expanded and moved west, it furnished a growing market for the rapidly increasing industry. This was, as Veblen notes, an era of free competition in production in the United States where it was roughly true that the expanding market could absorb all that industry could produce.

Among the new machines that the Industrial Revolution produced were the steam boat and the railroad. The steam boat was very important in the early years of the nineteenth century in America, but the railroad quickly became the dominant transportation technology. The railroad first followed the population westward and then led the migration, opening up new areas, and markets, as it went, and after the Civil War reaching the West Coast to create a national market. Businesses of course moved too, locating so as to maximize their access to population centers and natural resources. The transportation revolution expanded the markets that the local industries could reach, and so brought about competition among the regions. And with population distribution rapidly changing and new natural resources being discovered, businesses found themselves at risk in a competitive free-for-all. This was the situation in which the corporation rose to dominance in the American economy.

A corporation is created by the state, either by an act of the legislature or by an agency created by the legislature for that purpose. It is a real entity; it is immaterial and immortal, yet it can own property, buy and sell goods, sue and be sued, and can commit crimes such as fraud. It cannot be imprisoned because it is an immaterial being, but it can be punished by fine. It is not a biological person, but it is a person under the terms of the Fourteenth Amendment and is so entitled to due process. It has the right of free speech under the First Amendment, even though it cannot speak; it "speaks" through its designated representative. The corporation has many of the rights of a biological person and these allow it to operate in the world of business as if it were an enormously powerful biological person. Although it is immortal in the ordinary course of affairs, it can be "dissolved" by the court under certain conditions. The law giveth and the law taketh away. The medieval theologians who debated how many angels can co-habit on the point of a pin would be right at home with today's lawyers in arguments concerning the rights and powers of corporations.

The original purpose of the corporation was to raise money, which it does by the sale of stocks. There are various types of stocks, the most important being common stocks. Veblen regarded common stocks as credit instruments; such stock he says, "Effects a transfer of a given body of property from the hands of an owner who resigns discretion in its control to a board of directors who assume the management of it."[5]

Common stocks are not regarded as credit instruments today. In the present view they are investments in equity. Ownership of such stocks is ownership of a portion of the company. Such ownership gives the shareholder the right to vote in the election of the board of directors and accordingly a voice in the management of the corporation. Stock dividends are not interest payments; some corporations pay dividends, some do not, and some do so irregularly. In all of these respects, stocks are different from loans. Nevertheless, Veblen sees them as credit instruments, and one should bear this in mind in interpreting his statements about the "credit economy" and the role of credit in business.

It is one of the peculiar features of the corporation that the owners – the holders of the common stocks – usually do not manage the business. The stockholders do elect the board of directors, but the actual operation of the business is done by managers hired by the board for that purpose. The managers need not own any stock at all in the corporation, although it is generally policy to make them shareholders to ensure that their personal financial interest coincides with that of the corporation. Stockholders can of course take on the role of managers, and some do, but this is not the usual practice. Accordingly the corporation affects a separation of ownership from the control of the company. That fact aroused considerable discussion when Adolf A. Berle and Gardiner C. Means emphasized it in their 1932 book *The Modern Corporation and Private Property*.[6] Veblen had repeatedly discussed this separation years before; he considered it one of the important features of the corporation.

In Veblen's view, corporations are conspiracies entered into by businessmen (chiefly) for the purpose of generating private gains. They may do this by generating goods and services or by constricting the production of goods and services. The important thing in Veblen's eyes is that the owners seek to maximize their private wealth. Veblen calls the income they acquire from their ownership of corporate stocks "free income," signifying that no useful work has been done by the owners to justify receiving this income.[7] If the owner is actually engaged in the management or operation of the company, Veblen considers his income to be earned.

That natural resources should be held as private property has been accepted without question in America, and ownership from the beginning has been absentee ownership. Those resources have been exploited for private gain. Of course the owners had no part in "producing" such resources, but the rights of the owners to profit from them has been unquestioned. These resources are so great in extent that the American population might have "come in for an unexampled material abundance on unexampled easy terms."[8] What has prevented the realization of that possibility has been the restrictive use of the natural resources imposed by the absentee owners to further their private gain. The owners seek to maximize their "free income" which comes from forcing the population to pay dearly for access to the resources necessary for living. Yet no movement to terminate the hold of the absentee owners has made headway in America; the legitimacy of absentee ownership is taken for granted. It is of course true that natural products become resources only when so defined by the Industrial Arts and that the exploitation is made possible by the Industrial Arts, but as Veblen has noted this fact has been largely ignored.

America was in the beginning chiefly an agricultural country; its industry was largely auxiliary to its agriculture. The expansion of agriculture by the settlement of the West is one of the greatest American achievements. At the time the nation was founded, the greatest natural resource it possessed was its land. From the beginning the land was used to encourage rapid settlement; it was packaged for sale in quarter section lots of 160 acres and sold at prices that rapidly declined over the course of the nineteenth century until the Homestead Act of 1862 gave land free in return for settlement and development. Land was held in fee simple; no attempt was made to keep public control over the land once it was sold. As Veblen says, the plan involved the transfer of public wealth into private hands. Veblen does not discuss the political and policy factors that underlay this practice and treats it as an obvious result of the business culture. Such it became, so that when John Wesley Powell proposed a different policy for dealing with the arid lands of the West, his proposal was rejected out of hand.[9]

From the beginning, American farmers have regarded themselves as "independent" masterless men, and Veblen says they have been models of self-help and cupidity. Farming as practiced in America has been extensive, not intensive. Even after the slash and burn phase had passed, farmers have been concerned chiefly with quick profits and paid little attention to the long-run fertility of their land. As they moved West, farmers sought to acquire more land than they could cultivate themselves, understanding well that as the population of the area increased the value of their land would rise. Thus the farmer has been a speculator in real estate, and often a very successful one. As this suggests, American farmers have exhibited little devotion to the land itself; rather they have seen it as a resource to be exploited for the greatest gain.

The process of settlement has led to the wide dispersion of farmers across the land, with each farm household settled on its own farm. In an earlier day, each farm family was supposed to be self-supporting. But Veblen notes that today

> farming is teamwork. As it is necessarily carried on by current methods in the great farming sections, farm work runs on such a scale that no individual owner can carry on by use of his own personal work alone, or by use of the man-power of his own household alone.[10]

One might think that the situation would have inspired collective action among the farmers, given the common problems they faced. But with rare exceptions, this has not happened; the desire for individual independence has been too strong. Partly this is due to the persistence of the ideal of the independent farmer, partly to the belief that by hard work the farmer can acquire a "competence" which will enable him someday to take his place among the absentee owners of the land and so come in for an easy livelihood at the cost of the rest of the community, and also by "the persistent though fantastic opinion" that he himself is an absentee owner since he works his land with hired help, and partly to the migratory pattern of his life.[11]

Veblen points out that the independence of the American farmer is largely an illusion. The settlement pattern has left the farmer always at a considerable distance from his market. Communication and transportation facilities such as roads have been wretched. Farmers have been largely at the mercy of the railroad, a fact of which the railroads have taken full advantage. Moreover, although farmers themselves have not been able to achieve collusive control over their production, those to whom they sell their products have. At market the farmers are faced with prices set by the corporate buyers, with the result that farm income is modest, and with the mechanization of farm production, costs of farm machinery have further reduced farm livelihoods to very modest amounts indeed. Farmers are caught in the web of absentee ownership and have not been able to find a way out.

What binds the farmer to the rest of the economy is the country town. Veblen remarks,

> The country town is one of the great American institutions; perhaps the greatest, in the sense that it has had and continues to have a greater part than any other in shaping the public sentiment and giving character to American culture.[12]

The country town is located with an eye to its real estate value, and real estate continues to be the dominant interest of its inhabitants throughout its life history. This is actively promoted by its citizens who are "boomers" and "boosters" for the town. The objective is to inflate the value of the surrounding real estate often by as much as 200 percent or more of its actual value. Real estate is of course an enterprise in fiction designed, Veblen says, "to get something for nothing from the unwary," of whom Veblen says "there is one born every minute."[13] Veblen says the real estate is a rival of poker as the Great American Game.[14]

The principal business of the town, aside from real estate, is its traffic with the farm population. It is both a shipping station for farm produce, since the towns are always located with access to the railroad, and the distribution point for goods required by the local farmers. Would-be merchants clustered in the town in numbers in excess of what the available traffic can support; many fail while some become rich at the expense of the countryside. Given the settlement pattern with farmers scattered across the land, the town market has a virtual monopoly both as buyer and supplier. The distance to any neighboring town is too great to allow competition, so the country town has an iron grip on the local farm population. The competition is therefore confined to the town's businessmen who well understand that their mutual rivalries must never reach the point of interfering with their fleecing of the farmers. The real threat to the town system comes from mail order houses, and while these pose an increasing problem it is not enough to undermine the town's monopoly.

The monopoly hold of the town's business on the farmers opened the way for extortionate charges which Veblen says "were inordinately high."[15] At the same time, the town leaders understood that the exploitation of the farmers could not be pressed to the point where they would give up and move on, so the merchants had to walk carefully. The system led to extravagant amounts of waste and duplication, but some men emerged from the fray with substantial fortunes. This was not a situation that could last; large corporate businesses saw the opportunities provided by the country town and took advantage of them. The size and power of the wholesale business, the increase in transportation and communication facilities, the introduction of package goods, brands, trademarks, and advertising, chain-store methods, and the entrance of large financial houses all gradually reduce the role of the country town merchant to that of an agent for outside businesses. "The country town and the townsmen are by way of becoming ways and means in the hands of Big Business."[16] This has not dimmed the addiction to "self-help and cupidity" that has characterized the country town, but the larger profits have moved further up the chain of command.

"The country town and the businesses of its substantial citizens are and have ever been an enterprise in salesmanship,"[17] and salesmanship has always been an exercise in prevarication and duplicity. But "the dominant note of this life is circumspection."[18] One must be circumspect; "one must avoid offense, cultivate goodwill, at any reasonable cost, and continue unfailing in taking advantage of it; and, as a corollary to this action, one should be ready to recognize and recount the possible shortcomings of one's neighbors."[19] One's neighbors are potential rivals in trade; further, "in trade one man's loss is another's gain, and a rival's disabilities count in among one's assets and should not be allowed to go to waste."[20] The system of knowledge produced by the country town does not admit of anything that might offend another, "and so it becomes a system of intellectual, institutional, and religious holdovers."[21] This is, Veblen says, a system for standing pat with the views of the Civil War era. As a result, men so conditioned are supporters of Christian charity. Promoters of good works have learned that the support of the country town is essential and available. Whether such generosity springs from Christian commitment or the desire for prestige or underlying fear and guilt, the result is the same. "This system of innocuous holdovers, then, makes up what may be called the country-town profession of faith."[22] Whether it is altogether believed is perhaps a pointless question for "men and women come to believe in the truths which they profess, on whatever ground, provided only that they continue stubbornly to profess them."[23] And yet, Veblen says, the material conditions of life are taking such a form that "the plain country-town common-sense will no longer work."[24]

Veblen regards the country town as a "great American institution." The greatest population movement in the history of the United States has not been the movement from east to west but that from farm to city. Veblen sees the country town as the first stop for the farmers making their move to urban life. Most of the town's population are farm born and farm bred, and when they leave, it is for more urban destinations. It is through the country town that they acquire their Christian conservatism and competitive ruthlessness, their cupidity and eye to the main chance, their salesmanlike quickness to exploit others, their pious mendacity and shallow goodfellowship, and their firm conviction that a sucker is born every day just for them to exploit. These virtues they have carried with them as they moved into more urban settings. This function of the town was no doubt greater in Veblen's youth than it has since become, but he thought it important in shaping the character of the American people.

Farmland has been the greatest natural resource the United States has had and its exploitation has set the model for dealing with its other natural resources. Veblen is very well aware of the importance of such resources. America, he says, is now preeminent in the value of its natural resources. But in a passage of extraordinary foresight, Veblen remarks

> someday China and the Russian dominions will presumably outbid America in that way, both as to the abundance and the availability of the natural resources, and Brazil and Argentina come into the same class in this respect, as also other less well known regions in the low latitudes.[25]

At present, Veblen says, these countries are chiefly suppliers of raw materials to the industrial nations, but he foresaw accurately that this would change. But Veblen points out that what makes an environmental feature a natural resource is the state of the Industrial Arts. To the pre-Columbian Indians, coal was just another rock of no particular value; it is the Industrial Arts that have made it a priceless source of energy. As the Industrial Arts have made America resource rich, so as knowledge of the Industrial Arts spreads, it will make other nations rich too.

In the use of its natural resources, "This American plan or policy is very simply a settled practice of converting all public wealth to private gain on a plan of legalized seizure."[26] Veblen's first example of the results of this policy is the fur trade, which neatly illustrates how the exploitation of the trade made furs highly valuable, which led to the slaughter of the furbearing animals, which destroyed the trade. On the far grander scale, American agriculture illustrates the same pattern, although the value of farmland has so far survived our exploitive farming practices. But this leads Veblen to a consideration of southern agriculture – one of the few times he dealt with this subject. Peculiarities of climate and soil made large-scale agriculture with forced labor profitable in the South, and slavery provided the forced labor.

> Negro slavery has left its mark on the culture of that section so deeply etched into the moral tissues of its people that the bias of it will presumably not be outgrown within the calculable future. In the South that bias is still right and good which the exacting discipline enforced by this "peculiar institution" once made right and good to them and so ingrained it in their common sense; very much as the equally "peculiar institution" of the Country Town has made the moral bias and the spiritual outcome in the North.[27]

The chief natural resources that have been developed on the "American plan" are, according to Veblen, gold and other precious metals, timber, coal, iron and other useful metals, petroleum, natural gas, water-power, transportation (water-fronts, rights-of-way, and terminal facilities), and irrigation. Veblen picks gold as his first example; although the exploitation of gold has not been of great industrial importance, yet "it ranks in the popular esteem as the greatest and most glorious of them all, the most picturesque and the most affectionately familiar in men's minds."[28] The search for gold involved many able-bodied men, of whom a small fraction acquired great wealth, a larger fraction acquired very modest wealth, and most acquired nothing but debt for the equipment they wasted. The rich claims soon passed into corporate hands, and the free-wheeling prospecting days ended. Veblen believes that the money spent in the search for gold exceeded the value of all the gold found. The industrial use of gold is trivial and its main use has been to increase the amount of specie.

The results of increasing the amount of specie has been to depreciate the money-unit, to alter the terms of our banking laws in favor of the debtor, to redistribute goods to the disadvantage of the creditors, annuitants, and holders of securities drawn in terms of money, and "to lighten the burden of outstanding corporation securities, and thereby enable the corporations to increase the volume of their obligations and capitalization,"[29] and it has stimulated business activity (and industrial activity) by inflating prices. This will in turn mean that the corporations acquire new fixed obligations which must be covered by earnings, which in turn require sabotage to keep prices up. But whatever its effects on business, Veblen holds that

> in point of material usefulness, then, it seems fair to say that the production of gold is pure waste – more especially the production of more than is currently taken up in the arts – and that this waste commonly exceeds the total value of the product.[30]

Timber furnishes a second example of a natural resource that has been developed on the American plan. Veblen is not concerned with the picturesque episodes of the timber industry history but with the working out of the American system. In the colonial era where settlers cleared land simply to get at the soil and viewed the timber as an obstruction, it would be hard to say how much was due to absentee ownership. At first, timber was sought for immediate gain and without afterthought. The practice was to acquire timberlands in large tracts by any means necessary. The land was then clear-cut, taking the best trees for lumber and leaving "the slashings" on the ground. When this discarded material had dried out – after several years – it was fired, leaving the bare land exposed. Frequently, the fires escaped control and demolished stands that were intended for profitable use. Veblen says that at least half of the original stand of timber was lost in these fires, and that the lumbering practices used destroyed more timber than was utilized.

The assault on the nation's forests was not willfully destructive. The lumber men were simply following out the American plan of quick conversion of natural resources to private use with no thought for the future. What they did was not only legal but it was generally approved by their fellow citizens. The more successful of these men became leading citizens, with many parks, hospitals, schools, etc. named in their honor. Some have even become officers of the state and federal government; these are entrepreneurs honored by their fellow citizens.

As the end of the timber resources has become visible, some have taken a more prudent approach to the exploitation of the resource. Corporations have purchased timberlands, and begun management practices designed to make the timber supply renewable. This is of course designed to generate future profits for the companies, but the effect is to stabilize the supply of timber at a sustainable level. Control has taken a monopoly form to prevent further waste.[31]

The process illustrated by the history of timber is similar to those with other resources such as coal and iron but Veblen picks as his last example oil, because the process is less further along there. The discovery of the country's petroleum reserve is more recent, and so the working out of the American plan can be observed at an earlier stage. The older oilfields have already passed under the control of absentee owners, but new fields have been discovered, particularly at the time Veblen was writing, the Texas fields. As expected, there has been a rush of "independent" fortune hunters, many of them with inadequate equipment, and men who are running shoestring operations in the hope of a lucky strike. Some of those who entered the field are actually agents of established companies that handle refining and want to secure their sources of supply. The field is replete with those whose business practices border on larceny – for example, drilling at the borders of one's own claim in order to tap the pool under one's neighbors' land. Veblen comments,

> The clamorous waste and manhandling of the oil resources runs on quite as a matter of business routine, and the recital of any part of the story here may well seem a piece of aimless tedium. It runs on in this fashion from the outset, but it is plain that the enterprise is in all cases due to head up eventually in a collective control of the output by large absentee owners.[32]

The same story Veblen says could be told with respect to coal, iron, water power, transportation lines, and other natural resources; all of them fit the American plan.

In 1800, the United States was almost entirely an agricultural country. By 1900, it was an industrial powerhouse. Many factors were involved in this transformation – population growth, immigration, internal migration, urbanization, all were important contributors, but the most important factor was the development of industry. In 1800, the United States was still in the handicraft stage of industrial development. Manufacturing developed first in port cities or along the fall line where water power was available. But the Industrial Revolution, and particularly the invention of the Watt steam engine, freed industry from geographic constraints and made possible the use of larger and heavier industrial equipment powered by steam. The increasing cost of such equipment soon put them beyond the reach of even the master craftsmen. By 1840, manufacturing was developing in regional population centers.

Mechanization developed first in light industry like textiles, but it followed quickly in heavy industries such as the manufacture of steam engines, locomotives, rails, and other industrial work in iron and steel. These industries first developed in regional population centers such as Philadelphia and New York, and served local markets. But the rapid expansion of transportation soon brought these local industries into competition with each other, and made possible the development of companies spanning the continent. With population and markets rapidly expanding the economy was very nearly one of free competition in manufacturing. Although mechanized industries were at first a relatively small part of the American manufacturing scene, Veblen believed that they marked the course of future development. In his writings he focused on these industries almost entirely.

The productivity of the machine industry was, Veblen says, "inordinate." Business soon discovered that even the national market was not enough. At some point around 1850, markets began to close.[33] This happened at different times for different industries, but from 1850 on, the market closed for industry after industry, and in particular, Veblen said, the market closed in what he called the "'key industries' – those lines of production upon whose output of goods and services the continued working of the industrial system as a whole depended from day to day."[34] As examples, Veblen cited coal, steel, oil, transportation, and structural work. Upon these industries most of the rest of the economy depended in one way or another. Even agriculture, which at first glance would appear to be relatively independent, was dependent on the key industries – agricultural machinery (harvesters, plows, harrows, etc.) and transportation to and from market (the steamboat and the railroad) were now essential in farming, so if the key industries found themselves in difficult straits, the whole economy was affected.

The closing of the market after 1850 created a crisis for the key industries. As they saw the matter, they had two options – limit production or increase sales. They did both. Limiting production meant that competition in production had to end and furthermore required that means be found to reduce industrial output so that the smaller supply would raise prices, thereby restoring "normal" profits. Such a limitation was possible in several ways. As we have seen, the industrial process, at least in the key industries, resembled a massive integrated machine. But the various components of the machine were owned by different businesses.

Disrupting the relations among the components reduced the efficiency of the whole machine process and lowered output. The relations among these businesses were pecuniary relations and there were profits to be made from sabotage, as Veblen calls such deliberate disruptions, borrowing the term from the IWW. One firm might raise the prices at which it sold to another; competing firms may indulge in rate wars; false information about a firm might affect the value of its stocks, etc. A further way was to interfere with the firm's access to credit which would impair its operation. Veblen regarded labor practices such as strike, boycotts, slow-downs, or damaging machinery as also being sabotage. He believed that by 1914 the practice of sabotage had become so pervasive in the American economy that the key industries were not producing what they could. This he held was shown by the performance of these industries during the Great War when their production rose spectacularly. Veblen concluded that in peacetime these industries were operating at 50 percent of their capacity and in some cases at as low as 25 percent. In Veblen's view, the welfare of the community required that the industrial system should be run at full capacity; the amount by which it failed to do so was the amount by which business exploited the underlying population.

But the reducing of supply was only one way of dealing with the problem of "overproduction" – producing more than the market could absorb at an acceptable price. A second method was increasing sales. This took a variety of forms. One was to add features to the product that served no purpose but attracting the attention of consumers. Although such features were pure waste so far as the utility of the product was concerned, they were designed to appeal to the buyers' need for conspicuous consumption. Other methods included billboards, window displays, door to door salesmen, all were employed to induce consumers to increase their expenditures. The method of promoting sales to which Veblen gave the most attention was advertising. The point of advertising, Veblen said, was to create as near to a monopoly position as possible for the product advertised. Instead of the consumer being forced to choose among a variety of nearly identical kinds of soap, each advertiser sought to make his brand of soap unique – the "best," the "purest," the "most fragrant," the "gentlest," etc., of all soaps known to man. Such a celestial soap had no competitor; it stood alone at the summit of soapy perfection. The consumer simply had to buy it on pain of being thought smelly and foul. Of course, Veblen emphasized, truth was irrelevant in advertising; nobody cared if the consumer really stank as long as he bought the soap. Such practices traded on the consumer's fears of disease and of being shamed in society, and they worked. But Veblen pointed out that the most brilliant success in advertising – the gold standard – was the propaganda of the faith. The advertisements of the faith promised everything and delivered nothing, yet they sold their product to millions and had done so for two thousand years. But the failure to deliver the goods may in this case be fortunate.

Hell fire is after all a commodity the punctual delivery of which is not desired by the ultimate consumers; and according to such descriptive matter as is available the Kingdom of Heaven, on the other hand, should not greatly appeal to persons of sensitive taste, being presumably something of a dubiously gaudy affair, something in the nature of three rings and a steam-calliope, perhaps.[35]

By restricting production and promoting sales, the competition that had formerly existed in production was now transferred to sales, where companies competed furiously for larger shares of the closed market.

As lately noted, the corporation became the dominant form of business in the United States around the midpoint of the nineteenth century. At the time Veblen was writing, most economists held that the capital of the corporation was its tangible property – plant, equipment, etc. This was not Veblen's view. "In modern business practice," Veblen says, "capital is distinguished into two coordinate categories of assets, tangible and intangible."[36] Tangible assets are material items of wealth (capital goods); they yield an income stream and so are capitalized. These goods are generally involved in the production of items having some degree of serviceability to the population at large. But Veblen points out that such goods are not always serviceable; some are designed to obstruct the work of industry – for example, military equipment which is used by the owners in their efforts to capture the usufruct of the society's Industrial Arts.[37] There are also tangible assets that inflict damage on society, such as saloons, brothels, and gambling houses. And there are tangible assets whose effect on society is equivocal, such as newspapers, advertising enterprises, and fashionable goods. The existence of such assets, Veblen notes, shows that technological proficiency does not imply serviceability, though in general tangible assets are presumed to have serviceable uses.

For intangible assets, however, "there is no presumption that the objects of wealth involved have any serviceability at large, since they serve no materially productive work, but only a differential advantage to the owner in the distribution of the industrial product."[38] Some intangible assets may be indifferent with respect to serviceability, but in general they are presumed to be disserviceable to the general population.[39] Intangible assets are items that give the owners an advantage over their rivals in their efforts to increase their share of the output of production, whether in the form of goods, services, or money. They are thus factors that influence distribution rather than production. Intangible assets are usually classified as goodwill. Veblen describes this as follows:

Goodwill taken in its wide meaning comprises such things as established customary business relations, reputation for upright dealing, franchises and privileges, trade-marks, brands, patent rights, copyrights, exclusive use of special processes guarded by law or secrecy, exclusive control of particular sources of materials.[40]

Since tangible assets are involved in production, they serve to increase the wealth of the society; intangible assets, since they only affect the distribution of goods already produced, do not affect the wealth of the society. But Veblen considers intangible assets the most important assets of business companies since they affect their competitive position. The value of the company "is fixed for the time being only, by an ever recurring valuation of the company's properties, tangible and intangible, on the basis of their earning-capacity," that is, the expected earnings.[41] The evaluation of course is provided by the market. The corporate securities also serve as collateral for the extension of credit which is merged into the corporate capital, with the result that the value of the company rises. This leads to the issuance of more stock, which in turn becomes collateral for further credit, and the process has no limit.

The corporation, Veblen points out, "is organized for prosperity, not for adversity, and is somewhat helpless in the face of adversity."[42] One result of this is the practice of "trading on the equity"[43] – capitalizing every promising increase of earnings and covering it with new securities. The reason for doing this is the ever pressing need for more capital to meet the demands of the business. As lately noted, competition in production was sharply limited in the nineteenth century by fears of market gluts. One result of that was the intensification of competition in sales. Indeed, Veblen holds, salesmanship and sabotage have become pillars of the modern economy.

The goodwill of the company is covered by the common stock of the company. But there is another class of stocks that Veblen says first came into prominence in the funding of the railroads but is now (1904) in general use. These are debentures; a class of stocks of which preferred stocks are the most common. Debentures are significantly different from common stocks. They do not carry voting rights. They carry a fixed rate of dividends and cover the material property of the corporation. In case of liquidation, the holders of preferred stocks have priority over the holders of the common stocks. Veblen remarks,

> This method of capitalization, therefore, effects a somewhat thoroughgoing separation between the management and the ownership of the industrial equipment. Roughly speaking, under corporate organization the owners of the industrial material have no voice in the management, and where preferred stock is a large constituent of the capital this alienation of control on the part of the owners may be, by so much, irrevocable. Preferred stock is, practically, a device for placing the property it represents in perpetual trust with the holders of the common stock.[44]

Whatever control over the company the holders of the common stocks may have vanishes when the stock is preferred. Here the separation of ownership from control is complete.

The capital structure of the corporation is accordingly complex. The common stock covers the goodwill while the preferred stock covers the material property and sometimes somewhat more, and there are various types of bonds and loans. The value of the corporations is given, Veblen says, by the "earning capacity of the corporation as a going concern."[45] It is important to note that the "earning capacity" means the "expected earnings" – that is, the anticipated future earnings of the corporation. It has therefore a certain speculative character. The evaluation is given by the market, and so is variable from day to day. It may therefore happen that the expected earnings differ from the actual earnings as known to the management. This discrepancy creates an opportunity for the managers. If the expected earnings are substantially above the actual earnings, the managers may buy stock to profit from the rise; in the converse case, they may sell short, planning to buy back the stock at the lower cost.[46] But the managers need not wait for the market to produce such a situation. Since they control the corporation, they may manipulate the earnings to create a favorable situation of which they can then take advantage. Thus the interests of the corporate managers may conflict with the interests of the corporation, which in turn may conflict with the interests of the community. It is the interest of the community that the corporation should produce as large a supply of serviceable goods as possible, whereas the interest of the corporation is that whatever its output, it should be vendible at the greatest possible profit, while the interest of the managers lies in obtaining the greatest possible gain they can for themselves. It is rather obvious that this situation involves conflicts of interest.[47]

The corporation managers are not the only ones who can play games with corporate stocks. Any investor, Veblen says,

> is able, under modern circumstances, to make a secondary use of his investments for the purpose of trading in vendible corporate capital; but this secondary use bears no hard and fast quantitative relationship to the investments in question, nor does it in any determinate way interfere with the ordinary employment of this invested capital in the commonplace conduct of the corporation's business traffic. The capital employed, as well as the potential credit extension which it affords for the purposes of this higher business traffic, is therefore in a peculiar degree intangible, and, in respect of its amount, highly elusive.[48]

Above and beyond the ordinary market of goods, there is now a new market in corporate securities. Corporate stocks thus have a double life: in the lower level they are parts of the corporate capital that produces goods and services, while at a higher level they are themselves the goods bought and sold in the market for corporate securities. Needless to say, these two roles may conflict.

Historically, the function of the corporation has been to raise money by selling stock. The corporation can raise much more money than a partnership or private owner. The money value of the corporation constitutes its capital; thus on Veblen's theory the capital is a creation of credit – the money acquired depends on the price of the stock and the amount of stock sold. This investment for profit Veblen sees as the dominant fact about business finance. The corporation may produce goods or services, but its purpose is not serving the community, it is making a profit. Veblen notes that in current business there is an expected rate of profit that is considered "normal." This he says, is a new idea; traditionally no such expectation existed. But now not only is such a normal profit expected, but it serves as a standard for describing the state of the economy. If the normal rate is exceeded, times are said to be "brisk;" if it falls below the normal standard, times are said to be "dull." How well a business is doing is indicated, Veblen remarks, by the size of its turnover.

> If the general conditions of the trade and of the market are given, the two factors which determine the status and value of a given sound concern, as seen from the businessman standpoint, are the magnitude of the turnover [of capital] and the length of time it occupies.[49]

The greater the "volume" of the capital turned over in a given period of time, the more profitable the business; the shorter the period required to turn over the capital, the better for the business. It is therefore to the advantage of the business if the value of its capital can be increased. This is done, Veblen says, by credit – that is, by borrowing. Of course, borrowing money requires the payment of interest, which so becomes an overhead charge, but Veblen says, "The current rate of business earnings exceeds the rate of interest by an appreciable amount"[50] and so it is generally profitable for the businessman to employ credit. Once obtained, the borrowed funds are merged into the capital with the result that the volume of capital is increased. The gain so achieved is not great, but it is enough to make such a course of action mandatory.

> On the average, it may be said, the aggregate earning of the aggregate capital with credit extension are but slightly greater than the aggregate earnings of the same capital without credit extension would be in the absence of a competitive use of credit extensions. But under modern conditions business cannot profitably be done by any one of the competitors without the customary resort to credit. Without the customary resort to credit a "reasonable" return could not be obtained on the investment.[51]

So where one firm resorts to credit, its competitors must do so likewise, which means that all of them resort to credit extensions. As a result the competitive situation is not very different than it was before resort to credit extensions was begun.

The added funds so obtained are not usually used to increase the industrial equipment of the firm; rather they are employed for other business purposes such as sales promotion. But the increase in capital increases the value of the firm and raises the prices of its industrial equipment. The inflationary effect creates a "buoyancy" in industrial business as businessmen view rising prices as signs of brisk times ahead. "An enhanced value of the property affords a basis for further extensions of credit, and so on."[52] The result is an inflationary spiral in which the extension of credit leads to higher prices that increase the value of the firm and its property, and these become collateral for new extensions of credit. The inflation also raises the value of the earnings, "But the nominal magnitude (value) of the earnings is not increased in as large a ratio as that of the business capital."[53]

But the money value of the collateral is at the same time the capitalized value of the property, computed of the basis of its prospective earning capacity. These two methods of determining the value of the collateral must agree if the capitalization is to afford "a stable basis for credit." If they do not, then when the discrepancy is recognized there must be a rerating in which the rating on the basis of earning capacity must prevail, since earnings are the basis on which business rests. The result is a period of liquidation.[54]

There was a third way of dealing with the menace of competition. By the late years of the nineteenth century, competitive warfare among businesses had become a matter of serious concern for businessmen. Various steps were taken to try to remedy the situation; "rings" and "pools" were tried without much success, but "trusts" proved more effective, beginning with the Standard Oil Trust in 1882. A trust is formed when two or more corporations give controlling blocks of their stocks to a group of men and receive in return trust certificates. The trustees are so empowered to vote the stock entrusted to them, giving them control over the constituent corporations. Trusts rapidly proliferated, emerging in one industry after another.[55] The trust aroused immediate opposition from those who feared they would become monopolies, and antitrust campaigns led to the passage of the Sherman Antitrust Act in 1890 and numerous legal challenges.[56] But in 1889, New Jersey revised its incorporation laws to allow corporations to own the stock of other corporations; the holding company thus appeared upon the scene and in due course replaced the trust. Although legally distinct, the holding company could do all that the trust could do, and its legality was affirmed by the Supreme Court in *United States versus E. C. Knight Company* in 1895.[57]

The point of the trust movement was the elimination, or more accurately, the mitigation, of competition. The problem is well illustrated by the problem of competition among the railroads. A return that yielded normal profits for one railroad could mean bankruptcy if it was divided between two competing lines. Similar situations arose in other industries and in particular in the key industries. The capital invested in these businesses' plants and equipment was so great that the men who controlled the companies had no intention of allowing competition to drive them into bankruptcy. The large trusts, like the oil and sugar trusts, could control production and so output and adjusted them to a level that insured an adequate profit. Veblen's favorite example of this process was the formation of the United States Steel Corporation which illustrated the process beautifully.

By the late 1890s, the steel industry was in serious trouble owing to the competitive situation among the firms in the industry. Like many other businesses, steel companies had moved west with the great westward migration of the population and had located plants based on emerging population centers, access to natural resources, and access to transportation facilities. But people kept on moving and natural resources kept being discovered. Locations that had seemed promising at one time turned out to be less so as time passed.[58] Furthermore, steel was an industry in which the technology was costly and changed rapidly, and it was difficult for small companies to keep up. Obsolescence of equipment therefore became a major problem; so did obsolescence of men since some of the companies were run by men whose talents were no longer adequate to their task. Moreover, these companies had been developed in a time of fairly open competitive markets.

> [But] the period of competitive business in the key industries was closing. So that continued open competition among them became "cutthroat competition"; such as to entail present and prospective decline of their earning-capacity. As one consequence of this situation, they were greatly in need of additional credit for use in their businesses, at a time when their credit capacity was falling off and their liabilities were already becoming distressingly burdensome.[59]

The result was a series of mergers in the industry that by the late 1890s left a smaller number of firms but did not end competition.

What produced the crisis in steel were the changes in the strategies of the companies. The largest firm – Carnegie Steel – was protecting its position by integrating backward, acquiring control of sources of supply, raw materials, and transportation. Other companies followed suit to secure their own positions. The companies that became the United States Steel Company fell into two groups, based on the products they made. Carnegie Steel, the Federal Steel Company, and the National Steel Company were large producers of steel products that were not in final form for sale to the public but were sold to other companies that converted them to finished consumer goods. The second group National Tube, American Steel and Wire, American Tinplate, American Steel Hoop, and American Sheet Steel – bought their materials from companies of the first group and turned them in to finished products for consumers.[60] If the companies of the second group began integrating backward, or the companies of the first group began integrating forward, there would be a general war within the industry. In January 1901, Carnegie announced its intention to begin the production of tubes and sheets – both in finished form.[61] A disastrous war appeared to be inevitable. Furthermore, these companies were ill prepared for such a contest. In the late

1890s, the steel companies had paid ample dividends, with the result that their reserves were depleted. The costs of a general war within the industry would have been too great for them to bear.[62]

Such was the situation which led to the consolidation that produced the United States Steel Corporation. J.P. Morgan entered the field as a promoter, bringing with him the large amounts of credit necessary. The process of consolidation was not easy; Carnegie bargained very hard and delayed matters until his demands were met. But the deal was made; the ownership of the recapitalized industrial equipment and other property was distributed among the former owners, and the promoter. The former owners now appeared as creditors of the new corporation as well as owners. They acquired large holdings of preferred stock and other debentures at the same time that they held the common stock. The material equipment was not greatly changed from what it had been before, but the business capital was augmented by both the goodwill of the old corporations and that of the new, which in this case was increased by the new company's strategic position in the market. Savings that resulted from the combination came largely from the elimination of duplication.

> It is in doing away with unnecessary business transactions and industrially futile maneuvering on the part of independent firms that the promoter of combinations finds his most telling opportunities. So that it is scarcely an overstatement to say that probably the largest, assuredly the securest and most unquestionable, service rendered by the great modern captains of industry is the curtailment of the business to be done – this sweeping retirement of business men as a class from the service and the definitive cancelment of opportunities for private enterprise ... It is a casting out of business men by the chief of business men.[63]

The promoter was rewarded with a "bonus" which in this case was a large block of stock in the new company worth fifty million dollars. All of this, Veblen remarks, shows that "capital" as understood in current business means "putative earning capacity." The line between capital and credit often cannot be drawn. Both are shown by current market quotations which make no such distinction.[64]

The development of modern corporate capitalism has created a new situation, Veblen says. For the community, what is important is that business should produce serviceable goods and services in ample amounts at reasonable cost. For business, what is important is that the goods it produces are vendible at prices exceeding their cost of production, in other words, that they can be sold at a profit. But now there is a new market – the market for corporate securities. Traders in this market are not concerned with the serviceability of the goods produced by the companies in whose stocks they trade, nor are they concerned with the profits of these companies; they are concerned with the profits they can make by buying and selling securities and if they buy a company's stocks, it is usually not to hold but to sell at a profit. The interests of the securities trader may contradict the interests of the corporation whose interest may be contrary to those of the community but it is from the capital markets, Veblen says, that the great fortunes are now realized. Those, like Morgan, who are most successful in this new market require liberal supplies of credit but they receive such supplies because they have acquired a kind of goodwill of their own. This goodwill, Veblen says, is a peculiar kind. It seems to be inexhaustible in supply; investing it in one business does not diminish the amount available – indeed it may increase it. It can also be withdrawn without warning. It is, Veblen says, of a spiritual sort, capable of being present in many places at once, inexhaustible, immaterial, and somewhat mysterious. "Hence," Veblen says, "this traffic in vendible capital is the pivotal and dominant factor in the modern situation of business and industry."[65] The result is one in which,

> the fortunes of property owners are in large measure dependent on the discretion of others – the owners of intangible property; and the management of the industrial equipment tends strongly to center in the hands of men who do not own the industrial equipment, and who have only a remote interest in the efficient working of this equipment. The property of those who own less, or who own only material goods, is administered by those who own more, especially of immaterial goods; and the material processes of industry are under the control of men whose interest centers on an increased value of the immaterial assets.[66]

Veblen was intrigued by the power and wealth of magnates like Morgan who dominated the economy. The secret, Veblen concluded, was the possession of great wealth, no matter how acquired. Once acquired, the wealth could be used. The business magnate's wealth is held in the form of the securities of corporations. If this wealth is great enough, the magnate can, by concentrating his holdings in the securities of a particular company, take for himself a large fraction of the company's earnings. Accordingly, Veblen says that when the magnate finds a company which is doing well and whose stocks are increasing in value, he can by concentrating his holdings in the securities of that company reap the benefits of the success of its managers. Such a large-scale infusion of new capital into the company will of course further stimulate its operations and further increase the value of its stock. But as soon as the value of the company's stock ceases to rise, the magnate can sell out and shift his wealth to another target company.

> He does this by force of his large holdings of capital at large, the weight of which he can shift from one point of investment to another as the relative efficiency – earning capacity – of one or another line of investment may make it expedient; and at each move of this kind, in so far as it is effective for

his ends, he cuts into and assimilates a fraction of the invested wealth involved, in that he cuts into and sequesters a fraction of the capital's earning capacity in the given line.[67]

The owner-manager of the target company is reduced to the status of an involuntary servant of the magnate, loses his discretionary initiative, and becomes a collector and conveyor of revenue from the community at large to the magnate. Thus while ordinary business captures the usufruct of society's Industrial Arts, the magnate captures the usufruct of ordinary business. Even the parasites have parasites.

Veblen then turns to the question of the business cycle. The pattern of business booms, followed by depressions, to be followed by another boom and another depression, etc. has, Veblen notes, become a recognized but unwelcome feature of capitalist economics. But Veblen draws a distinction between the crises of the first three-fourths of the nineteenth century and those since. The early crises were commercial crises, he says, and had limited effects on the society as a whole. The economy of that time was too loose in the joints for the crisis to spread throughout the system. It is only with the depression of 1873 that he believed the industrial depression has appeared, and this is the type of event he wants to consider. But Veblen does not believe this phenomenon to be cyclic in the manner claimed by other writers such as his sometime student, Wesley Mitchell. Veblen argues that booms are followed by crises and then depression, but he thinks the American economy since 1873 is characterized by chronic depression.[68] The "booms" that have occurred during this period are chiefly due to exogenous factors such as the Spanish-American War; it is chronic depression that has become the normal state of the economy.

The phenomena of booms, crises, and depressions are business phenomena; Veblen says, they affect industry only through the business control of industry; fundamentally, they concern prices. Accordingly, the causes of these phenomena are to be found in the business system, and the remedies, if there are remedies, are also questions of business. Booms, crises, and depressions have important effects on the community at large, but there are only secondarily industrial effects.[69]

Booms begin, Veblen says, when businesses in some particular line receive a stimulus, such as the outbreak of a war. As a result of this stimulus, the businessmen concerned see profitable opportunities ahead; they expand production and raise prices. Owing to the close interconnections within the business system, this change is communicated through the entire system. Those businesses most closely linked to the first responders react first, raising their prices in expectation of brisk times ahead. How rapidly and how extensively the effects of the stimulus spread depends on how tight the articulation of the system is. Some areas may be only slightly affected – e.g., agriculture – but all will show some effects. The rising expectations lead to large-scale credit extensions; contracts are drawn, goods and equipment purchased, materials contracted for, orders are placed, workers are hired, etc. One effect of this is to bid up the value of the company's assets which serve as collateral for the further issuance of credit. Insofar as the effect of the stimulus takes time to spread the first responders will enjoy a differential advantage in dealing with their suppliers, so profits rise. Wages generally do not rise until the boom is nearly over, which affords another differential advantage to these businesses. On the basis of these developments the capitalization of the stimulated businesses are increased as the expected earning capacity rises.[70]

At some point, the original stimulus ceases to function. That will not immediately end the boom; businessmen's expectations do not change at once. Contracts have been drawn that carry the boom into the future, plans have been made and put into effect, equipment has been bought and men hired, all on the assumption of continued brisk times. As the impulse of the original stimulus decays, rapidly or slowly, earnings decline. Businessmen find their capitalizations, inflated by the boom and the rising expectations of gain, exceed their actual earnings. There is nothing for it but to recapitalize at a lower figure. But the businessmen resist doing so; they perceive doing so as a defeat; their self-esteem and the esteem of others will suffer from such a course. And often they cannot make the required readjustments; they have acquired contractual obligations that cannot be changed, they have creditors who demand payment in full, and they cannot meet these demands. The result is liquidation; there is a fall of money values, unemployment is increased, and there is a redistribution of property.[71]

As the economy falls into depression, a further factor becomes crucial. The Industrial Arts develop continuously; new inventions and improvements continue to appear, regardless of the depression. One result of this is that the efficiency of the productive process increases, and as this happens, increasing industrial efficiency leads to greater output at lower costs. As the depression wears on, new companies enter the market with new and more efficient productive equipment, with the result that the new companies (and old companies that are emerging from bankruptcy) can produce more goods more cheaply than the older companies, and can sell at lower prices. The older companies still have obligations contracted before the crisis that they cannot shed; their technology is less efficient than that of their new competitors, and their cost of production are consequently higher. These companies find that they cannot compete with the newcomers, and are gradually forced out of the market.

One should note here Veblen's assumption that the rate of growth of the Industrial Arts is not affected by the depression. He gives no argument for this claim. But one would think that the incentives to discovery, invention, and innovation would decline as the general prosperity declines, since less money would be available for new product development or for the retooling of factories. He does hold that calamities that reduce the population can adversely affect the culture, but he says little about the cultural effects of depressions.

It was in terms of this process that Veblen saw the explanation to chronic depression. Given that technological progress is continuous, any company's technological plant begins to become obsolescent the day after it opens for business. To keep pace with the resulting decline in his costs and his increasing output, the businessman needs some way to keep prices up or else he must accept a decline in his profits. The former alternative is embraced by the introduction of planned waste accompanied by intensive selling. Both are used, but Veblen thinks they are not enough. The businessman is unwilling to reduce his profits and so he finds himself continually "overproducing" – that is, producing more goods than he can sell at a price that will yield a "fair" return. From this situation, competition offers the businessman no escape.

What then is to be done? Veblen thinks the answer is obvious – output and prices must be controlled so as to yield suitable profits. The way to do this, Veblen thinks, is by the establishment of a monopoly – a trust or holding company that controls the whole system, or at least all but a negligible fraction of the system. A monopoly can set output and prices at such a level that adequate profits will be assured. Competition in production must go; "the exercise of free contract and the other powers inhering in the natural right of ownership, are incompatible with the modern machine technology."[72] Such a consolidation will bring virtually all businesses into a single company, with the result that the "general body of owners are necessarily reduced to the practical status of pensioners dependent on the discretion of the great holders of immaterial wealth."[73] The ordinary businessman now becomes a bureaucrat serving the giant company and the population in general becomes "raw material of industry."[74] So Veblen concludes "when the last step in business consolidation has been taken, there remains the competitive friction between the combined business capital and the combined workmen."[75] The workers are not owners, so they have no place in the final company.

Veblen points out that the consequences of a depression, particularly the elimination of a large number of business firms from the market, are similar to the consequences of a consolidation. In both cases, the number of firms in a given line of production is reduced, and property is redistributed. The obvious conclusion is that large-scale consolidations are in some ways substitutes for the liquidation resulting from a depression. To the extent that competition drives the behavior that led to the depression, consolidation can achieve the pruning of the industry that would otherwise be done by the liquidations caused by the depression. "The trust-maker is in some respects a surrogate for a commercial crisis."[76]

Veblen believed that about 1897 the American economy entered a new phase that he called the "new order."[77] The changes leading to this new order were gradual but he thought them sufficient to justify a new designation. Veblen had previously emphasized the mechanical character of the industrial process, but in the late nineteenth century chemical science began to play an increasingly important role in industry, to be followed shortly thereafter by electrical science.

This increased the scientific knowledge required of the engineers who actually operate the industrial system. But this also rendered the technology still more opaque to its business masters whose concentration on business and finance left them little time or inclination to keep up with the growing demands of the scientific competence among the technicians of industry. So rapid was the expansion of science and technology that Veblen remarked,

> Chemical and electrical engineers and appliances have been multiplying on the face of the land like the frogs of Exodus until the only remaining certainty is that if there is any root or branch of industry that is free from these today they will invade it tomorrow.[78]

Veblen likens the contrast between the simple mechanical system of the 1850s and the complex system of today (1923) to the relation of a cube to a square or of a three-dimensional figure to a two-dimensional one.[79] He also stresses that the advance of science and technology has created new natural resources as uses have been discovered for items of the environment that had been regarded as useless before. Yet the final management of this marvelously complex system lies, Veblen notes, in the hands of absentee owners whose government runs on "certain broad principles of ignorance, neglect and sabotage."[80]

Veblen apparently chose the date 1897 as the beginning of the new order because it marked an explosion in the formation of trusts and holding companies. It is with the trust and the holding company that "Big Business" appears upon the scene.

> The holding-company and the merger, together with the interlocking directorates, and presently the voting trust, were the ways and means by which the banking community took over the strategic regulation of the key industries, and by way of that avenue also the control of the industrial system at large. By this move the effectual discretion in all that concerns the business management of the key industries was taken out of the hands of corporation managers working in severalty and at cross-purposes, and has been lodged in the hands of that group of investment bankers who constitute in effect a General Staff of financial strategy and who between them command the general body of the country's credit resources.[81]

So emerged the investment bankers who Veblen believed had now become the rulers of the economy. The original incentive for bankers to undertake this rationalization of business has been the bonus paid to the banker or the banking house at the completion of the reorganization – a bonus usually paid in stock of the new company resulting from the mergers and restructuring. The new business entities are capitalized at a figure substantially above the sum of the capitalizations of the businesses merged. Since no new tangible assets are created in this process, the result is a creation of new values out of credit. In many cases the new companies undergo repeated recapitalizations, each marked by the issuance of new securities. But despite charges of "stock watering," the new companies have generally made good on their obligations. The rate at which such new obligations will appear depends on the amount of credit already outstanding and what Veblen calls the "tensile strength" of the business, by which he means the willingness of the business community to undertake new liabilities and obligations.[82]

The "Captains of Solvency," as Veblen calls the investment bankers, extend credit to those companies paying a good return. These companies, so advantaged, are able to use their increased purchasing power to buy, thereby bidding up prices, since the supply of vendible goods is not similarly expanded. Access to credit confers a temporary advantage on a business, so that its competitors will at once seek to augment their credit to stay abreast of the competition. The result is a scramble for credit, which in the long run leaves matters pretty much as they were before, but with businesses more dependent on the providers of credit than they were.

The nation's credit resources have now (1923) been drawn together under the surveillance of a half dozen "massive credit institutions at the fiscal center of all things."[83] Evidently, Veblen says, "the country's assets should, at a progressively accelerated rate, gravitate into the ownership, or at least into the control of, the banking community at large,[84] and within the banking community into the hands of the massive credit institutions that dominate the field. The stability of the system of credit is fairly guaranteed by the fact that "the chief banking-houses and their chief clients are now identical in point of their business interests; to a very appreciable extent identical in point of ownership."[85]

What is happening in the economy is therefore a steady increase in the ownership of the nation's resources and businesses by the masters of credit, or when actual ownership is not achieved, usufruct is. Veblen notes the situation of the prairie farmers who have "fallen into a state something like effectual client-ship and usufruct at the call of the implement makers, commission man, warehouse men, millers, packers, and railways."[86] A very similar situation exists for the country's businesses as a whole. The economy functions on the basis of credit instruments, of which banknotes are one example. Its banknotes are issued far beyond specie reserves; this is fiduciary money in which the gains and losses of businesses are calculated. "This fiduciary currency is of the nature of certified make-believe, in the main; being a volume of intangibles hypothecated on the sound sense of the banking community and the Federal Reserve Board."[87] As Veblen sees it, the government has joined the bankers.

The success of the present system requires the continual inflation of money values (or the depreciation of the currency). In an earlier era, this would have been seen as a dangerous course, but Veblen holds that the present system is stable enough so that no such danger exists. In fact, Veblen believes, prices have been rising for decades. At the same time, the advance in the Industrial Arts has meant a steady decline in the cost of producing the goods the community wants, but this has been offset by the inflation. Obviously, the system of business involves a double use of credit: on the one hand, businesses employ their assets to make a profit by selling goods to customers who constitute the general population, but these same assets serve to provide the income necessary to pay the overhead charges due to credit and to support the captains of solvency. "The whole fabric of business is built on and about this double use of assets, and its movements are regulated by the circumstances which govern this double use."[88] Veblen describes this as follows.

> The one line will be financial, in the nature of investment banking, occupied with the creative use of credit resources, capitalizations and flotations; while the other line will be commercial or industrial business of the corporate sort, perhaps more frequently the latter, occupied with the output and sale of vendible goods or services.[89]

As was clear in the case of steel, mergers and reorganizations lead to recapitalizations which involve the issuance of new securities. But these mergers did not involve the creation of new tangible assets. The result was inflation which meant rising prices. The value of the company's tangible assets is thus increased, and since these assets serve as the collateral for credit, further credit is acquired based on the now more valuable collateral. Rising prices increase purchasing power which further boosts prices. There is therefore a circular process in which credit increases the value of assets which leads to more borrowing that raises prices that raises the value of collateral which leads to more borrowing, and so on. Veblen comments, "The fabric of credit and capitalization is essentially a fabric of concerted make-believe resting on the routine credulity of the business community at large."[90]

Business interests dominate the government, so they dominate foreign policy and foreign relations. These relations have come to be competitive pecuniary relations among nations. Given the view of the businessman as the hero of the community, businessmen have been able to secure popular support for their policies by appeal to patriotism. This peculiar doctrine, Veblen says, takes its rise from barbarism, but it is strong enough even now to command unreasoning support among the public. Hence nations become as it were businesses seeking competitive advantages against each other. That in turn has led to the building up of national armies and armament, since it is widely believed that trade follows the flag, but that it will not follow it very far unless it is backed by military might. This Veblen sees as particularly true in the dealings of the more advanced nations with those on the "lower levels of culture." It has proven necessary to use more than sweet reason to convince these people of the beneficence of the European powers in removing their natural resources, but they can be intimidated if not convinced. It is in their dealings with each other, however, that the powers feel the necessity of military might most acutely. Veblen notes that (as of 1904) Germany,

France, and Italy are furiously building their military establishment at enormous cost to their economies while Britain and even the United States are following the same path though not yet as rapidly. Veblen remarked in 1904,

> Barring accidents and untoward cultural agencies from outside of politics, business, or religion, there is nothing in the logic of the modern situation that should stop the cumulative war expenditures short of industrial collapse and consequent national bankruptcy, such as terminated the carnival of war and politics that ran its course on the continent in the sixteenth and seventeenth centuries.[91]

There was of course another possibility – war.

The effect of the machine has been profound and has affected all of society, but the greatest impact has been on the working class – the upper classes, being more sheltered from contact with the machine, have been less powerfully affected. But Veblen is careful to point out that the machine has not affected all workers equally; its greatest impact has been on the skilled workers who direct the operations of the machine. They have had to learn to think in terms of the machine process, of efficient causal process and natural forces. These men must be intelligent to do the work they do; they are engineers or highly skilled men who understand the forces involved and can guide their action. But workers who merely tend the machine need not understand its workings as do those who plan and direct the machine's activities. Yet even here, Veblen notes, the hold of the pecuniary culture is still present. Engineers work for wages; they buy in the market; they pay rent; they are not exempt from the influence of business. But this business influence is to some degree mitigated by recent developments in business itself. Wage scales are increasingly set by grade rather than by bargaining. Those who shop in department stores confront fixed prices for standard goods – there is no haggling here. Most of those who work in business bureaucracies do routine work that does little to inculcate business values. Even the engineers are still part of the business culture, but the influence of the machine is powerful.

The influence of the machine extends to the whole society. We have seen in an earlier chapter how Veblen believed that the machine had led to the standardization and regimentation of society. Today, we are so accustomed to this sort of regimentation that it is hard to imagine how else there is to live. But to Veblen and the people of his time, this regimentation and standardization was a new and unwelcome intrusion.

We have seen that there is a division in points of view (world views) between the business classes and those who have learned the lesson of the machine. The foundation of the business point of view is natural rights; the ownership of property was considered a Natural Right like life and liberty. The laws governing property and ownership are held for true and right. Court decisions are by precedent; facts are warped to fit the decisions of past courts. Even personal relations are often expressed now in pecuniary terms, and many types of obligations are now fulfilled in pecuniary terms. There are many things that exist only *de jure* – corporations being a prime example. Interpersonal relations tend to be those of status. Purposes are imputed to events and entities. This view is anthropomorphic; it holds that there are purposes guiding nature and human affairs and that all things will eventually work out to the benefit of mankind. It is patriotic; Veblen sees this is a survival of higher barbarism. It is deeply conservative, opposed to change, and devoted to today's eternal truths.

The point of view inculcated by the machine is very different. It rejects anthropomorphism in favor of a matter-of-fact view. It is materialistic, and looks to the cause and effect relations for explanations. It is skeptical of things that exist only *de jure*; the *de facto* world is the only world it knows. It is skeptical of precedent and abstract rule. In this perspective, laws must be adapted to the facts, not the converse. It views the world in impersonal objective terms; it is democratic and suspicious of conventions and conventional entities, and conventional obligations. It is irreligious and favors peace rather than war. Quite obviously, the children of the machine do not fit well into the world of ownership and pecuniary relations.

Veblen remarks that, in current society, workers are believed to be disinclined to saving or thrift. There are, Veblen thinks, several reasons for this. But among these Veblen believes that the influence of the machine is one of the most important. The prosy matter-of-fact manner of thought that he attributes to the discipline of the machine has, he thinks, undermined the institution of ownership. For these men, ownership has lost its charms and diminished their desire for possessions.

A further, and more striking, evidence of the influence of the machine, Veblen believes, is the growth of trade unions. This phenomenon is largely one of the urban industrial scene. It is particularly where workers are involved in the heavy industries that trade unions have grown. Veblen says,

> Hitherto the movement has shown a fairly uninterrupted growth, not only in the numbers of its membership, but in the range and scope of its aims as well; and hitherto it has reached no halting-place in its tentative, shifty, but ever widening crusade of iconoclasm against the received body of natural rights. The latest, more mature expressions of trade-unionism are, on the whole, the most extreme, in so far as they are directed against the natural rights of property and pecuniary contract.[92]

Veblen sees unionism as a denial of the owners' right to do as they want with their property, to pay what they choose, to set the conditions of employment as they like, and to hire and fire at will. Court decisions have shown that the law favors the owners; the law as Veblen has emphasized is devoted to the protection of property. It holds wages to be matters of free contract between employer and employee, although they are obviously nothing of the kind.

Veblen points out that there is a still more radical movement demanding change in the established pecuniary culture – socialism. Veblen sees socialism as a natural outcome of trade unionism but it is a rather long step ahead. Socialists do not want to redistribute the ownership of property; they want to abolish the ownership of property. Veblen notes that the socialist program is not very clearly formulated. While the demand for an end to ownership is clear, the socialists are very vague about what form the post-ownership society is to take. This criticism he urges against the Marxists but also against the other forms of socialism. Nevertheless, Veblen thinks socialism is a growing movement, for which there was good evidence in the pre-war period.

There are further changes that Veblen attributes to the discipline of the machine. The patriarchal family, Veblen believes, is losing its appeal among those most influenced by the machine; male dominance in the family seems less plausible to those that the machine has touched. He also believes that religion is losing its attraction among the same group and he says that the spectacular growth of the sciences is a reflection of the same causes. Veblen admits that the origins of science lie well before the industrial revolution but he holds that the development of science has accelerated since then. Earlier scientists were still touched with animism; they held such doctrines as "nothing appears in the effect but what is contained in the cause" and the effect must be quantitatively equivalent to the cause.[93] Both of these dicta reflect an anthropomorphic view of causation and are now defunct. As usual, Darwin is his favorite example of the great scientist. Darwin rejected the taxonomic and anthropomorphic approaches of his predecessors. He does not mention God; like Pierre-Simon LaPlace, he has no need of that hypothesis. He focused on evolution as a cumulative causal process, operating impersonally and without purpose – a purely natural phenomenon. Such a view Veblen believes is not consistent with the ideology of business. Thus even while business still rules the culture, Veblen sees it as being eaten away by the machine process.

In the last chapter of his 1904 book, *The Theory of Business Enterprise*, Veblen looked to the future of the institution of business. The discipline of the machine, Veblen holds, disintegrates the conventional institutional basis on which the business system rests but at the same time, business depends on the machine process; without the machine process, modern business could not survive. Business requires goods to be sold; it is the machine process that produces these goods. So business as a social institution cannot survive without the machine process. We have then two competing cultural systems – the business system and the machine system. Which will triumph? On the one hand, the machine discipline is affecting an ever increasing percentage of the population. Although most of the huge businesses in the country are now based on machine technology, much of the economy has yet to reach this level of development. Veblen thinks industry will become increasingly mechanized in the future, but he also believes the business ideology is being inculcated in a decreasing percent of the population. Those who work in large firms are mostly reduced to performing bureaucratic routine which hardly encourages the views of the business system. It is true that the US educational establishment, at least the endowed schools, is dedicated to furthering business principles. The schools are often headed by businessmen; they seek funds by catering to the views of men rich enough to make large grants, and they are of course run by businessmen. Similarly, the press and periodical literature are devoted to the business ideology; they are businesses themselves; they depend chiefly upon advertising for their revenue and advertising is a systematic propaganda machine for business principles. Moreover, the content of these publications must be pleasing to the audience that the publication targets. "They must also conform to the fancies and prejudices of this class as regards the ideals – artistic, moral, religious, or social – for which they speak."[94] But despite this control of such influential institutions, Veblen thinks the business system as a whole is losing its ideological contest with the machine.

But business has an apparent way to reverse this trend; national politics are business politics, run by businessmen for business interests. The current direction in national politics, Veblen held, in 1904, is toward war and military prepared-ness. Hence businessmen can mobilize the populace on the basis of patriotism and the claim that business interests are national interests. And military training is training in subservience, fealty, and credulity, with the results, Veblen says, that are not what businessmen hope for.

> The barbarian virtues of fealty and patriotism run on national or dynastic exploit and aggrandizement, and these archaic virtues are not dead. In those modern communities whose hearts beat with the pulsations of the world-market they find expression in an enthusiasm for the commercial aggrandizement of the nation's business men. But when once the policy of war-like enterprise has been entered upon for business ends, these loyal affections gradually shift from the business interests to the warlike and dynastic interests, as witness the history of imperialism in Germany and England. The eventual outcome should be a rehabilitation of the ancient patriotic animosity and dynastic loyalty, to the relative neglect of business interests. This may easily be carried so far as to sacrifice the profits of the business man to the exigencies of the higher politics.[95]

The defenders of business are caught between the discipline of the machine on the one hand and the discipline of militarism on the other. Neither is compatible with the business ideology of Natural Rights. So Veblen concludes,

> It seems possible to say this much, that the full dominion of business enter-prise is necessarily a transitory dominion. It stands to lose in the end whether

the one or the other of the two divergent cultural tendencies wins because it is incompatible with the ascendancy of either.[96]

But by 1923, when Veblen published *Absentee Ownership*, he had changed his mind about the future of business. Veblen claimed that the economy had changed in the last three decades, developing into what he called a "new order."[97] This was not, Veblen said, a radical break from the past but a development from within which had progressed to the point where it required a separate designation. The companies that constituted the economy Veblen divided into three groups: the key industries, the rest of the industries, and agriculture.[98] What made certain industries "key" was of course the fact that their products were necessary for the functioning of the other industries. Hence control of the key industries meant control of the entire system. And such control, Veblen said, had now been achieved by what he called the "One Big Union" – a term which had been a rallying cry of the IWW that he used ironically to refer to the union of investment bankers and absentee owners who, by controlling the nation's credit resources, were able to control the key industries. Veblen saw the Federal Reserve as a member of this union which helped to guarantee its stability and power. The lesson of consolidation had been learned by the absentee owners and bankers who now control the economy and so regulate industrial output and prices as to make sure that no unwelcome fluctuations would occur. While the one big union was not quite a monopoly, its control was sufficient to guarantee steadily rising prices without crises.

> The price level at large will rise progressively in response to that progressively enlarged volume of purchasing-power which arises out of the progressive creation of credits in the ordinary course of investment, merchandising, and corporate finance. The expansion is self-propagating. Each successive advance of the price-level calls for a corresponding increment of the working-capital of all those concerns that do business within its scope, which includes virtually all of the business community. The needful increase of working capital is got by a creation of new credits; which goes to increase the volume of purchasing-power; which goes to increase the general level of prices, etc. It is a matter of workday routine, and is, in effect, to be broken into only by such a general liquidation of credits as is no longer to be apprehended, since the Federal Reserve and the One Big Union of the interests have taken over the stabilization of credits on a reasoned plan.[99]

The management of the economy has now been reduced to a question of impersonal routine run by absentee owners and investment bankers with the help of the government.

At the same time, the advance of the Industrial Arts has brought the sway of the machine process to include virtually the whole economy. The machine process itself has become more complex and more productive than it was. Technology and applied science have merged, enormously increasing the complexity and the power of the industrial system. Only men schooled in the sciences can now deal with the industrial system intelligently, and the absentee owners are not so schooled. The result is that despite the vastly increased productive power of industry sabotage has increased sufficiently to offset it.

But the workers have not been included in the One Big Union; the workers do not own – therefore, they do not belong. The workers have turned to unions in an effort to gain bargaining power against the absentee owners. The tactics of the unions are business tactics; they argue for better wages and better hours, rather than attacking the legitimacy of the system in which they are caught. The only real weapons the workers have are the strike, that is, sabotage. But the owners of the One Big Union regulate the economy so as to keep a certain fraction of the workers unemployed, and the threat of unemployment suffices to keep the workers in line. Even when the workers win an increase in their wages, the victory is temporary at best. Workmen are not owners, and the steadily rising price level means that the workers' gains are overrun by the rising cost of living; thus the workers find themselves in a game of catch-up in which they never succeed. Much of the same is true for the farmers, although the methods used are different. The farmer is dependent on the One Big Union for the credit necessary for the machines he uses and for the transportation of his crop to market. As Veblen points out, the workers and farmers are, from the standpoint of the absentee owners, "The species of natural resources which the business community holds in usufruct, in the nature of inert materials exposed to the drift of circumstances over which they have no control, somewhat after the analogy of bacteria employed in fermentation."[100]

When the workers have tried to use legal action against their employers, they have generally failed. Not being a corporate entity, the workers find their organization labeled a conspiracy whereas the absentee owners, bonded together with a corporate charter, are not held to be a conspiracy. Since the absentee owners own the plant and equipment, they can deny access to the workers who are then unable to enforce its idleness.[101] Whenever a case goes to court, it is almost certain that it will be decided in favor of the absentee owners. A democratic government, Veblen says, is a business government; its elected officials are usually drawn from the ranks of business.[102] It is no surprise that the government, the courts, and the One Big Union generally stand together. The state has in effect joined to the One Big Union.

> [The state] is a residual derivative of the predatory dynastic state, and as such it still continues to be, in the last resort, an establishment for the mobilization of force and fraud as against the outside, and for a penalized subservience of the underlying population at home.[103]

It is a government of businessmen, by businessmen, and for businessmen. The national interest has become identified with the interests of the large businesses domiciled within its borders. And national policy is constructed on the old mercantilist principle that one nation's gain is another nation's loss. This of course flies in the face of the fact that the industrial system has become international, embracing all the nations of Christendom. As the articulation of the industrial system grows tighter, the national frontiers with their "customs-duties, shipping-subsidies, trade-concessions, counselor services, passport regulations, national protection and enforcement of the claims of foreign parts"[104] have become barriers. These frontiers have become obstructions to the smooth running of the industrial system that the community of Christendom requires.

One should note here how Veblen's view of democratic government has changed. In 1892, he saw a constitutional democracy as the desirable alternative to the business system. But by 1923, he saw it as just another business institution, dedicated to the achievement of business ends. The hostile view he had asserted toward the Dynastic State he now extends to all governments. The hope of progressive reform that the government could be the champion of ordinary people against the power of business had vanished.

The international cooperation that the industrial system requires has not been achieved; in his place the

> national pursuit of warlike and political ends has come to be a fairly single-minded chase after unearned income to be produced by intimidation and intrigue. It has been called imperialism; it might also, in a colloquial phrasing, be called national graft.[105]

The result is that the national integrity becomes ever more closely identified with the success of the business interests in operating in foreign lands.[106] These activities, Veblen notes, are pursued under cover of "night and cloud" by "such a texture of prevarication as may well serve to keep the national left hand from knowing what the right hand is doing."[107]

The harmony achieved between the absentee owners and the national establishment is sufficient, Veblen believes, to ensure the business control of industry for the foreseeable future. The dream of 1904 that the discipline of the machine would undermine the business system had vanished by 1923. What Veblen saw ahead was disaster.

> The drift of workday discipline, as well as of deliberate instruction, sets in the conservative direction. For the immediate future the prospect appears to offer a fuller confirmation of the faith that business principles answer all things. The outlook should accordingly be that the businesslike control of the industrial system in detail should presently reach, if it has not already reached,

and should speedily pass beyond that critical point of chronic derangement in the aggregate beyond which a continued pursuit of the same strategy on the same businesslike principles will result in a progressively widening margin of deficiency in the aggregate material output and a progressive shrinkage of the available means of life.[108]

There is no suggestion here that the discipline of the machine can undermine business even in the long run. Rather Veblen foresees an ever tightening grip of business on the industrial system until the whole system collapses. What comes then Veblen does not say; presumably he did not believe that the outcome could be predicted.

The Corrupting Influence of Business

In Veblen's view, business is a perversion of industry. The purpose of industry is the production of goods that satisfy the needs of society in sufficient quantities so that these needs are fully met. But business corrupts industry so that it serves primarily the needs of the wealthy, leaving an inadequate remainder for the general population. This corruption is not confined to industry; business corrupts other portions of the culture as well. Representative democracy is supposed to yield a government of the people, by the people, and for the people, but in the United States it has become a tool of the business interests in their search for profits. But nowhere is the perversion more obvious than in the case of the university.

The university was of recent birth in the United States in Veblen's time. Before the Civil War, American colleges were almost all church schools. There were exceptions – University of Virginia, for example – but in the vast majority of cases the church was the founder of the college and controlled its curriculum. College presidents were almost all ministers. The only advanced degrees available in the United States were in medicine and divinity. Those who sought advanced training in other fields had no recourse but to attend a European university.

After the Civil War, as industrialization powered up here, the demand for access to advanced education grew, especially in the sciences. Some colleges had tried to meet the demand by establishing separate advanced schools – the Lawrence Scientific School at Harvard and the Sheffield Scientific School at Yale were founded in the 1840s. Then in 1876 the Johns Hopkins University was established in Balti more with the announced intention of creating a true university in America. Hopkins brought together a distinguished group of scholars, some of whom were European, such as the English mathematician J.J. Sylvester, and launched a full scale graduate program. Other colleges followed suit – Harvard and Yale, and in due course many others. At the same time this development was taking place, the leadership in American education began to change from the ministry to businessmen. And new universities were founded such as Stanford and the University of Chicago, with large endowments given by business leaders such as John D.

Rockefeller. These were joined by the new state colleges, established by the Morrill Act in 1862, to provide agricultural and mechanical training. These were vocational schools though many of them aspired to be universities and began shaping their programs toward that goal. The presidents were not ministers but men of business.

In a book that he began in 1899 and finally published in 1918, Veblen undertook to examine "The Higher Learning In America: A Memorandum on the Conduct of Universities by Business Men." Veblen began by saying that

> in any known civilization there will be found something in the way of esoteric knowledge. This body of knowledge will vary characteristically from one culture to another, differing both in content and in respect of the canons of truth and reality relied on by its at adepts.[109]

The existence of such a body of knowledge is a culture universal, though its content and standards will vary from one culture to another.[110] The esoteric knowledge is held by "a select body of adepts," and is regarded by the members of the culture as of "great intrinsic value."[111] The universality of this phenomenon, Veblen says, is due to its instinctive basis – the instincts of workmanship and idle curiosity. But this knowledge takes its color from the nature of the culture in which it is born; in our time from the conditions imposed by the state of the Industrial Arts.

> The modern technology is of an impersonal, matter-of-fact character in an unexampled degree, and the accountancy of modern business management is also of an extremely dispassionate and impartially exacting nature. It results that the modern learning is of a similarly matter-of-fact, mechanistic complexion, and that it similarly leans on statistically dispassionate tests and formulations.[112]

This learning has so far become an avowed "end in itself" that "the increase and diffusion of knowledge among men is now freely rated as the most humane and meritorious work to be taken care of by any enlightened community or any public-spirited friend of civilization."[113] In our present culture, Veblen says, the university is the only institution entrusted with the holding, increasing, and diffusing of this knowledge.[114] The quest for knowledge is the prime duty of the university; it is a duty owed to the truth and to civilization.

But what exactly is the university? It is, Veblen says, a group of men who are fully and solely engaged in "scientific and scholarly inquiry" and "the instruction of students."[115] The university men are engaged in research, which means they are actively seeking the truth about some matter of interest. Each pursues his own quest as he thinks best, though cooperation in research is frequent. This body of men is self-governing; each is free to pursue his own work at his own pace and in his own way. If they have students, the relation of the student to the scientist/ scholar is that of an apprentice to his master. The students learn by watching what the master does and helping him do it. The master passes on his own knowledge by allowing the student to become his aid. This sort of teaching is one on one, and its effectiveness depends on the relation between master and student. It cannot be translated into "courses" or "units" or subjected to schedules. It will vary from one apprentice-master pair to another; there is no rule here for everything depends on the personal relation between the two. And, Veblen believes, nothing more is needed. Of course there must be buildings and equipment of whatever sort the master requires, but these things are not the university; the university is the master and apprentices.

Veblen's definition of the university is clearly an idealization; no modern university has this form. Why then does Veblen propose this ideal as the standard for what the American university ought to be? As lately noted, Veblen demands this freedom from practical purposes for two other factors – for science and for idle curiosity. The basic claim is for idle curiosity. Veblen believed that since action under the instincts of workmanship and the parental bent is teleological, our views of the world, as a result of the apperceptive mass, will be teleologically organized. That takes him back to Kant's Antinomy of the Reflective Judgment. If human thought is teleologically organized but the world runs by efficient causality, how are we to acquire knowledge of the world without imputing final causes where they do not belong? The answer is idle curiosity, an instinct that allows us to gain matter-of-fact knowledge organized on the basis of efficient causality. And to avoid contamination, idle curiosity must remain free of all utilitarian considerations. The same considerations led Veblen to hold that the men of the university – true scholars and scientists – must also be free of self-serving or practical considerations.

But like everything human, the university requires a place and that place, in the United States, has come to be the college. The two coexist in the same proximate physical facilities. More important, they are both divisions of the same corporation, for in America educational institutions are usually corporations. Typically, the university is distinguished as the "graduate" division and the college as the "undergraduate" division, but they are subject to the same corporate form. And the corporate form has consequences, for it means that there is a board of directors who have legal jurisdiction over both the undergraduate and graduate divisions. As academic institutions are now (early twentieth century) structured, the members of the board are not drawn from the university faculty but are chiefly businessmen. And as things run in America, membership on such a board is viewed as an honor and so is given to men who have achieved some distinction in business – that is to say, who are wealthy and no longer young. Such men are usually conservative in their social, political, and economic views. They are also men who know little or nothing about the research being done in the university that now falls under their legal control. These men are not likely to interfere directly with the work of the university men, but they control the budget, and he who controls the budget controls all.[116]

The board appoints the chief executive, usually styled as "president;" he is the central figure in the business university. The board normally selects someone in its own image. "The new incumbents are selected primarily with a view to give the direction of academic policy and administration more of a businesslike character."[117] Sometimes the alumni have a voice in the choice of a president, but their choices usually go along the same line as the board's, since it is widely held in America that "pecuniary success is the final test of manhood."[118] The qualifications are businesslike efficiency in management, a fluent command of language suitable for impressing a popular audience, and

> serene and voluble loyalty to the current conventionalities and a conspicuously profound conviction that all things are working out for good, except for such untoward details as do not visibly conduce to the vested advantage of the well-to-do businessmen under the established law and order.[119]

The president need not be a scholar or scientist of distinction, but he must be able to present himself to a vulgar audience as an academic leader and spokesman for the faculty. Of course, the faculty will know better, but within the university the president has the power to hire and fire and so can enforce his will. In speaking to the public he must deliver attractive homiletics and avoid topics that might give offence, bearing in mind that his audience will contain well-to-do women, who are potential donors. It will help if he has already acquired experience as an academic administrator, such as a dean, and has a coterie of supporters within the faculty. Such a figure ought to appeal to the governing board, to the wealthy from whom donations may be expected, such of the faculty as have business sympathies, and to the public at large. He will fit the view of the board that

> the university is conceived as a business house dealing in merchantable knowledge, placed under the governing hand of a captain of erudition, whose office it is to turn the means in hand to account in the largest feasible output. It is a corporation with large funds, and for men biased by their workday training in business affairs it comes as a matter of course to rate the university in terms of investment and turnover. Hence the insistence on business capacity in the executive heads of the universities, and hence also the extensive range of businesslike duties and powers that devolve on them.[120]

The new president comes to his task armed with the power to hire and fire members of the faculty and staff. The chief task he faces is the college. This will be by far the largest component of the corporation. Not only does the college account for the majority of the students, but these are also students whose families pay the tuition that is the chief source of income to the university. Moreover, the students are minors and can be expected to behave irresponsibly. While some of them may actually be interested in their studies, a large fraction if not the majority are chiefly interested in various forms of dissipation. It is therefore necessary to provide sufficiently enticing activities for them that will channel their energies into less hazardous pastimes. Hence the importance of fraternities, clubs, and particularly sports.

To bring order to this herd of cats, the president must introduce methods of accountancy and evaluation. Instruction is divided into units each of which earns a certain number of credits. Requirements for graduation are defined by credits earned. Classes are scheduled for particular times in particular places for particular lengths of time. Times and places for sports and other activities are specified. All of this regimentation is required to permit the specification of a standard sequence of academic units, complete with an evaluation of performance at each point so that the students' progress or lack thereof can be monitored and suitable discipline administered where and when necessary. To run this organizational structure, a bureaucracy has to be created. There will be records of each student's various activities – of credits earned and grades received of course, but also of disciplinary actions, sporting activities, fraternity memberships, etc. All of these require clerks, files – all the paraphernalia necessary to monitor large numbers of people in an era before electronic records became available. Not surprisingly, the president's time and attention will be focused on the undergraduate division far more than the graduate one.

None of these regulations and organizational tactics have any application to university's work. But once the undergraduate domain has been organized, the extension of the methods to graduate work takes on an irresistible allure. Teaching by apprenticeship is inconsistent with teaching large numbers of students. That requires classes and course units. With the credits and grades system, the administration can monitor what each student is doing, whereas with apprenticeships the administration is forced to rely on the masters evaluations which are not subject to statistical methods. One can say one has x number of graduate students, but where they are in their training is at best only vaguely knowable. So of course the corporation tries to extend the undergraduate system of accountancy to the graduate division where it does not apply and to subvert the difference between undergraduate and graduate work. In this process the administration finds support among undergraduates who consider themselves qualified to take graduate "courses." This interferes with graduate teaching and so with the university's work, since apprentices play an important part in research.

In addition to organizing the students, the president has to organize the faculty. The faculty is divided into departments on the model of a department store and each department specializes in some "field" reflecting an arbitrary classification of subject domains. Since the department must cover its field, instructors are often required to teach courses that are not in their specialties. Departments compete with each other for resources and appointments, which are always said to be in short supply. The president finds among the faculty men whose views are similar to his own and builds up a following who are loyal to him. Since he has the power to hire and fire, to promote and reward, there are faculty who are very glad to become his supporters. But many faculty do not share the businesslike views of the president, and since it is well understood that the university is dedicated to the increase and diffusion of knowledge, the faculty must include dedicated scientists and scholars. The result is a compromise: men of both types will be appointed. But men who have wealth, particularly inherited wealth, will be preferred. "Leading" faculty will represent the university at public affairs where they will mix with potential donors, and it is easier for men who are wealthy to socialize with men who have money than it is for impecunious scholars. Such men will be accomplished in conspicuous consumption; their domestic establishments will be consonant with those of the Leisure Class, and their expenditures will be appropriate for their station. For those faculty not so graced with money, there are "many committees for-the-sifting-of-sawdust" into which the faculty of a well-administered university is organized. These committees are in effect, if not in intention, "designed chiefly to keep the faculty talking while the bureaucratic machine goes its way under the guidance of the executive and his personal counselors and lieutenants."[121]

It is well known that academic salaries are lower than those of men who have devoted equal time to training in other fields. But the standard of expenditure applies to wealthy and poor academics alike. Those who cannot afford to meet the standards must resort to devious means. They reduce expenditures for things that are private in order to present a suitable public face or they seek ways to supplement their incomes. Many work part-time at other jobs, or take on administrative duties that pay additional money, or teach summer school or night school.

> By consequence of this pressure of bread-winning and genteel expenditure, these university men are so barred out from the serious pursuit of those scientific and scholarly inquiries which alone can, academically speaking, justify their retention on the university faculty, and for the sake of which, in great part at least, they have chosen this vocation. No infirmity more commonly besets university men than this going to seed in routine work and extra-scholastic duties.[122]

The overall effect of business principles is to convert academic remuneration from a salary to piece-work "designed to procure class-room instruction at the lowest practicable cost."

Business in the United States is competitive; to men trained in business, it is axiomatic that universities must be competitive, and where a given university stands in the competition is taken to be a measure of the academic executive's success. Competition focuses on endowment and enrollment, size and complexity; the model is the business trust. The larger the endowment the more the size and activity of the college/university can be expanded. The larger the enrollment, the larger the staff will be and the more varied their activities will be. Publicity becomes a sign of success and notoriety is sought. The audience for whom competition is performed is the laity, including donors and potential donors. But the proper work of the university is in research and research is largely invisible. What is visible is buildings; "to the laity a 'university' has come to mean, in the first place and indispensably, an aggregation of buildings and other improved real-estate."[123] The result is that large sums are spent on buildings while the real work of the university – research and teaching – go underfunded. University buildings are meant to impress the laity; not only are they large but there is a preference for archaic architectural styles such as the Gothic, together with modern touches to show that the university is up-to-date. Typically, great attention is given to the exterior and its decoration but this attention to detail often is not carried over to the interior.

> In recent scholastic edifices one is not surprised to find lecture rooms acoustically ill designed, and with an annoying distribution of light, due to the requirements of exterior symmetry and the decorative distribution of windows; and the like holds true even in a higher degree for libraries and laboratories, since for these uses the demands in these respects are even more exacting. Nor is it unusual to find a waste of space and weakness of structure, due, e.g., to a fictitious winding stair, thrown into the design to permit such a façade as will simulate the defensive details of a mediaeval keep, to be surrounded with embrasured battlements and a (make-believe) loopholed turret.[124]

Such buildings, built chiefly for show, are often cheaply constructed, so that they become obsolete rapidly – a process helped by the underfunding of maintenance. Yet it is for such buildings that it is easiest to raise funds.

The president of the university has the authority to hire and fire faculty. Of course he will prefer people who share his own point of view – people wise in the ways of business. Scientists and scholars generally are not wise in the ways of business. There will be among his faculty some men who are genuinely devoted to research and do not conform to the requirements of business principles. Science and scholarship, Veblen says, are not competitive activities; quite the contrary they require cooperation among men so engaged. Such men pose a delicate problem for the executive head of the university. Those scientists and scholars who have made major achievements have a notoriety that the president can use to further the prestige of his university, particularly if those achievements are such as to allow profitable applications to some branch of business; here the president has something of great advertising value. But such men are likely to be strong advocates of the university's mission of advancing knowledge and not inclined to compromise. The ideal solution would doubtless be to fire them, but such a move may bring criticism. Veblen suggests that there are better ways to solve the problem. It may be possible to so harass these men that they will resign; if this does not work, carefully handled defamation of their domestic establishment or their views on religion or politics or economics may be sufficient to permit their removal without an adverse public reaction.

Problems also arise where faculty members teach or publicly espouse doctrines that create public outcry. This is less likely with those who work in the physical sciences. The problem usually comes with those in the social and moral sciences. The president must keep a sharp eye on the laity; men who make substantial gifts to the university are wealthy; they tend also to be businessmen grown old. "These select and substantial elements are on the whole more conservative, more old-fashioned in their views of what is right, good and true, and hold their views on more archaic grounds of conviction, than the generality of the vulgar."[125] The difficulties arise, Veblen points out, where scientists and scholars in the social sciences conduct investigations into the institutions of our current society. "No faithful inquiry into these matters can avoid an air of skepticism as to the stability or finality of some one or other among the received articles of institutional furniture."[126] The problem so created is largely solved by the fact that "a large and aggressive mediocrity [is] the prime qualification for a leader of science in these lines, if his leadership is to gain academic authentication."[127] Judicious appointments can do wonders.

Veblen then turns to the subject of vocational education – more exactly, of professional schools as parts of the university. Veblen's view is that such schools have no relation to the university or the higher learning. He thinks that they are a capitulation to the demands for practical education, and represent an outgrowth of the elective system that allowed undergraduates to begin specialization early. Some of these schools, for example, engineering schools, draw upon the results of the research done by the university but none of them contribute to the pursuit of knowledge, and so have no place in the university. Veblen finds "schools of commerce" to be the most offensive, followed closely by law schools. Such schools provide training in the ways and means of competitive gain; they contribute nothing to the community but more men devoted to making money for themselves. The higher learning, Veblen says, has nothing to do with individual competitive gain. They therefore represent a perversion of the mission of true university. "As related to the ostensible purpose of the university, therefore, the support and conduct of such schools at the expense of the universities is to be construed as a breach of trust."[128] Veblen insists that such schools damage the university. If they are to have competent faculties, they will have to recruit faculty from among those in their vocations who are the most successful. But the incomes of leading businessmen or leading lawyers are far higher than academic salaries. To recruit such faculty will therefore divert university resources from their proper end but not to recruit such faculty will be to offer a second rate program that will ill-equip the students. Either way, the university will suffer.

Why then are such schools being established? In the competition among universities, the two chief points of comparison are enrollments and endowments. The establishment of schools of commerce or business is an obvious appeal to wealthy businessmen of the type that fund the endowment and the claim that they prepare their students for success in business is an appeal to well-to-do middle class men who are prepared to invest in their children's futures. On both counts, the university suffers either by loss of students or loss of donations. Vocational education endangers the universities and contributes nothing to the community.

It is, Veblen says, widely believed among businessmen that "learning is of no use in business."[129] It is also believed, though less widely, that "what is of no use in business is not worthwhile."[130] Yet to businessmen our society entrusts the running of the sole institution that is "dedicated to the increase and diffusion of knowledge."[131] It is not a surprise that under these conditions the university suffers. The surprise is that it survives at all. For many men of business, the question is what is the use of the higher learning? To answer this, Veblen turns to that champion of the practical, Benjamin Franklin.

> Benjamin Franklin – high-bred pragmatist that he was – once put away such a question with the rejoinder: What is the use of a baby?[132]

The baby is not a means; it is an end. The same Veblen holds is true of the higher learning. Knowledge, understanding, is valuable in itself. Idle curiosity impels us to seek knowledge for its own sake. And it happens to be true that knowledge so acquired turns out to have marvelously practical uses. It is an achievement in spite of the corruption of the university.

Is there a remedy for this situation? Veblen says there is. "All that is required is the abolition of the academic executive and of the governing board."[133] If this were done, the various components of the university (which Veblen refers to as the trust) would separate; the vocational schools would go their own ways, the college would revert to its proper role as a school for adolescents, and the university – unhindered by the competitive obsession and the megalomania of the executive – would be able to pursue its true mission.[134]

At the end of the book, Veblen adds a paragraph in which he says there is of course no chance that the remedial action he has proposed will be taken. "All that is here intended to be said is … that, as seen from the point of view of the higher learning, the academic executive and all his works are anathema, and should be discontinued by the simple expedient of wiping him off the slate."[135] A similar fate should be given to the governing board.

But Veblen has a further goal in this description of how business subverts the university. His point is that business principles will corrupt any enterprise that is created to serve non-business ends. The university, as Veblen defines it, is devoted to the search for truth, and secondarily to the service of mankind. No such institution can survive uncorrupted in a business culture. The fact that it is organized as a corporation is itself sufficient to subvert the true mission of the university, and the appointment of businessmen to the controlling positions makes its subversion certain. Veblen proposes as a remedy eliminating the board and the president – changes that he knows will never happen. But in a business culture there is no alternative to the corporation as an institutional form, and the corporation carries with it the board and the executive. In a business culture, business principles must rule, and there is no escape from their corrupting influence.

Notes

1 Thorstein Veblen, *The Theory of Business Enterprise* (New York: Charles Scribners, 1935), 4.
2 John Locke, *Of Civil Government and Toleration* (London: Cassell and Co., 1905), 23.
3 Thorstein Veblen, *Absentee Ownership: Business Enterprise in Recent Times – The Case of America* (New York: B. W. Heubsch, 1923), 50–51.
4 Thorstein Veblen, "On the Nature of Capital," in *The Place of Science in Modern Civilization*, intro. Warren J. Samuels (New York: Cosimo, 2007), 340.
5 Veblen, *Theory of Business Enterprise*, 114.
6 Adolf A. Berle and Gardiner C. Means, *The Modern Corporation and Private Property* (New York: Macmillan, 1932).
7 Veblen, *Absentee Ownership*, 126.
8 Veblen, *Absentee Ownership*, 124.
9 John Wesley Powell, *Report on the Lands of the Arid Regions of the United States* (Washington DC: US Government Printing Office, 1878).
10 Veblen, *Absentee Ownership*, 131.
11 Veblen, *Absentee Ownership*, 130.
12 Veblen, *Absentee Ownership*, 142.
13 Veblen, *Absentee Ownership*, 134, 143.
14 Veblen, *Absentee Ownership*, 143n1.
15 Veblen, *Absentee Ownership*, 149.
16 Veblen, *Absentee Ownership*, 155.
17 Veblen, *Absentee Ownership*, 157.
18 Veblen, *Absentee Ownership*, 159.
19 Veblen, *Absentee Ownership*, 159.
20 Veblen, *Absentee Ownership*, 159.
21 Veblen, *Absentee Ownership*, 159.
22 Veblen, *Absentee Ownership*, 163.
23 Veblen, *Absentee Ownership*, 164.
24 Veblen, *Absentee Ownership*, 165.
25 Veblen, *Absentee Ownership*, 165–166.
26 Veblen, *Absentee Ownership*, 168.
27 Veblen, *Absentee Ownership*, 170.
28 Veblen, *Absentee Ownership*, 172.
29 Veblen, *Absentee Ownership*, 177.
30 Veblen, *Absentee Ownership*, 177.
31 Veblen, *Absentee Ownership*, 186–201.
32 Veblen, *Absentee Ownership*, 200.

33 Veblen, *Absentee Ownership*, 76–77.
34 Veblen, *Absentee Ownership*, 77.
35 Veblen, *Absentee Ownership*, 323.
36 Veblen, "Nature of Capital," in *Place of Science*, 352–353.
37 Veblen, "Nature of Capital," in *Place of Science*, 356–357.
38 Veblen, "Nature of Capital," in *Place of Science*, 364.
39 Veblen, "Nature of Capital," in *Place of Science*, 365.
40 Veblen, *Business Enterprise*, 139.
41 Veblen, *Business Enterprise*, 138.
42 Veblen, *Absentee Ownership*, 93.
43 Veblen, *Absentee Ownership*, 93.
44 Veblen, *Business Enterprise*, 146.
45 Veblen, *Business Enterprise*, 137.
46 Veblen, *Business Enterprise*, 154–157.
47 Veblen, *Business Enterprise*, 158–159.
48 Veblen, *Business Enterprise*, 164.
49 Veblen, *Business Enterprise*, 93.
50 Veblen, *Business Enterprise*, 96.
51 Veblen, *Business Enterprise*, 99.
52 Veblen, *Business Enterprise*, 105.
53 Veblen, *Business Enterprise*, 108.
54 Veblen, *Business Enterprise*, 106.
55 Edward Sherwood Meade, *Trust Finance: A Study of the Genesis, Organization, and Management of Industrial Combinations* (New York: D. Appleton, 1920), 31.
56 Meade, *Trust Finance*, 31–36.
57 Meade, *Trust Finance*, 42.
58 Veblen, *Absentee Ownership*, 335.
59 Veblen, *Absentee Ownership*, 337–338.
60 Meade, *Trust Finance*, 198.
61 Meade, *Trust Finance*, 206.
62 Meade, *Trust Finance*, 193–198.
63 Veblen, *Business Enterprise*, 47–49.
64 Veblen, *Absentee Ownership*, 334–350.
65 Veblen, *Business Enterprise*, 168.
66 Veblen, *Business Enterprise*, 175–176.
67 Thorstein Veblen, "Industrial and Pecuniary Employments," in *The Place of Science in Modern Civilization*, intro. Warren J. Samuels (New York: Cosimo, 2007), 383.
68 Veblen, *Business Enterprise*, 184–186.
69 Veblen, *Business Enterprise*, 180–182.
70 Veblen, *Business Enterprise*, 194–200.
71 Veblen, *Business Enterprise*, 200–209.
72 Veblen, *Business Enterprise*, 266.
73 Veblen, *Business Enterprise*, 266–267.
74 Veblen, *Business Enterprise*, 266.
75 Veblen, *Business Enterprise*, 266.
76 Veblen, *Business Enterprise*, 128.
77 Veblen, *Absentee Ownership*, 329–332.
78 Veblen, *Absentee Ownership*, 266.
79 Veblen, *Absentee Ownership*, 271.
80 Veblen, *Absentee Ownership*, 274.
81 Veblen, *Absentee Ownership*, 338–339.
82 Veblen, *Absentee Ownership*, 339–350, 354.
83 Veblen, *Absentee Ownership*, 362.

84 Veblen, *Absentee Ownership*, 362.
85 Veblen, *Absentee Ownership*, 362.
86 Veblen, *Absentee Ownership*, 366.
87 Veblen, *Absentee Ownership*, 369.
88 Veblen, *Absentee Ownership*, 378.
89 Veblen, *Absentee Ownership*, 375–376.
90 Veblen, *Absentee Ownership*, 383.
91 Veblen, *Business Enterprise*, 301.
92 Veblen, *Business Enterprise*, 330.
93 Veblen, *Business Enterprise*, 364.
94 Veblen, *Business Enterprise*, 388.
95 Veblen, *Business Enterprise*, 394–395.
96 Veblen, *Business Enterprise*, 400.
97 Veblen, *Absentee Ownership*, 210.
98 Veblen, *Absentee Ownership*, 233.
99 Veblen, *Absentee Ownership*, 390.
100 Veblen, *Absentee Ownership*, 401.
101 Veblen, *Absentee Ownership*, 433.
102 Veblen, *Absentee Ownership*, 429.
103 Veblen, *Absentee Ownership*, 442.
104 Veblen, *Absentee Ownership*, 441.
105 Veblen, *Absentee Ownership*, 442.
106 Veblen, *Absentee Ownership*, 444–445.
107 Veblen, *Absentee Ownership*, 443.
108 Veblen, *Absentee Ownership*, 445.
109 Thorstein Veblen, *The Higher Learning in America: A Memorandum on the Conduct of Universities by Business Men* (New York: B. W. Huebsch, 1918), 1.
110 Veblen, *Higher Learning*, 1.
111 Veblen, *Higher Learning*, 1.
112 Veblen, *Higher Learning*, 7.
113 Veblen, *Higher Learning*, 10.
114 Veblen, *Higher Learning*, 15–16.
115 Veblen, *Higher Learning*, 16.
116 Veblen, *Higher Learning*, 65–82.
117 Veblen, *Higher Learning*, 82.
118 Veblen, *Higher Learning*, 82.
119 Veblen, *Higher Learning*, 245.
120 Veblen, *Higher Learning*, 85.
121 Veblen, *Higher Learning*, 253.
122 Veblen, *Higher Learning*, 166.
123 Veblen, *Higher Learning*, 139.
124 Veblen, *Higher Learning*, 144–145.
125 Veblen, *Higher Learning*, 184.
126 Veblen, *Higher Learning*, 180–181.
127 Veblen, *Higher Learning*, 186.
128 Veblen, *Higher Learning*, 210.
129 Veblen, *Higher Learning*, 73.
130 Veblen, *Higher Learning*, 73.
131 Veblen, *Higher Learning*, 116.
132 Veblen, *Higher Learning*, 200.
133 Veblen, *Higher Learning*, 276.
134 Veblen, *Higher Learning*, 285.
135 Veblen, *Higher Learning*, 286.

7

THE GREAT WAR

Biographical Note

When Veblen joined the Stanford faculty, President Jordan let it be known that he did not expect a repetition of the behavior that had made it necessary for Veblen to leave Chicago. His expectations were disappointed. When a female friend arrived in Palo Alto and took up residence with Veblen, his friends warned him that she was trouble. But Veblen's reply was, "What is one to do if the woman moves in on you?"[1] He apparently did nothing and the president was not pleased. Veblen told a friend, "The president doesn't approve of my domestic arrangements. Nor do I."[2] The woman stayed, and the University acted. In December of 1909, Veblen was forced to resign.[3]

Given the circumstances under which he had left Chicago, and now Sanford, finding a new academic post was a matter of some difficulty. The problem was not just that Veblen attracted women; the problem was that he was still married to Ellen Rolfe, so he was guilty of adultery. The issue was at last partially settled in 1911 when Ellen finally agreed to his requests for a divorce.[4] That meant that his liaisons were at least not illegal. But Veblen also had the help of some former students who were loyal friends – particularly of Herbert Davenport who was dean of the School of Commerce at the University of Missouri. Davenport managed to secure Veblen's appointment as a lecturer – an appointment that required annual renewal.[5] There is a certain irony in this appointment, given Veblen's views of business schools. Veblen stayed at Missouri for seven years. His marriage to Anne Fessenden Bradley in 1914 seems to have solved the problem of his "domestic arrangements."

During the early years of his stay at the University of Missouri, Veblen wrote his book entitled *The Instinct of Workmanship* – a work that he said was his only important book.[6] In preparation he published several articles on the origins of the blond race. *The Instinct of Workmanship*, the title suggests, was based upon the instinct psychology he had long held. But Veblen remarked that the concept of instinct was now (1914) no longer regarded as a proper scientific term by psychologists. Veblen did not abandon the use of the term "instinct"; he held that it could still be properly employed in studies such as his.[7]

The concept of instinct has a long history in psychology where it had been quite respectable only a few years before. Psychologists as highly regarded as William James and William McDougall had used it without hesitation. But psychology was undergoing a major revolution that brought behaviorism to the dominant position in academic psychology. Behaviorists rejected the notion that human behavior was determined by innate factors and claimed that learning, based on conditioning, could explain human behavior without the use of instinct or introspection. Whether in the crude form championed by John B. Watson or in the sophisticated form advanced by Clark Hull, the behaviorists rejected nature for nurture. At the very time when Freudian psychology came to dominate American psychiatry, behaviorism ruled academic psychology departments. From a behaviorist standpoint, Veblen's instincts were nonsense.

Times change. The day of behaviorism has past. Psychologists now recognize that much human behavior is "hardwired," and using techniques less subject to bias than introspection, the cognitive revolution has brought renewed interest to the study of the innate determinants of human behavior. This does not mean that the instinct psychology has been resurrected; the term "instinct" is still regarded as radioactive. But it does mean that Veblen's claims that there are innate determinants of human behavior should not be rejected out of hand. Whether Veblen's instinct theory is tenable is an empirical question; it is not one that can be settled *a priori*.

The Great War – Germany

Through 1914, Veblen's attention was focused on the development of his theory of evolutionary economics and on its application, particularly to the United States and England. In his prior writing, he had dealt with early European history and prehistory, but not much with modern Europe. As the likelihood of European war increased, he turned his attention more to the roots of the emerging conflict, and in 1915 published one of his most brilliant books, *Imperial Germany and the Industrial Revolution*. This was in some respects a test case for Veblen's theory: could he, as he said in his Preface, "account for Germany's industrial advance and high efficiency by natural causes, without drawing on the logic of manifest destiny, Providential nepotism, natural genius, and the like" – that is, in terms of his own theory, without recourse to the rubrics of standard political and economic history.

Given the emphasis Veblen had placed on race, the first question he had to answer was whether the differences between Germany on the one hand and France, England, and the United States on the other could be accounted for on racial grounds. His argument, based on the theory of race we have already examined, was that they could not. From a racial perspective, Veblen argued, there was no difference at all between the nations of northern Europe; Germany and England were indistinguishable on racial grounds.[8]

He then turned to the issue of borrowing. He had touched on this issue before in discussing the borrowing proclivities of Neolithic Europeans and the fact that hybrid populations were able to assimilate items by borrowing more easily than non-hybrids, and again in describing the industrial rise of England, but now he gave the phenomena a detailed treatment. Cultures borrow items from one another, as neolithic Europeans had borrowed animal husbandry from Asia. To see what the consequences of this are, Veblen first examined how innovations are assimilated into a culture, regardless of their source. The introduction of an innovation usually begins on a small scale with the inventor and perhaps a few more, and it is gradually adopted if it proves to be useful to people within the society.[9] Its adoption will displace or alter existing features of the culture, which must be revised to accommodate the new factor. Such readjustments are concessive, and involve the retention of the existing system so far as possible, even at the cost of mitigating the effectiveness of the new item.[10] But once established, the innovation becomes embedded in a matrix of beliefs and practices – a "fringe" as Veblen calls it. This fringe includes laws and customs, "class distinctions," magic and religious rituals, "occupational divisions, standardization of methods and products, together with trade routes, trade relations and settled markets," and other items as well.[11] The growth of this fringe takes time, but it signifies the integration of the new item into the cultural system.

When an item is borrowed by one culture form another, its entrance into the new culture will follow the same course as that of any innovation. But it will not carry with it the fringe of beliefs and practices it had in the old culture, and this will be particularly true where the borrowing involves the crossing of cultural and linguistic frontiers. The new item comes into its new home as it were naked and alone, and it will take time for it to be integrated into the culture of its new host.[12] As a result, it may be put to new and different uses in the host culture than it had in its original culture, and to the extent that the fringe it carried in its culture of origin may have restricted the realization of some of its possibilities, it may prove to be more effective in its new context than it was in the old. Borrowing therefore offers a potential advantage to the borrower; not only is a new item acquired, but it may be possible to employ the new item more adequately in its new home than it was employed in its old home, at least until a new fringe of beliefs and practices grows up in the host culture marking its full assimilation. There is then a window of opportunity between the time the item is borrowed and the time it becomes encultured when the possibilities of its exploitation are at a maximum.[13]

Veblen then turns to the comparison of the process of industrial development in England and Germany. At the beginning of the sixteenth century, England was just emerging from feudalism and was substantially behind continental Europe industrially. But the English borrowed heavily from the continent in their development of the handicraft system, and particularly from the Dutch in respect to shipbuilding and navigation.[14] They also began extensive development of their natural resources.[15] Given the advantages of island isolation and peace that Veblen had discussed before, the English were able to develop steadily and rapidly, and caught up to Europe in the early part of the seventeenth century. With the Industrial Revolution, England moved into the industrial leadership of the world. This rapidly developing technology acquired a cultural "fringe."[16] The fringe included the private ownership of technological equipment, its private control, and its use for private profit in a system of private enterprise. Given the central role of the Industrial Arts in English life, the whole capitalist system is incorporated in the fringe of the technology, including the restriction of output, the production of conspicuous waste, and hyperstimulated sales, unemployment, wage relations, and workers' discontents. Veblen does not stop there. The slow English drift to democracy and a skeptical and a matter-of-fact point of view he considers to be part of the fringe of the machine technology. Although the philosophical doctrines of Natural Rights and Natural Law are products of the handicraft system, Veblen notes that they have continued to hold throughout the nineteenth century and are the foundation of much British law. And the machine technology is also credited with the slow drift of England toward democratic government, although it is a government still encumbered with a crown and nobility, with "gentlemen," sports, servants, and other survivals of bygone times.[17] The enthusiasm for democracy that Natural Rights spawned led to the establishment of democratic governments in America and France.

The development of modern Germany took quite a different course than that of England. At the end of the Napoleonic wars, "Germany" was fragmented into a number of small principalities, among which Prussia was the leader. From the time of the Great Elector,[18] Prussia had been the exemplar of the German Dynastic State. Just what the Dynastic State is, Veblen admits, is not easy to say in English:

> It is neither the territorial area, nor the population, nor the body of citizens or subjects, nor the aggregate wealth or traffic, nor the public administration, nor the government, nor the crown, nor the sovereign; yet in some sense it is all these matters, or rather all these are organs of the State. In some potent sense, the State is a personal entity, with rights and duties superior and anterior to those of the subjects.[19]

As something above and beyond the people, "it does not ask how the people is disposed; it demands obedience."[20] For the German people, obedience to the demands of the state, in the form of duty, is the mark of correct conduct. This holdover from Feudalism characterized not only Prussia but all the German states, but Prussia was the place where it achieved its fullest development.[21]

The industrial development of Germany Veblen dates from the end of the Napoleonic wars, though its acceleration after the founding of the new Reich in 1871 is dramatic.[22] In the second quarter of the nineteenth century, Germany was still in the handicraft era.[23] From an industrial perspective, its economy was about at the stage reached by England in the Elizabethan era. But after the formation of the Customs Union, economic development picked up. Germany borrowed the Industrial Arts from England.[24] But in the process, the cultural fringe that surrounded technology in England was left behind. And with German unification into the German Empire under the Hohenzollern crown, the Industrial Arts were put to work in the service of the Dynastic State.

Veblen holds that the objective of the Dynastic State is war and conquest. Accordingly, the German state embarked on a program of development for Germany designed to prepare the nation for war. One aspect of this program was a drive to make Germany self-sufficient in all the industries whose output was essential for war. This involved the development of Germany's natural resources. Germany's endowment of natural resources, Veblen says, is about the same as that of other northern European countries; it is liberal but not sufficient for the long-run needs of the nation at war. To shield the industries developing its natural resources, the German State invoked the tariff which was employed generally to bar the import of goods and materials that the government wanted produced at home.[25] But protection against foreign competition was not enough; Germany required new sources of supply. This led to a policy of colonial acquisition and development, believing that although Germany alone was not self-sufficient, the German Empire could be. The general trade policy was mercantilist, aimed at building national strength rather than at low consumer prices. Of course, Veblen points out, this policy is inconsistent with the requirements of the machine industry for which international free trade is the optimal policy.

The actual borrowing and assimilation of British technology was not difficult. Veblen comments,

> No great difficulty need be experienced and no great interval of time need be consumed in assimilating the working elements of this technology when once they are presented. What is required to a sufficient understanding and an intelligent employment of the appliances and processes of the machine industry is nothing more recondite than a certain body of matter-of-fact information as to the physical behavior of certain material objects under given conditions.[26]

The management of this equipment was undertaken by what Veblen calls the "German adventurers in the field of business [who] being captains of industry rather than of finance, were also free to choose their associates and staff with a

view to their industrial insight and capacity,"[27] and Germany provided an edu-
cated and intelligent labor force accustomed to work at quite low wages. The
standard of living being low, pressures from the workers for higher wages were
not a severe problem.[28] The result was a considerable margin between prices in
the market and wages, leaving a very comfortable margin of profit. These profits
are now threatened by rising costs of production and rumblings among the
workers, but German business remains highly profitable.[29]

The problem of obsolescence is not yet severe in Germany, but it is growing,
in this case not so much as a question of deterioration but rather one of rapid
changes in technology. The advantages of pioneering in technological inventions
are obvious. If the invention yields an improved product, the pioneer can not
only outsell his competitors, but his advantage will last for some time. Utilizing
the invention will be expensive, but if the estimated working life is, say, a dozen
years, the profits in a clear field should exceed the cost by a significant margin.
His competitors will of course try to borrow (steal) the invention, and it is an
unpleasant truth about inventions that once the prototype is in use, other inven-
tors will find ways to improve it. As a result, the pioneer may well find that in, let
us say, five years, a new and more efficient model is developed by a competitor.
The pioneer then faces a difficult problem. If he does not adopt the new model,
his competitor will undersell him and steal his market. But if he does adopt it, not
only must he pay the cost of the new model but he will have to forego the
profits he expected from the pioneer version over the last seven years of its
working life, and all of the adaptations he developed that are specific to the pioneer model but not to the new one will be wasted. Veblen points to the "silly
little bobtail carriages used in the British goods traffic."[30] The British
railroads were among the first ever built. Accordingly, the equipment first used
was not always well fitted to actual requirements and quickly became obsolete.
The early railroad cars were of course first modeled on the familiar horse-drawn
carriages; it took time for more suitable rail cars to be designed and built, making
the "bobtailed carriages" obsolete. Such problems are the penalties for being
pioneers in the technological field; where change is rapid it will affect all businesses employing costly technology, as the Germans are just beginning to
discover.[31]

The goal of the Dynastic State is, Veblen says, "a place in the sun."[32] This
involves military dominance in the wars that are expected to occur, but it also
involves a need for territorial expansion to accommodate Germany's increasing
population, and it involves the preservation and expansion of German culture.
It is the conviction of the German leaders that the German language is superior
to all others and should be universally adopted. Veblen, who was fluent in
German, compares the German language to the English language and finds no
ground for believing German superior. It can hardly be held the German technology is superior to all others since it has only recently been borrowed from
England. But superiority is also claimed for German philosophy, a claim that

Veblen denies. German philosophy is a holdover from the romantic era. Veblen notes,

> The peculiarly German philosophy is peculiarly ineffectual for the purposes of modern science, and peculiarly incapable of articulating with or illuminating any of the questions with which modern scientific inquiry is occupied. It is an idealistic philosophy; that is to say, at its nearest approach to the domain of fact it is a theoretical construction in terms of sufficient reason rather than of efficient causes, in terms of luminous personal valuation rather than of opaque matter-of-fact.[33]

And where German culture is said to lie in its system of government, Veblen describes it as arbitrary, bureaucratic, and authoritarian.[34] It is in Veblen's view a reaction against the trend to increasing democratization that has been clear in modern European history across the last several centuries. German culture is out of date, particularly with respect to its governmental system.[35]

The Great War erupted while Veblen was writing this book on imperial Germany. In the last chapter he drew certain conclusions of a more general kind. Speaking of Christendom Veblen says,

> The modern civilization, in high or low degree, is what has, in the simplest terms hitherto given it, been called the mechanistic conception. Its practical working-out is the machine technology, of which the intellectual precipitate and counterpart is the exact sciences.[36]

This, Veblen says, is the conceptual system of technology and science, and it now dominates the culture of the occident. He holds that Germany represents a regression toward a form of culture now archaic. "Coercion, personal dominion, self-abasement, subjection, loyalty, suspicion, duplicity, ill-will – these things do not articulate with the mechanistic conception."[37] Rather obviously, Veblen has here abandoned any pretense of impartiality. The war, he says, will have devastating effects, but he points to two respects in which he thinks the results may not be as calamitous as is generally believed. First, Veblen notes that the war will almost certainly result in widespread destruction of property, but, picking up a theme he has developed before, he says that so long as the Industrial Arts remain unimpaired, material property can be relatively rapidly rebuilt. And there is no reason to believe that the war will impair the Industrial Arts.[38] Second, the loss of life will no doubt be very great, and so far as the non-commissioned soldiers are concerned, the loss will be spread more or less evenly across the population. But the officer corps is usually a self-selected group, drawn chiefly from men who are the most pugnacious and bloodthirsty. Disproportionately high losses from the officer corps may therefore be beneficial.[39] Finally, he notes that since wars are fought on credit, the result of this one will be a redistribution of property in favor of the creditors.[40]

Imperial Germany and the Industrial Revolution is a remarkable book. Veblen presents the book as a theoretical investigation intended to solve the problem: how can England and Germany have the same technology yet be so different in general culture? Implicit in this formulation of the question is the assumption that cultures must exhibit a high degree of integration, and the assumption that technology (including science) is the dominant factor in determining a society's culture. Veblen presents this book as a scientific investigation; he says, "It is believed to be the first attempt yet made at an explanation, as distinct from description or eulogy, of this episode in modern economic history."[41] His explanation is in terms of the process of borrowing.

Veblen's analysis of borrowing is brilliant. Assuming, as he does, that all cultures are highly integrated, every component of the culture, material or immaterial, is embedded in a cultural matrix. This matrix, or "fringe" as Veblen calls it, may consist of laws, customs, magic, or religious rituals, but whatever its composition, it governs the uses to which the item is put. Consider for example a flush toilet. Its use in our culture is well defined and quite specific. But it could be used as a washtub, or for any activity that involved holding a liquid with the ability to make a rapid change of the contents – perhaps a punch bowl. In our culture, it is not so used. But there is nothing in the nature of the device itself that prevents such alternative uses.

If someone from another culture borrows the toilet, what he will get is the device; it's matrix, Veblen says, will not be borrowed with it, presumably because the more encumbered with cultural baggage the item is the more difficult its assimilation to another culture will be. Accordingly, upon entrance into the new culture, a new matrix will gradually form governing the proper use of the item in its new home. It will take time for the new matrix to develop, and in that time window between the item's first entrance into the new culture and the jelling of its new matrix, the item is open to a variety of new uses undreamed of in the old culture. Thus the toilet might be used as a baptismal font – a use to which it has never been put in our culture. But however it comes to be employed, its introduction will occasion readjustments in the new culture which may be extensive. And during this process of assimilation, the item may acquire an importance it never had before, for example if the toilet is used as a receptacle for holy water.

It is this theory of borrowing that solves Veblen's problem. He holds that the technology/science borrowed from England can be turned to the services of the state in Germany, and so to preparations for war, conquest, and slaughter. For example, English railroad lines were laid out to further trade. But in Germany the railroad lines were laid out to facilitate the movement of troops and military supplies. Veblen believes conflict is inevitable between the borrowed technology and the culture of the Dynastic State. But while the time-window is open, conflicts may be tolerated that would not be acceptable once the new matrix has become rigid. So for the present (1915) the Dynastic State and the borrowed technology can work together, though according to Veblen this will not be true in the long run.

Veblen's argument about the consequences of the introduction of the machine technology into Germany offers one of the clearest indications of the degree to which he believed technology/science determines culture. In his account, German culture will in the long run become more and more similar to the culture of the English-speaking countries. This is not due to the technology carrying those cultural features with it when adoption takes place, for Veblen holds that the old cultural matrix is left behind; it is due to the causal effects of science and technology in the new culture. Veblen is usually very careful in his statements about how the machine technology influences culture; but it is clear here that he thinks the process is more deterministic than he actually says it is. And in his description of how it will reshape German culture, the causal power that he attributes to the machine technology is clear.

For Veblen, science and technology will destroy the Dynastic State. In his theory of knowledge, it is science and technology that further the satisfaction of the true instincts. The culture of the Dynastic State is for him a creation of the contaminated instincts; it is therefore a make-believe phenomenon. The Dynastic State exists only as an imputation of power to a metaphysical figment. What will destroy this system of make-believe is the general change in the point of view of the German people due to the discipline of the machine. As men come to think in matter-of-fact terms of efficient cause, the Dynastic State will melt like the Wicked Witch of the West, leaving only her broomstick behind.

Finally, it should be noted what Veblen does not do. A Marxist writing on this subject would no doubt focus on the inevitable strife caused by a rising capitalist power challenging the position of an older established capitalist power. This line of argument is obvious and many besides Marxists have seen the Great War in these terms. But Veblen does not deal with the problem in this way. His approach is in terms of the theory of economics that he had developed before the war. Those who think Veblen is a closet Marxist should note the difference; Veblen is no Marxist – he has his own theory.

Japan

In an article also published in 1915, "The Opportunity of Japan,"[42] Veblen drew a striking parallel between the case of Germany and that of Japan. Like Germany, Japan remained a feudal Dynastic State until its rude awakening in 1868. Like the Germans, the Japanese are a hybrid people whose instinctive flexibility made borrowing a viable option. And like Germany, since it emerged from isolation Japan has borrowed the Industrial Arts of the West on a massive scale, resulting in an extraordinarily rapid industrial development. Here too the cultural fringe has been left behind in the process of borrowing, with the result that industrial power has been harnessed to the imperial Dynastic State. "It is in this unique

combination of a high-wrought spirit of feudalistic fealty and chivalric honor
with the material efficiency given by the modern technology that the strength of
the Japanese nation lies."[43] But Veblen goes on to argue that the time window
will not last. The machine process brings with it a cultural discipline that is not
compatible with the feudal culture of Japan. Accordingly, "Japan must strike, if at
all, within the effective lifetime of the generation that is now coming to maturity."[44] The same conclusions apply to Germany. In fact, Veblen thought Germany had waited too long. He believed the disintegrating effect of the machine
process was already detectable in Germany and that other European nations –
France, Italy, Russia – had also borrowed English technology and were rapidly
developing their industrial power so that the German advantage was already on
the wane. Many people have noted Veblen's prediction of the Japanese attack
that came in 1941. It should be noted that Veblen was not the only person to
make such a prediction. Homer Lea also foresaw the Japanese attack.

Peace

In 1917, Veblen published *An Inquiry into the Nature of Peace and the Terms of its
Perpetuation.*[45] In a two-page preface, he cites Kant's famous essay, *Zum ewigen
Frieden.* Kant held that the pursuit of peace is an intrinsic human duty[46] and one
which will be successful in the long run, not so much as a human achievement
but as the result of the divine plan. Much has changed since Kant wrote, but
Veblen believes the quest for perpetual peace is still a human duty but not one to
which divine guidance will lead us. His inquiry is an attempt to determine what,
in the world of 1917, are the possibilities of such a peace. Specifically, Veblen
says, "The main point of the inquiry being the nature, causes, and consequences
of such a preconception favoring peace, and the circumstances that make for a
contrary preconception in favor of war."[47]

War, Veblen points out, is the work of states or governments. The governments of Europe, Veblen says, are all descendants of the feudal establishments of
the Middle Ages. At one extreme among those descendants are the dynastic states
such as Prussia and now Germany, and possibly Russia whose status Veblen
considered indeterminate, showing the discomfort which the democracies felt in
having that autocratic monarchy as an ally. The list also includes Japan, although
Japan's feudalism was not European. At the other extreme are the democratic
commonwealths such as England, France, and the United States. The rest of
Europe's states lie between these two "type-forms."[48] All of them command the
loyalty of their subjects, even to the extent of being willing to wage defensive
wars. During the eighteenth and nineteenth centuries, the nations of Western
Europe and notably England enjoyed relative peace; this was the era of natural
rights and natural liberty. (One wonders how Napoleon fits into Veblen's
scheme.) But this is also a time of rapid technological advance, of the industrial
revolution, the revolution in transportation, and in weapons. One consequence

of this transformation is the realization that "no corner of the earth was any longer secure by mere favor of distance and natural difficulty, from eventual aggression at the hands of any provident and adventurous assailant – even by help of a modicum of defensive precaution."[49] Since then, Veblen says, it has been clear that the advantage lies with offense, and every nation has found it necessary to prepare for defense, though the line between defense and offense has become blurred. Veblen was ahead of his time. It took World War II and the atomic bomb to convince most Americans of the futility of isolation.

Prussia in particular became the leader in "preparedness," and this role was inherited by the German Empire. Veblen believes that Germany started the Great War. He holds that once a modern state becomes involved in a war, it can count on the fervent support of its population, regardless of how the war began, since all wars are now claimed to be defensive. Veblen holds that present-day wars are started chiefly by businessmen for business interests, while the common people pay the cost. And when the war fails to receive the expected popular support, making the issue one of national honor usually does the trick.

Patriotism, Veblen says, may be defined as "a sense of partisan solidarity in respect of prestige."[50] Patriotism involves both emulation and solidarity; it is a type of sportsmanship. It seeks the humiliation of a rival and finds its full expression in wars where it seeks "the death, damage, discomfort and destruction of the party of the second part."[51] Patriotism can be made to embrace any cause; a threat to the foreign investments of American business can be construed as an insult to the national honor, but in all cases, the cause called patriotic must be morally blessed. Patriotism is also an invidious spirit; it pits one nation against others. But in this it contradicts modern culture. Veblen holds that much of Western culture is shared among the nations of Christendom; in particular, science and technology are cosmopolitan. Modern industry crosses borders with impunity. In this cosmopolitan modern culture, the patriotic spirit fits "like dust in the eyes and sand in the bearings."[52] Why, then, do we have it?

The first question Veblen tries to answer is what patriotism is: is it a habit or is it an instinctive proclivity? He calls it "a frame of mind."[53]

> It so involves a concatenation of several impulsive propensities [presumably hereditary]; and that both the concatenation and the special mode and amplitude of the response are a product of habituation, very largely of the nature of conventionalized use and wont … the underlying aptitudes requisite to this patriotic frame of mind are heritable, and that use and wont as bearing on this point run with sufficient uniformity to bring a passably uniform result.[54]

The description makes patriotism capable of uniform persistence over generations, but it does not rule out the possibility of change. Note what Veblen does not say. In earlier writings, he had argued for an instinct he called the parental bent which was an instinctive impulse to further the welfare of the community at large. There is no mention here of the parental bent – indeed, no mention of instinct at all. Patriotism has to be more than a habit if it is inheritable, as Veblen says it is. It looks very much like a result of contamination of the parental bent, just as emulation is the result of a contamination of the instinct of workmanship. But in this book Veblen does not mention instincts. This does not mean that he had abandoned the theory of instincts; in *Absentee Ownership* in 1923 he has no hesitation in using his theory of instincts. Veblen does not explain why he did not invoke instincts in this book. One may conjecture that his decision not to invoke the theory of instincts was determined by the choice of the audience he hoped to reach. In the *Instinct of Workmanship* Veblen had admitted that the concept of instinct was no longer acceptable in the biological sciences. I think Veblen hoped that this book, *The Nature of Peace*, would have a significant impact on those who would determine the outcome of the war and the nature of the peace, and he therefore omitted anything that he thought would give his critics an opening to attack his proposals. I can think of no other reasons for his omission of the theory of instincts here.

Patriotism, Veblen says, existed in savagery as an impulse to group solidarity; what undermines this group solidarity is the introduction of ownership in severalty. It is ownership and the resulting desire for property that makes individual gain more attractive than group welfare. As technology develops and the community becomes larger and more diversified, individual interests come to dominate; and specialization becomes increasingly necessary with the result that there are fewer common concerns among the individuals. As these changes occur, the older bonds among people disintegrate and new groupings appear based on property – those who own on the one hand and those who don't on the other. So arises a division of classes. Governmental policies come to favor some groups against others. The protective tariff is a good example; it benefits some while others pay the cost. "The substantial interests of these classes in the common welfare is of the same kind as the interest which a parasite has in the well-being of his host."[55] The government of each nation undertakes to further the interests of its own country understood as meaning the interests of the business leaders of the country. Patriotism here serves to rally the common people to the support of business interests. The state therefore becomes the protector of the business interests of the nation, and "preparedness" is sought as a preparation for war. States try to become self-sufficient, fearing that war may cut of their access to needed resources, despite the fact that industry requires worldwide trade.

The objective of the national governments is "the Kingdom, the Power and the Glory"[56] to be achieved by peaceful means if possible, by war if necessary. Each nation promotes its own economic interests, whether by tariff or subvention or force of arms. The material gains do not accrue to the common man but to the holders of the nation's wealth. The mobilization of patriotism is sufficient to persuade the common man that by supporting such policies of business he is protecting the honor of the nation.

If there is to be peace, it must be a peace among the "powers," that is, the major nations of Europe and America: England, France, Germany, the United States, and Japan. Spain and Italy do not count as powers; Austria should be considered a part of Germany and Russia has questionable status. The patriotic spirit is strong in these nations. Given the strength of patriotism and its ubiquity, any peace will be a mere armistice – a peace until a fresh opportunity for aggression arises. Germany and Japan are dynastic powers and cannot be counted on to keep the peace. The other nations will fight if attacked but will not initiate war. Given this situation, peace can be maintained in either of two ways: submission to Germany and Japan or the elimination of Germany and Japan as dynastic powers. But there are those who believe there is a third alternative; advocates of this point of view hold that incorrigible though the rulers of Germany and Japan may be, the common people of these nations are only misinformed. If they can be re-educated to see that the dynastic ambitions of their rulers hold no promise of advantage for them, then the danger posed by these states can be put aside.

Is such a plan of reeducation possible? Veblen observes that the German people "are, notoriously, in a state of obsequious loyalty to the dynasty, single-minded devotion to the fortunes of the Fatherland, and uncompromising hatred of its enemies."[57] This "frame of mind" is not new. The early history of Germany is obscure, Veblen says, but it is clear that the country was taken over by the barbarians who, when they "moved into the territories of the Fatherland, they moved in as invaders, or rather as marauders and made themselves masters of the people already living on the land."[58] This rough society of conquerors gave way to Feudalism. For one thousand years, Veblen says, the German people have lived under autocratic rule. The difference between the Germans and the English-speaking peoples is marked. But, Veblen says, this is a differential in development.

> It is not of the nature of a divergence, but rather a differential in point of cultural maturity, due to a differential in the rate of progression through that sequence of institutional phases through which the civilized peoples of Europe, jointly and severally, have been led by force of circumstance.[59]

Veblen says that the English and French "have left behind and partly forgotten that institutional phase in which the people of Imperial Germany now live and move and have their being."[60] Note that Veblen is here assuming a linear sequence of "phases" through which the European peoples have moved to reach civilization; the problem of the Germans is that they have not come as fast as their neighbors and are still traversing phases that Britain and France have already left behind.

Veblen believes that the Germans can complete the journey, but it will take time. One thousand years of habituation cannot be overcome in a day or a year or a decade. Any hope the German people can be quickly re-educated so as to become suitable partners in the work of making and keeping the peace is just fanciful. And so Veblen returns to the other two alternatives: unconditional surrender to the imperial powers, or their elimination.

Veblen first considers the possibility of unconditional surrender to Germany. To illustrate what this would involve, Veblen discusses several comparison cases: American government of the Philippines, Japanese governance of Korea, Turkey's governance of the Armenians, Germany's treatment of the Belgians, British treatment of India, and everybody's treatment of China. None of these examples are adequate to show what life would be like under imperial rule, but they are instructive. Most Americans, Veblen says, will reject the idea of submission, but Veblen holds that this alternative needs to be considered rationally. So considered, the great difficulty is "a difficulty of the psychological order" – namely, the patriotism and allegiance that people feel toward their nation.[61] As lately noted, patriotism is ubiquitous. One is born into a nationality and accepts it as a matter of course. But legal citizenship is not always decisive; Veblen cites the hyphenated Americans who are legally citizens of the United States but whose hearts he thinks are elsewhere. Citizenship can be changed, as the massive immigration into the United States demonstrates. The people of the southern states renounced their citizenship in the United States, were conquered, and have now resumed it. Patriotism is a habit and like all habits it is subject to change. What keeps up the patriotic spirit is the threat from outside – i.e., from other nations. If this threat can be reduced, patriotism – at least of the bellicose sort – should fade and as it does so the prospects for an enduring peace should improve.

Note here Veblen's equivocation on the nature of patriotism. Earlier in the book, he said it was inheritable, which means that it must be something more than a habit. Here he says that it is a habit and therefore changeable. I think the inconsistency reflects the rapidity with which he wrote the book. So far as one can tell, *The Nature of Peace* was written between December of 1916 and February of 1917,[62] which for a volume of 367 pages means very rapid composition. Veblen had a message that he wanted people to hear; events were moving very fast; his book was published in April – the month in which the United States entered the war. He hoped to make a difference in the post-war settlement; and so he rushed composition in order to reach his audience before other plans for the peace made his contribution irrelevant.

Assuming that national pride can be set aside, the prospects under the rule of the Dynastic State are surprisingly good. Since there is no longer a threat of attack, the costs of military preparedness would be drastically reduced. There would be the cost of the imperial establishment, to which the conquered people would of course contribute, but at the same time they would be relieved from supporting their own governmental establishments, and the total cost of the former might be less than that of the latter. Pecuniary waste generated by Imperial rule will no doubt be considerable, and Veblen remarks that such costs are "infinitely extendable" and so he thinks that their amount is impossible to estimate. American society divides into two classes: those who own much and those who own little. Roughly, Veblen says, 10 percent of the population own 90 percent of the wealth. It is not clear that the common man would be worse off under imperial rule than he is under the rule of business. Veblen then describes the capitalist economics of the nations of Western Europe and America, emphasizing their exploitation of the common man. Should this political and economic system be taken over by an imperial power, he thinks the condition of the common man might be improved.

> This excessively long, and yet incomplete, review of the presumptive material advantages to accrue to the common man under a regime of peace by unconditional surrender to an alien dynasty, brings the argument apparently to the conclusion that such an eventuality might be fortunate rather than the reverse; or at least that it has its compensations, even if it is not something to be desired.[63]

But regardless of such material advantages, Veblen holds, such a surrender is impossible for the people of the West. "Man lives not by bread alone."[64] The ends for which men will die are intangible, Veblen says; certain "principles" of personal liberty and opportunity for creative self-direction and an intellectually worthy life have become part of the creed of the democratic people, and, "on these and the like intangible ends the common man is set with such inveterate predilection that he will, on provocation, stick at nothing to put the project through."[65]

For the people of the democratic commonwealths, he says, freedom means freedom from restraint by obedience to any authority not constituted by the express advice and consent of the governed.[66] This, Veblen says, is bedrock and from it civilized men will not move. Hence, peace by surrender is impossible.

Why does Veblen insist on exploring this alternative if it is simply to be rejected? He contrasts what life would be like for the common man under the rule of Imperial Germany with what life is actually like under the rule of Big Business and concludes that the common man might be better off under the former than he is under the latter. His point is that the common man is ruthlessly exploited by Big Business. Given the way Imperial Germany was portrayed in the English, French, and American press at the time and the rising anti-German feeling in the countries of the Entente, the identification of Big Business with Imperial Germany was a clever ploy.

The remaining alternative is the destruction of Imperial Germany. This will require the conquest of the Fatherland. Unconditional surrender must be obtained; no arrangement short of unconditional surrender will allow the destruction of the Dynastic State. What further should be done to Germany Veblen spells out as follows:

(1) The definitive elimination of the Imperial establishment, together with the monarchical establishments of the several states of the Empire and the privileged classes; (2) Removal or destruction of all warlike equipment, military and naval, defensive and offensive; (3) Cancelment of the public debt, of the Empire and of its members – creditors of the Empire being accounted accessory to the culpable enterprise of the Imperial government; (4) Confiscation of such industrial equipment and resources as have contributed to the carrying on of the war, as being also accessory; (5) Assumption by the league at large of all debts incurred, by the Entente belligerents or by neutrals, for the prosecution or by reason of the war, and distribution of the obligation so assumed, impartially among the members of the league, including the peoples of the defeated nations; (6) Indemnification for all injury done to civilians in the invaded territories; the means for such indemnification to be procured by confiscation of all estates in the defeated countries exceeding a certain very modest maximum, calculated on the average of property owned, say, by the poorer three-fourths of the population – the kept classes being properly accounted accessory to the Empire's culpable enterprise.[67]

One should note that the terms Veblen proposed here are more severe than those imposed by the Treaty of Versailles, terms that Keynes *fils* judged too severe.

The reference to the league here is of course to the League of Nations, proposals for which were already being discussed even as early as 1917. Veblen became a strong supporter of the idea of a league of pacific nations, for reasons that are interesting. Veblen believed that alternative efforts to keep the peace had failed.

The ideal of the nineteenth-century statesmen was to keep the peace by a balance of power; an unstable equilibrium of rivalries, in which it was recognized that eternal vigilance was the price of peace by equilibration. Since then, by force of the object-lesson of the twentieth-century wars, it has become evident that eternal vigilance will no longer keep the peace by equilibration, and the balance of power has become obsolete.[68]

Furthermore, the nature of war has changed.

Technology and industrial experience, in large volume and at a high proficiency, are indispensable to the conduct of war on the modern plan, as well as a large, efficient and up-to-date industrial community and industrial plant to supply the necessary material of this warfare.[69]

More clearly than most, Veblen saw that modern warfare depended on modern industry. It was not just the requirement of modern weaponry that required the industrial base, but the maintenance and supply of huge armies in the field was only possible if the nation at war had a fully developed industrial system. The mechanization of warfare has further consequences.

[The state of the Industrial Arts] is of such a character that a judiciously prepared offensive launched by any Power of the first rank at an opportune time can reach and lay waste any given country of the habitable globe.[70]

The United States was in January of 1917 the largest neutral and most of its citizens believed that it was safe from attack because it was protected by the two largest oceans in the world. But the American situation was actually precarious since on both the East and the West it faced Dynastic States – Germany on the East and Japan on the West. The recognition of the changing situation, Veblen says, is only slowly dawning upon the American people,[71] but the reality of the threat is becoming clearer to them. Veblen believed that the Wilson administration was now (by 1917) moving away from isolation and toward "a taking of sides,"[72] and in doing so he says, "The administration appears to be speaking for the common man rather than for the special interests or the privileged classes."[73] Veblen thought American entry into the Great War was clearly the direction in which events were moving.

Given this analysis of the overall situation, Veblen thought it obvious that no nation could guarantee peace for itself alone. He therefore concluded that the only way such a peace could be guaranteed was through a league of nations united in their determination to keep the peace. The core of such a league, he believed, must be England with all its dominions. The United States was also critical, since it would bring in Latin America. Other nations would of course join: France certainly, Belgium and probably the rest of Europe, and China should be members. The fundamental fact is the need to eliminate the threat of aggression by Imperial Germany and Imperial Japan, and the recognition by the other nations – neutrals and at war – that no nation is secure alone. Whether Russia should be included among the dynastic powers Veblen thinks it is impossible to say at that time (early 1917). It is clear, Veblen says, that Germany and Japan must be included in the league, but their inclusion with the present governments would be like admitting "a drunken savage with a machine gun."[74] The current German and Japanese monarchies and governments must be eliminated; so must the German and Japanese military and any other elements of the ruling class that are incorrigible. The strength of the imperial governments lies in the devoted loyalty of their peoples. This loyalty must be changed to permit the formation of democratic commonwealths. Clearly this will require massive intervention in the internal affairs of Germany and Japan; a massive program of reeducation will be necessary. Accordingly, Veblen says, the war must be prosecuted to a complete and final victory culminating in unconditional surrender; only so will the victors be able to establish the regime of surveillance and tutelage that will be necessary. Note that this proposal contradicts his earlier assertion that a swift reeducation of the German people to accept democracy was impossible.

Veblen proposes several steps the league could take to help remove the causes of wars. One issue that has generated conflict among nations in the past is the issue of international shipping. The solution, Veblen says, is to neutralize all international shipping. If all ships involved in such commerce are declared neutral, the disputes over whose ships carry what will be avoided. This is a small step, but it leads Veblen to propose a much larger one – the neutralization of citizenship among nations. If this were done, many issues that now become issues between nations would be transformed into issues between citizens in which nations would have no part. Such a move would undercut patriotism at least of the bellicose kind and further knit together the nations involved.

There is a further issue with which Veblen believes the league will have to deal, at least in due course. The nations of Christendom either are, or are rapidly becoming, industrialized nations. Industrial capitalism is creating a situation in which the fundamental division in society is between those who own and those who do not. Already in the more highly industrialized nations, this division is leading to strife between the two classes, much of which is being waged in terms of sabotage that disrupts the working of the machine technological system There is every reason to believe that as industrial integration increases, this situation will become more disruptive.

Given this situation, Veblen thinks the division between those who have and those who have not will become a class division, and one which will lead to unrest within the nations so constituted. Such strife may become an issue for the League of Nations. The development of the Industrial Arts has led to economic integration that transcends national borders, so the disruption of industry in any one nation will spread to others. This may become such an issue that the desire to preserve the peace will justify an intervention by the league in the internal affairs of its members. Since the governments of all the nations of Christendom are staffed by members of the owning class, equitable solutions are not in evidence.

Meanwhile, the war is having effects on the belligerents. Veblen says that the British governing class is a class of "gentlemen"; it is, he says, "a government by gentlemen, for gentlemen and of gentlemen."[75] But the war has shown that the British gentlemen are incompetent to run the war. The war is now very much an industrial affair where the industrial capacity for the production of war materials is crucial to success and gentlemen are not equipped to manage such an enterprise. Accordingly, Veblen notes, positions of power and trust are passing to the "underbred," with the result that there is a certain vulgarization of the ruling group. Veblen believes the present gentlemen will be less interested in the elimination of the German ruling class than will the underbred English.[76]

In short, there is in this progressive vulgarization of effectual use and wont and of sentiment, in the United Kingdom and elsewhere, some slight ground for the hope, or the apprehension, that no peace will be made with the dynastic Powers ... until they cease to be dynastic Powers and take on the semblance of democratic commonwealths, with dynasties, royalties and privileged classes thrown in the discard.[77]

The war was also having unexpected effects on the Central Powers. While the populations of the Imperial states are steeped in loyalty and bellicose patriotism, and a semi-feudal system of subservience, the material base on which they depend is one of science and technology. The result, Veblen holds, is a mismatch, since he believes that exposure to science and technology creates habits of thought that are not consistent with the conceptions of the feudal world view. The dynastic states therefore face a contradiction; they cannot successfully wage modern war without a fully developed industrial base to support the enterprise, yet the discipline of the industrial technology renders the conceptual foundations of the dynastic state obsolete. But, Veblen says, the erosion is slow, being a matter of habituation, and in the meantime the dynastic states are formidable.

But Veblen did not really believe his conditions would be met. Great Britain was the nation he thought most indispensable to the league, and as lately noted he believed the war had undermined the hold of the English upper class on the government. But he did not really believe that the English would disestablish their monarchy, nor did he think it likely that they would agree to neutralize international trade. How far they might go, he thought, depended on the amount of power gained by the underbred and he was not optimistic. The league would have to conform to English demands. Veblen did not think American membership in the league was as indispensible as British membership, but it was clearly very important, and he doubted whether the business government of the United States would go as far as he hoped. If America did not join, he thought the league would become little more than a defensive alliance.

So far as can be judged from present (1917) indications, the league of nations that will be formed after the war will seek as its objective the restoration of the situation that existed before the war but with the threat of Germany reduced. Suppose this plan is carried out; what will the consequences be? Since the governments of these nations are staffed by men from the owning classes, the policies that will be followed will be conservative. "This nineteenth century scheme it is proposed to carry over into the new era; and the responsible spokesmen of the projected new order appear to contemplate no provisions touching this scheme of law and order, beyond the keeping of it intact in all substantial respects."[78] The new era will bring an increase of the population of the peaceful world and further advances in the Industrial Arts. The rights of property will be strengthened, and the dominance of the price system will increase. Business consolidation may be expected to continue. In short, the new era will become very similar to the Victorian era in England. There will be a substantial middle class whose members will identify their interests with those of the upper class. The middle class man will delude himself with the belief that he has "independent means" or will aspire to that state if he has not. Veblen offers the example of the American farmer who believes himself to be an independent owner which in fact he once was, but he is now subject to the market.

In a capitalist society, stratification by wealth is inevitable and so is the emergence of the Leisure Class on the model of the English gentlemen of the Victorian era. The features of this Leisure Class Veblen has already drawn in *The Theory of the Leisure Class*. This class will establish the norms of gentility for the society, and the patterns of conspicuous waste that will absorb the money of the common people that is not required for their livelihood. These standards will become fixed upon the lower classes whose incomes barely cover subsistence; any excess beyond that will be absorbed in conspicuous consumption and conspicuous waste – the "decencies" of life. Those who pursue reform will not come from the working class, who have neither the time nor the energy nor the education required, but from those in the Leisure Class whose interests are broader than those of the usual members. Assuming that the Leisure Class contains 10 percent of the population, which Veblen thinks is an overestimate, only a small fraction of those will develop interests so at variance with the norms of the Leisure Class. The "cultural consequences to be looked for, therefore, should be quite markedly of the conservative order."[79] If this is to be the likely outcome of peaceable societies, the future is not bright.[80]

But Veblen believes the progress of the Industrial Arts will continue in spite of such cultural retardation, at least in this sense, that the scope of the mechanical industry will broaden and the discipline of the machine will become more pervasive. Since the pecuniary system of business depends on the technological system, its spread under business rule is certain and Veblen believes that the impact of the experience of working with machines will progressively call in question what he calls "superstitions." Veblen claims this is evident in the decline of religion. "The recent past offers an illustration, in the unemotional progress of decay that has overtaken religious beliefs in the more civilized countries, and more particularly among the intellectually trained workmen of the mechanical industries."[81] So too Veblen believes decay will overtake the belief in ownership.

> So soon, or rather so far, as the common man comes to realize that these rights of ownership and investment uniformly work to his material detriment, at the same time that he has lost the "will to believe" in any argument that does not run in terms of the mechanistic logic, it is reasonable to expect that he will take a stand on this matter; and it is more than likely that the stand taken will be of an uncompromising kind.[82]

This division will be "between those who own and those who do not," and Veblen warns that it will come to a trial by combat. Those who own will not relinquish what they have without defending their property "by force of arms."[83] Veblen believes that those who do not own will be no less determined.

All of this Veblen thinks is the logical outcome of the establishment of enduring peace on the model of Victorian England, which in time will permit the universal triumph of the business culture. Accordingly, he suggests that those who are seeking enduring peace through the league of peaceful nations should take steps now to forestall this march of events.

Before 1914, Veblen had carefully avoided identification with any particular reform movements. He had been solicited by socialists and liberal reformers to join their organizations or at least to allow them to use his name, but he had refused. Apparently he felt that such advocacy would betray the stance of being a disinterested and impartial observer that he maintained in his writings. But the outbreak of the Great War changed things. Veblen regarded Germany as the aggressor in the Great War; he saw the war as a contest between a totalitarian dynastic state and the democracies. He believed from the start that the United States ought to join Britain and France in the war. Unlike many liberals who opposed intervention and attacked President Wilson, Veblen supported Wilson whom he believed voiced the sentiments of the American people. And these views became increasingly clear in his writings as the War went on.

As lately noted, in 1915, Veblen published his book on *Imperial Germany*. The book was framed as a theoretical investigation of the phenomenon of borrowing which happened to be illustrated by the careers of England and Germany. At a deeper level, he posed the question as, how could two nations with the same Industrial Arts and equipment be so different in their cultures? This way of posing the issue revealed his preconception that a nation's Industrial Arts and equipment have a determining effect on its general culture. This method of approach was not a ruse behind which to launch a partisan attack; these really were important questions for Veblen and he did devote the book to answering them. But along the way, Veblen made clear his hostility toward Germany. No reader could be in any doubt about which ending of the War Veblen favored.

Working for the Government

In 1916, Davenport's position at the University of Missouri became uncomfortable and he resigned to take a position at Cornell. Without Davenport's protection, Veblen recognized that his days at Missouri were numbered. On April 2, 1917, President Wilson asked Congress for a declaration of war against Germany. That same month, Veblen's book on *The Nature of Peace* was published and his partisanship was made more explicit. As *The Nature of Peace* showed, Veblen wanted to play an active role in the war and the framing of the peace that would follow it. In late 1917, Veblen wrote two memoranda for Colonel House's committee on the peace settlement. In the first, entitled "Suggestions Touching the Working Program of an Inquiry into the Prospective Terms of Peace,"[84]

Veblen focused on four issues. First, Veblen said a decision should be made as to whether the peace was to be essentially an armistice that would produce a temporary peace while the signatories prepared for the next war, or the establishment of a "neutral League" that might create a truly lasting peace. Second, he called for open diplomacy so that the public response to the emerging agreement could be monitored and guided during the negotiating process. Third, he said a decision should be reached as to whether the treaty would favor the vested interests or require a "realignment of the county's available resources designed to keep the peace even at the cost of some appreciable derangement to these vested interest."[85] And fourth, assuming that the peace would result in the formation of a "Pacific League," Veblen held that the United States should take the lead in the establishment of the League.

The second memo was entitled "Outline of a Policy for the Control of the 'Economic Penetration' of Backward Countries and Foreign Investments."[86] Veblen begins by saying that he is taking as his major premise "the need of peace is paramount."[87] Hence, policies or projects that endanger the peace must be eliminated. He takes it as established that the peace will involve the formation of a Pacific [i.e., peaceful] League of Nations which is to serve as the chief instrument for keeping the peace.

> The abiding purpose of the projected League is to be the keeping of the peace at large; not the furtherance of commercial enterprise, nor the pursuit of national ambitions. Therefore the latter are necessarily and unreservedly to be subordinated to the former.[88]

This requires that the League must have broad powers, and so the surrender of the corresponding powers by those nations who join the League.

Wilson set the goal of the war as making the world safe for democracy. Democracy, Veblen says, "may be described as that frame of mind by virtue of which a people chooses to be collectively fortunate rather than nationally formidable."[89] It will therefore be the duty of the League to eliminate those nations who choose to be formidable. The core of the League must be France and the English-speaking nations. To these Veblen adds the Chinese whom, he believes to be irremediably peaceful, and a large part of the nations of Latin America and Western Europe. But the League must also contain "the backward peoples of what are now the colonial possessions of these belligerents and of what have been the colonial possessions of their opponents in the war; and the undemocratic peoples at present comprised in the warlike coalition of the Centrals."[90] The organization of these peoples that Veblen projected is based on that of the United States: territories becoming self-governing and territories that are wards of the Union to be "held in tutelage and administered under discretionary control."[91] For the League the corresponding groups would be the Allied belligerents and nations deemed qualified to share their status, those nationalities now held by the

Central powers and their allies, and finally "the wards of the League, would comprise those characteristically backward peoples that inhabit Colonial Possessions."[92] Veblen then proposes the abolition of frontiers with the current national units replaced by administrative districts with boundaries fixed by topography, climate, and language. If this proposal is too extreme, Veblen proposes instead a neutralization of all relations.

Veblen then takes up the issue the memo was supposed to address – the economic penetration of the "backward nations." Veblen says that the natural resources already available in the developed nations are adequate not only for the current needs of the modern nations, but for the foreseeable future as well. There are, Veblen admits, some few natural resources not so available, but these he thinks can be obtained from nations not in the League by trade. With respect to the natural resources of the "backward peoples,"

> who so come under surveillance [they] should in no case be alienated; that they should at the farthest concession be worked under lease, for a short term only, and under such control and power of revision and revocation as would lower the inducements offered to private enterprise to the practicable minimum ... and, in general terms, no encouragement should be extended to private enterprise to enter this field, no discrimination is to be countenanced, and no vested interest must be allowed to take effect in these premises.[93]

And what about international relations of trade and investment? Veblen holds that

> all extra-territorial jurisdiction and all extra-territorial enforcement of pecuniary claims, both among the several peoples of the League and as between these peoples and the outstanding nations; in short, all pecuniary claims and obligations should be neutralized, with the effect of throwing their adjudication unreservedly under the local jurisdiction in whose territory they come up.[94]

The objective here, Veblen holds, is that no community should promote or safeguard any private enterprise seeking private gain beyond its own borders. Should members of the League violate its rules, Veblen proposed to punish the offender by interfering with its trade, either by embargo or by a tariff on all goods bound for the naughty member.

On April 25, 1918, Veblen published an article in *The Dial* with the title "The Passing of National Frontiers."[95] Veblen holds that the people of Christendom now face a revolutionary situation. The basis upon which the traditional system of law and order rested has shifted in a way that has made the received cultural system obsolete. The question is not whether there will be a significant change in the culture but what direction the change will take.

What has produced this critical situation are changes that are basically techno-logical. Modern industry has become increasingly a mechanical system. Not only is the production of goods now done by machines, but the interlocking of dif-ferent industries has taken on the character of a single mechanical process. Industry today (1918) is so constructed that the output of one machine is the material upon which the next machine operates in so complex and inter-connected a system that the whole system resembles a single machine that oper-ates from raw material to finished goods. "The modern industrial system is worldwide, and the modern technological knowledge is no respecter of national frontiers,"[96] and "as an industrial unit," Veblen says, "the nation is out of date."[97] National frontiers serve chiefly to obstruct the flow of materials and goods from one stage of the industrial process to another. Frontier duties make as little sense as imposing a tax on the fitting of the propeller to the plane in the manufacture of an aircraft or the joining of the wheels to a cart. So far as industry is concerned, the nation is an obstruction.

But, Veblen says, it is otherwise with the businessmen and their vested inter-ests. As Veblen has argued in great detail in his previous writings, the objective of businessmen is private gain, and this objective is pursued through competition in which each seeks advantage against the others. For businessmen, the integration of the industrial system provides an opportunity to make money by obstructing the activities of their competitors. And for this purpose, national frontiers are splendidly effective. Tariffs, duties, quotas, informal agreements among nations – these are all ways in which the vested interests can extort money from the industrial process, ultimately from the common people. The more integrated the system, the more effective industrial sabotage becomes, and the more profitable its disruption becomes for the vested interests.

On April 13, 1918, Veblen gave a speech before the Institute of Social Sciences in New York which he entitled "A Policy of Reconstruction."[98] Veblen claimed that the country is now (1918) caught between the vested interests of business and those of labor. Businessmen claim the right to hire and fire workers as they please, to set wages as they choose, to hire as many or as few men as they wish, and to limit output as they find most profitable. The workers, Veblen says, claim a right to a job, a right to strike or quit their jobs, and to choose who shall be their workmates. Each side seeks to promote its position by carefully directed sabotage. It is obvious, Veblen holds, that the interests of the community are adversely affected by this sort of industrial sabo-tage, regardless of which group carries it out. The war, he holds, has revealed how inefficient our present system is. Veblen points to the fact that the gov-ernment has had to take over the railroads because their private owners could not run them well enough to meet the needs of the country at war. Similar problems, he says, have arisen with oil, steel, copper, and other industries where businesses working at cross purposes to further private gains have failed to produce what is required.

The mischief appears to arise out of, or in concurrence with, the disjunction of ownership and discretion from the personal direction of the work; and it appears to take on an added degree of mischance so soon as the discretionary control vested in ownership comes to be exercised by an employer who has no personal contact with the employees, processes employed, or with the persons whose needs these processes are presumed to serve – that is to say, so soon as the man or staff in control passes into the class of supernumeraries in respect of the mechanical work to be done, and retains only a pecuniary interest, and exercises only a pecuniary control.[99]

Veblen holds that when such a business has reached the point where the distance of ownership from control allows the business to be managed by accountants far removed from the scene of the work, it should be taken over and run as a public utility by administrators with no pecuniary relation to the business. If the operation of the business has become routine, there is no reason why a public administrator cannot run it.

Veblen believes that the disruption of the system by sabotage – regardless of who carries out the sabotage – has put the public interest at risk. And he closes with a warning. "Current events in Russia, for instance, attest that it is a grave mistake to let a growing disparity between the vested rights and the current conditions of life over-pass the limit of tolerance."[100]

In 1917 and 1918, the government faced a danger of a shortage of food. Not only was the country faced with its usual needs, but European agriculture, particularly that of France, had been disrupted by the war and American imports were desperately needed. To make matters worse, the Selective Service had issued its first draft call for young men to serve in the army. Protests from Midwestern farmers were immediate, claiming that the drafting of young men would leave farmers with insufficient workers to harvest their crops. Furthermore, the rapidly expanding war industries needed workers who found urban living more attractive than farm labor. In February of 1918, the Food Administration employed Veblen as a special investigator to find out what was needed in the north Midwest.[101] What Veblen found was a complicated tangle of problems. The labor shortage was real, but it was not the only issue. In 1915, the Non-Partisan League had been founded – an organization that brought together reformers and radicals behind a program of progressive reform. The League captured the North Dakota Republican Party in 1916, and in 1918 captured control of the state government. The following year, the League was able to enact its program. This was the most important insurgency in the history of North Dakota. It is not a surprise that it met with bitter opposition, not only from private organizations but also from the federal government.

Veblen reported that the Treasury Department was refusing loans to farmers that were needed for the purchase of seed. The Department of Agriculture and the Department of Labor were actively trying to undercut the League. Veblen wrote,

To get the seed into the farmers' hands the Food Administration will have to disregard formalities and go over the heads of the Farm Loan people as well as of the representatives of the Agricultural Department. It appears to be not a question of placing Farm Loans and of the purchase of the seed by the farmers, so much as it is a question of distributing the seed and getting it planted, and then patching up the monetary questions involved afterward.[102]

Veblen recommended that the Food Administration should go over the heads of the Department of Agriculture and the Treasury and advance the needed funds. But that left the problem of the labor shortage. Veblen recommended that the federal government should immediately cease its prosecution of the IWW [Industrial Workers of the World] and recruit the IWW members for the needed farm labor. The IWW membership was largely composed of migratory farm workers who could fill the need for hands at once. Veblen also pointed out that the legal charges that were pending against the leaders of the IWW were in most cases without merit and should be dropped in any case. It was, Veblen believed, stupid to ignore a large group of men ready and able to solve the crucial problem of the labor shortage because of hysterical and baseless fears of radicalism. Veblen even intervened with the Department of Justice in his efforts to get the charges against the IWW men dismissed. His appeals had no effect. One hundred and one IWW leaders were brought to trial in Chicago on the charge of obstructing the draft. Veblen joined John Dewey, Carleton Hayes, James Harvey Robinson, and others in trying to raise money for their legal defense. The men were convicted and given severe sentences by Judge Kenesaw Mountain Landis.[103]

The problem of labor shortages was an important concern of the government. The calls for more men coming from the military led to real shortages of workers. Veblen addressed the issue in several reports. In May of 1918 he published an article in *The Pulse* entitled "Menial Servants During the Period of the War."[104] Veblen held that "the chief use of menial servants is to put in evidence their employer's ability to pay."[105] For anyone familiar with *The Theory of the Leisure Class* this claim was immediately recognizable. Such invidious employments Veblen believed should yield to the needs of the war economy. He therefore proposed that those employed as such servants should be "freed" to meet the economy's need for workers. Rather than drafting them, Veblen proposed to accomplish this objective as follows.

Beginning with the lowest-paid servants in households not exempt … it is proposed to impose a tax equal to 100 percent of the wages paid such servants, or their wages and keep in case the servant's keep is included in the terms of employment. Beyond this, the second taxable domestic would be taxed at the rate of 200 percent on his cost, the third at 300 percent, etc., each successive step in the series going to the next higher-paid employee, and the rate increasing by 100 percent of the employee's wages at each successive step.[106]

Such taxes Veblen believed would result in the freeing of a large number of able-bodied men for other work. There would of course have to be exemptions – e.g., a servant caring for a disabled person. But Veblen believed the exceptions could be managed, and offered suggestions as to how that might be done.

In a further memo, lately noted, "Farm Labor in the Period of the War," he proposed using the country town as a source for farm workers.[107] Veblen noted that a large percentage of the population of the country town consisted of men who had been raised on farms; hence they would not have to be retrained for farm work, which for the duration of the War was the important consideration. Veblen noted that such reforms as those he was proposing had been strongly opposed by the vested interests, but he held that winning the war was the primary problem facing the country, and that the needs of the war must prevail over all other considerations.

The country town, Veblen says, is "an organization of 'middlemen'"[108] who buy farm produce from the farmers and sell commodities to the farmers. He lists thirty-four types of retail businesses that are to be found in such towns. The number of establishments to be found in the towns is far greater than is necessary to meet the needs of the surrounding farm population. "This class of wasteful duplication will foot up to about three-fourths of all the equipment and workmen employed."[109]

> Taking one retail concern with another, one third of this retail trade is to be written off as being productive of nothing but waste; which leaves two thirds of the whole to be counted in as being of some use; and of this remaining two thirds, again, an amount running between one half and three fourths – say two thirds – is further to be written off as being mere wasteful duplication of equipment and work among the concerns that are doing partly useful work.[110]

Veblen concludes that seven-ninths of the town's population could be removed without impairing the town's function in shipping farm produce and supplying consumer goods to the farm families. These people could profitably be put to farm labor to ease the present shortage. But just how are these people to be convinced to change? Veblen has an answer. "The obvious line to take is to reduce the margin of profits in this retail trade to such a figure as to make it unprofitable for the full number of establishments to continue in business."[111] Hitherto, Veblen says, the regulation of local markets has been entrusted to the state authorities. But it is widely believed by the farmers that these authorities are too intimately related to the Commercial Clubs of the towns.

Veblen holds that to avoid this sort of political influence, the regulation must be taken over by the federal government. The greater the number of times that the goods are bought and sold between the farm and the mill or the packing house, or between the mill or factory and the farm, the greater the number of business profits to be deducted from the price which the famer gets for his produce, or to be added to the price which he has to pay for his necessary supplies, and the greater the uncertainty, miscalculation, and retardation to which the whole traffic is liable.[112] To remedy this situation, Veblen proposes that, for the period of the War, the whole traffic should be conducted on a non-profit basis, with goods priced at cost. The whole trade to and from the farm could then be handled by the methods developed by the Parcel Post, chain stores, and mail order houses. These are well-established instruments for collecting and distributing goods whose efficiency has been demonstrated. The Post Office's Parcel Post division should take over the mail order houses "with so much of the equipment, stocks, and personnel as may be useful for the purpose."[113]

> It is here proposed that the local post office act as agent of the central bureau of distribution, through its office employees and its carriers; to take orders and transmit them with the least possible annoyance or delay; to accept payment, and to make any necessary refunds or adjustments; with no unnecessary writing of instruments or transmission of funds, beyond what is comprised in the ordinary routine of accounting between the local office and the Federal Headquarters.[114]

Since the post office will handle both the purchase of farm goods and the sale of commodities to the famers, "the local office will carry a two-sided account with the central office, running roughly even in the long run, as between receipts and disbursements, but with a variable balance to be adjusted from time to time."[115] And this arrangement, Veblen believes, will pretty well eliminate the need for local banks. Of course various officers will be required to monitor the functioning of the system to ensure that standards of quality are met and prevent theft and delays, but Veblen believes the post office personnel can perform these duties.

But there is another step necessary if this system is to work. The great business concerns that supply the consumer goods the farmers need must be held to the standards of "quality, purity, cost and the like,"[116] and the goods they produce must conform to the requirements of the postal distribution system. Moreover, Veblen holds, "It is now becoming plain beyond debate that it will not do to allow these great industrial enterprises to be managed by their owners for profit, even under the most stringent standardization and inspection."[117] There are more ways to cheat than any set of mere rules can deal with. So, Veblen says, "The great industries which turn out staple goods for the market will on this plan, and for the period of the war, have to be taken under administrative control."[118] In other words, Veblen wants the entire system from the factory to the farm to the consumer goods the farmer buys to be brought under government control. The resulting efficiency, Veblen holds, would release most of the population of the present country towns and make it available for farm work or other work necessary for the winning of the war.

Veblen presents this proposal as a temporary measure required by the exigencies of the war. But it is fairly obvious that the plan he has laid out could be extended far beyond the war. Veblen has not previously dealt in any detail with issues of distribution. In doing so here under cover of a war-time plan, he is describing how he thought the problems of distribution could be dealt with if only business considerations could be set aside. The proposal fills a gap in Veblen's theory of business enterprise.

Veblen submitted a further report to the Food Administration dealing with the problem of farm labor.[119] Based on his travels in the north Midwest, he estimated that the labor shortage would amount to 15 to 18 percent for the prairie states west of the Mississippi, and varying from near zero percent in the South to 20 to 25 percent in the North. The problem was being aggravated, he said, by the draft calls for able young men and the calls for workers in the other defense industries. The farm labor available consisted of settled farm hands who are permanent residents of their states and a large number of migratory workers who did farm labor during the summer until the harvest was over and spent the winter working in the timber industry. Veblen believed that "a large majority" of these migrant workers were members of the Agricultural Workers Industrial Union of the IWW. Most of the farmers of the area, Veblen said, were supporters of the Non-Partisan League, and although there was no formal relation between the IWW and the Non-Partisan League, the former was generally sympathetic with the latter.

> The IWW men had agreed on the terms under which they would work. These were (a) freedom from illegal restraint; (b) proper board and lodging; (c) a 10 hour day; (d) a standard wage of $4.00 for the harvest season; and (e) tentatively, free transportation in answering any call from a considerable distance.[120]

If these terms were not met, the men would not refuse to work, "but, quite unmistakably, they are resolved in that case to fall short of full and efficient work."[121]

The opposition to the IWW comes, Veblen says, from the "vested interests," meaning in particular the Commercial Clubs of the towns which represent the local business interests, and a variety of organizations such as Councils of Defense, Security Leagues, Committees of Public Safety, etc. These, Veblen says, are generally regarded as business organizations determined to use the war to advance business interests. These business interests control the police, the courts, and the local and state governments. This has given them the ability to appeal to the federal government, which has generally taken their side. As a result, one

hundred and fifty members of the IWW have been arrested on charges of dis-
loyalty, with bail set at figures they cannot reach.

Veblen argues that the IWW men provide the solution to the problem of the
farm labor shortage. These men are experienced farm workers, and they are
ready and willing to work if their terms are met. Veblen claims that the legal
charges against them are largely bogus and should be quashed. These are not
foreign agents; 80 percent of them are native born. Veblen proposed that the
Administration enter into direct and official relations with the workmen through
their organizations:

> That a scheme of regimentation be put into effect by which the workmen
> will be enrolled, under officers of their own choice, as members of a col-
> lective labor force to be distributed and employed at the discretion of agents
> of the Administration with suitable powers – always with the proviso that
> these agents be vested with advisory rather than coercive powers and be
> enabled to offer inducements sufficient to give effect to such advice as they
> may offer; that facilities be constantly afforded for men to enroll in these
> regiments of workmen, without other necessary qualifications than a will-
> ingness to work and to submit to majority rule within their own regiment;
> and that board, lodging, and needed transportation be provided for the men
> so enrolled, on the sole condition that they do the work in hand and submit
> to majority rule.[122]

Veblen further proposed that the government agencies involved be the War
Department and the Food Administration. The Labor Department, Veblen said,
was too involved with the AFL that was hostile to the IWW, and the Department of Agriculture was too close to the local business interests. It hardly needs to
be noted that Veblen's proposal was not followed.

Veblen left the Food Administration, and government service, by the early
summer. As he had suspected would be the case, his recommendations were largely
ignored. But the fact that he undertook this work is an indication of his desire to
support the war effort, and of his general support of the Wilson Administration.
This is the only period of his life in which he was willing to become involved in
what he considered to be political action. But he had hopes – hopes of what might
come out of the Great War if the Allies won. Veblen regarded the Great War as a
cataclysmic event that he thought would bring about a real period of fundamental
reform, and he wanted to contribute to that outcome.

Notes

1 Joseph Dorfman, *Thorstein Veblen and His America* (Clifton, New Jersey: Augustus M.
   Kelley, 1972), 295.
2 Dorfman, *Veblen and His America*, 272.

3   Dorfman, *Veblen and His America*, 295.
4   Dorfman, *Veblen and His America*, 304.
5   Dorfman, *Veblen and His America*, 306–307.
6   Dorfman, *Veblen and His America*, 324.
7   Thorstein Veblen, *The Instinct of Workmanship And the State of the Industrial Arts* (New York: The Viking Press, 1946), 1–8.
8   Thorstein Veblen, *Imperial Germany and the Industrial Revolution*, intro. Joseph Dorfman (New York: The Viking Press, 1946), 8.
9   Veblen, *Imperial Germany*, 24ff.
10   Veblen, *Imperial Germany*, 25–30.
11   Veblen, *Imperial Germany*, 24.
12   Veblen, *Imperial Germany*, 38–39.
13   Veblen, *Imperial Germany*, 39, 101.
14   Veblen, *Imperial Germany*, 96.
15   Veblen, *Imperial Germany*, 96–97.
16   Veblen, *Imperial Germany*, 25.
17   Veblen, *Imperial Germany*, 140–146.
18   Veblen, *Imperial Germany*, 150–151.
19   Veblen, *Imperial Germany*, 161.
20   Veblen, *Imperial Germany*, 156.
21   Veblen, *Imperial Germany*, 164.
22   Veblen, *Imperial Germany*, 60–63.
23   Veblen, *Imperial Germany*, 64.
24   Veblen, *Imperial Germany*, 85.
25   Veblen, *Imperial Germany*, 184.
26   Veblen, *Imperial Germany*, 191.
27   Veblen, *Imperial Germany*, 194.
28   Veblen, *Imperial Germany*, 192–197.
29   Veblen, *Imperial Germany*, 194–210.
30   Veblen, *Imperial Germany*, 130.
31   Veblen, *Imperial Germany*, 128–130.
32   Veblen, *Imperial Germany*, 216.
33   Veblen, *Imperial Germany*, 227.
34   Veblen, *Imperial Germany*, 224.
35   Veblen, *Imperial Germany*, 240–248.
36   Veblen, *Imperial Germany*, 268.
37   Veblen, *Imperial Germany*, 269.
38   Veblen, *Imperial Germany*, 271–272.
39   Veblen, *Imperial Germany*, 276–278.
40   Veblen, *Imperial Germany*, 273–275.
41   Veblen, *Imperial Germany*, v.
42   Thorstein Veblen, "The Opportunity of Japan," *Essays in Our Changing Order*, ed. Leon Ardzrooni (New York: The Viking Press, 1945), 248–266.
43   Veblen, "Japan," in *Changing Order*, 251.
44   Veblen, "Japan," in *Changing Order*, 266.
45   Thorstein Veblen, *An Inquiry into the Nature of Peace and the Terms of its Perpetuation* (New York: Viking, 1945).
46   Veblen, *Nature of Peace*, vii.
47   Veblen, *Nature of Peace*, 3.
48   Veblen, *Nature of Peace*, 9–10.
49   Veblen, *Nature of Peace*, 18.
50   Veblen, *Nature of Peace*, 31.
51   Veblen, *Nature of Peace*, 33.

52 Veblen, *Nature of Peace*, 40.
53 Veblen, *Nature of Peace*, 45–46.
54 Veblen, *Nature of Peace*, 46.
55 Veblen, *Nature of Peace*, 57.
56 Veblen, *Nature of Peace*, 64.
57 Veblen, *Nature of Peace*, 89.
58 Veblen, *Nature of Peace*, 95.
59 Veblen, *Nature of Peace*, 100.
60 Veblen, *Nature of Peace*, 100–101.
61 Veblen, *Nature of Peace*, 133.
62 Dorfman, *Veblen and His America*, 356.
63 Veblen, *Nature of Peace*, 177.
64 Veblen, *Nature of Peace*, 178.
65 Veblen, *Nature of Peace*, 181.
66 Veblen, *Nature of Peace*, 183.
67 Veblen, *Nature of Peace*, 271–272.
68 Veblen, *Nature of Peace*, 301.
69 Veblen, *Nature of Peace*, 304.
70 Veblen, *Nature of Peace*, 220.
71 Veblen, *Nature of Peace*, 221.
72 Veblen, *Nature of Peace*, 224.
73 Veblen, *Nature of Peace*, 224.
74 Veblen, *Nature of Peace*, 238.
75 Veblen, *Nature of Peace*, 248.
76 Veblen, *Nature of Peace*, 238–241.
77 Veblen, *Nature of Peace*, 257.
78 Veblen, *Nature of Peace*, 334.
79 Veblen, *Nature of Peace*, 358.
80 Veblen, *Nature of Peace*, 344–346.
81 Veblen, *Nature of Peace*, 362.
82 Veblen, *Nature of Peace*, 364.
83 Veblen, *Nature of Peace*, 365–366.
84 Thorstein Veblen, "Suggestions Touching the Working Program of an Inquiry into the Prospective Terms of Peace," in *Essays in our Changing Order*, ed. Leon Ardzrooni (New York: The Viking Press, 1945), 355–360.
85 Veblen, "Suggestions," in *Changing Order*, 358.
86 Thorstein Veblen, "Outline of a Policy for the Control of 'Economic Penetration' of Backward Countries and of Foreign Investments," in *Essays in our Changing Order*, ed. Leon Ardzrooni (New York: The Viking Press, 1945), 361–382.
87 Veblen, "Economic Penetration," in *Changing Order*, 361.
88 Veblen, "Economic Penetration," in *Changing Order*, 363.
89 Veblen, "Economic Penetration," in *Changing Order*, 364.
90 Veblen, "Economic Penetration," in *Changing Order*, 365–366.
91 Veblen, "Economic Penetration," in *Changing Order*, 367.
92 Veblen, "Economic Penetration," in *Changing Order*, 367–368.
93 Veblen, "Economic Penetration," in *Changing Order*, 374.
94 Veblen, "Economic Penetration," in *Changing Order*, 376.
95 Thorstein Veblen, "The Passing of National Frontiers," in *Essays in our Changing Order*, ed. Leon Ardzrooni (New York: The Viking Press, 1945), 383–390.
96 Veblen, "National Frontiers," in *Changing Order*, 385.
97 Veblen, "National Frontiers," in *Changing Order*, 388.
98 Thorstein Veblen, "A Policy of Reconstruction," in *Essays in our Changing Order*, ed. Leon Ardzrooni (New York: The Viking Press, 1945), 391–398.

99   Veblen, "Reconstruction," in *Changing Order*, 395.
100   Veblen, "Reconstruction," in *Changing Order*, 398.
101   Dorfman, *Veblen and His America*, 383–384.
102   Dorfman, *Veblen and His America*, 384.
103   Dorfman, *Veblen and His America*, 386.
104   Thorstein Veblen, "Menial Servants During the Period of War," in *Essays in our Changing Order*, ed. Leon Ardzrooni (New York: The Viking Press, 1945), 267–278.
105   Veblen, "Menial Servants," in *Changing Order*, 270.
106   Veblen, "Menial Servants," in *Changing Order*, 274.
107   Thorstein Veblen, "Farm Labor for the Period of the War," in *Essays in our Changing Order*, ed. Leon Ardzrooni (New York: The Viking Press, 1945), 279–318.
108   Veblen, "Farm Labor, War," in *Changing Order*, 286.
109   Veblen, "Farm Labor, War," in *Changing Order*, 287.
110   Veblen, "Farm Labor, War," in *Changing Order*, 289–290.
111   Veblen, "Farm Labor, War," in *Changing Order*, 295.
112   Veblen, "Farm Labor, War," in *Changing Order*, 300.
113   Veblen, "Farm Labor, War," in *Changing Order*, 302.
114   Veblen, "Farm Labor, War," in *Changing Order*, 305.
115   Veblen, "Farm Labor, War," in *Changing Order*, 306.
116   Veblen, "Farm Labor, War," in *Changing Order*, 308.
117   Veblen, "Farm Labor, War," in *Changing Order*, 309.
118   Veblen, "Farm Labor, War," in *Changing Order*, 310.
119   Thorstein Veblen, "Farm Labor and the IWW," in *Essays in our Changing Order*, ed. Leon Ardzrooni (New York: The Viking Press, 1945), 319–336.
120   Veblen, "Farm Labor, IWW," in *Changing Order*, 321.
121   Veblen, "Farm Labor, IWW," in *Changing Order*, 321–322.
122   Veblen, "Farm Labor, IWW," in *Changing Order*, 331.

8

REVOLUTION

The October Revolution

Like many others, Veblen saw the Great War coming. His attitude toward Germany was made quite clear in his book *Imperial Germany*; he saw Germany as a dynastic state for which war was normal and he held Germany responsible for starting the Great War. From the beginning, he saw the war as a conflict between democracy – England, France, and the United States – and autocracy – Germany and Austria.

The view of the Entente as an alliance of democratic nations faced a problem in that Russia was a member of the Entente. Europe could boast no more autocratic monarchy than that of the Romanovs; there was nothing democratic about the rule of the Czar. Had the war really been a conflict between democracy and autocracy, Russia should have been allied with Germany rather than France. Accordingly, the first Russian Revolution of February 1917 was welcomed in the West. The Kerensky government claimed that it was establishing a democracy in Russia, and promised to continue as a combatant in the war. The American press applauded the revolution and the new government, as did those of England and France. The democracies were caught by surprise in October of 1917 when the second Russian Revolution overthrew the Kerensky government and the Bolsheviks took power. The Bolsheviks were something new; there had never been a communist state before. Bolshevik doctrine was anathema to America's business leaders, as it was to those of England and France. The situation was made worse by the Russian decision to abandon the war. The Brest-Litovsk treaty cost Russia dearly but the Bolshevik leaders signed it; for Germany, it was not just a victory over Russia – it meant that Germany no longer had to fight a war on two fronts.

Germany was now able to concentrate its military power on the Western front, which did not bode well for the Entente.

Veblen was at first distressed by the October Revolution. As Dorfman describes his response,

> Veblen welcomed the [first] Russian Revolution, which he had predicted not only before the war but again in *The Nature of Peace*. But when the Kerensky regime was overthrown by the Bolsheviks, he was disheartened, particularly after the signing of the treaty of Brest-Litovsk, for he feared that as a consequence Germany might win the war.[1]

The October Revolution surprised Veblen. It created an entirely new situation. Veblen was not a Marxist. He had given his opinion of Marx in his Harvard lectures; while he praised Marx's originality, he did not subscribe to his theories. But Veblen was in some sense a socialist – certainly not an orthodox socialist, but a socialist nonetheless. Throughout his career, he had made private ownership in severalty his *bête noire*; now he was confronted by a government that proclaimed its intention to abolish private ownership. If at first he was not supportive of the new Russian government, he was certainly not opposed to it.

On November 15, 1919, Veblen published an editorial in *The Dial* that marked a change in his views. Veblen condemned the Armistice as premature.

> A prostrate and completely discredited German military establishment, such as another three months would have left, and a broken and emptied imperial organization, such as the same three months would have left – with such an outcome of the war the German states would have gone Red and would have been fit to make trouble for none but themselves. Germany in that case would have been of no use for stabilizing things on the basis of the *status quo ante*. ... The elder statesmen sorely needed the bulwark of a practicable German Empire to serve as a bar against the spread of Bolshevism out of Soviet Russia, and they likewise needed the active use of a practicable German military establishment to defeat Bolshevism by fire, sword, and famine, in and out of Soviet Russia.[2]

Veblen's final view of the Treaty of Versailles is spelled out most clearly in his review of John Maynard Keynes's *The Economic Consequences of the Peace* in 1920.[3] Earlier, he had castigated the leaders who wrote the Treaty for their efforts to re-create the *status quo ante* but by 1920 he had changed his mind. He now took the Treaty to be an agreement to destroy Soviet Russia.

> The events of the past months go to show that the central and most binding provision of the Treaty [and of the League of Nations] is an unrecorded

clause by which the governments of the Great Powers are banded together for the suppression of Soviet Russia – unrecorded unless record of it is to be found somewhere among the secret archives of the League or the Great Powers. Apart from this unacknowledged compact there appears to be nothing in the Treaty that has any character of stability or binding force. Of course, the compact for the reduction of Soviet Russia was not written into the text of the Treaty; it may rather be said to have been the parchment upon which the text was written.[4]

This interpretation of the Treaty offered Veblen answers to a number of problems. First, like many others, Veblen thought the armistice had come too soon; he had wanted Germany to be forced to agree to an unconditional surrender that would allow a radical reconstruction of the German government and society. But now he concluded that the armistice had been made so early just to make sure that no such reconstruction could take place. Second, Veblen interpreted what he viewed as the leniency of the Treaty as due to the fact that the Great Powers wanted to prevent any Bolshevik party from developing in Germany and further wanted the German government, and particularly the German military, as allies in their efforts to destroy the Soviet Russian government. The fear that Germany might go Communist was not an illusion. Following the revolt of the sailors at Kiel, the revolution spread to Hamburg and Lübeck, and then to other cities. The German Communist Party was founded on December 31, 1918, and for a time there was a chance that the Communists might win. The reaction against them was swift in coming, but they had made a sufficient show to frighten many people.[5]

Third, Veblen's new view of the Treaty explained Wilson's behavior at the peace conference. In January 1918, Wilson had presented a fourteen-point program for what the final peace settlement ending the war should be. That program had led to high expectations that the peace treaty would establish a new world order based on justice and freedom. That was not what the Treaty of Versailles offered and Wilson was roundly criticized – by Keynes *fils* among others – for having failed to stand by his principles at Versailles. But, Veblen argued, once it was recognized that the Treaty was designed to bring about suppression of the Soviet government, Wilson's performance made sense.

The President was committed to the preservation of the existing order of commercial imperialism, by conviction and by his high office. His apparent defeat in the face of this unforeseen situation, therefore, was not so much a defeat, but rather a strategic realignment designed to compass what was indispensable, even at some cost to his own prestige – the main consideration being the defeat of Bolshevism at any cost – so that a well-considered view of the President's share in the deliberations of the Conclave will credit him with insight, courage, facility, and tenacity of purpose rather than with that

pusillanimity, vacillation, and ineptitude which is ascribed to him in
Mr. Keynes's too superficial review of the case.[6]

Veblen had thought Wilson a leader who accurately reflected the views of the
American people; unlike many liberals, he would not criticize Wilson's
performance; he believed that Wilson had acted courageously, sacrificing his own
prestige to defend his country against the threat of Bolshevism.

Veblen had little to say about the Bolshevik regime in Russia. He said
repeatedly that the strict censorship made it extremely difficult to get an accurate
picture of what was going on in Russia, and the situation in Russia was
sufficiently chaotic that accurate knowledge of it was not easily obtained.

> He became particularly interested in Bolshevism, anxiously read the news-
> papers as to its successes, and began learning Russian. During the summer of
> 1919 he followed with interest the military movements against [Lieutenant
> General Anton Ivanovich] Denikin and [Commander Alexander Vasilyevich]
> Kolchak.[7]

He pointed out that the fact that the Bolshevik government was able to stay in
power despite the efforts to overthrow it indicated that it must have considerable
popular support. So did the success of the Red Army which to the surprise of
many succeeded in holding its own against a variety of White Russian attacks
seeking to overthrow the Bolshevik government. Military efforts by the allies
fared no better. It did appear that the Bolshevik government was there to stay.
Veblen also expressed an interest in the Soviets, which he saw as a possible
alternative to representative democracy, in which he had now lost faith.

> In its elements, the Soviet appears to be very closely analogous to the town-
> meeting as known in New England history. The dictionary meaning of the
> word is "counsel" and "council." But to let a self-justified town-meeting
> take over all items of absentee ownership within its jurisdiction would plainly
> be revolutionary innovation, a subversion of law and order.[8]

What seems to have interested Veblen was the possibilities of the Soviets as a
form of direct democracy.

The American Response

What particularly engaged Veblen's attention was the American reaction to the
second Russian Revolution. That Bolshevism created a "nerve-shattering fear" in
this country, particularly among the better off, struck him as amusing. As he
remarked, "Bolshevism is a menace." But Veblen asks to whom is it a menace?
His answer of course was that it was a menace to the absentee owners and the

vested interests. But what sort of menace? No one seriously believed that Russia posed a military threat to the United States. Given the performance of the czar's army against the Germans, and its subsequent collapse, there was nothing to fear there. As Veblen pointed out, Russia was not an industrialized country; its structure of self-supporting agricultural villages made it very difficult to conquer, but it also made aggressive action impossible. The threat, Veblen said, is of infection. "There prevails among the astute keepers of law and order in other lands an uneasy statesmanlike dread of 'Bolshevik infection,' which it is considered will surely follow on any contact or communication across the Russian frontiers."[9]

The infection feared was that the working class of America might come to believe the Bolshevik propaganda, and follow the example of the Russian workers. Veblen regarded such fears as lunacy, but they were widespread and led to action by the local, state, and federal authorities against so-called "radicals." These developments led Veblen to write a book in which, while pretending to be demonstrating that Bolshevism posed no threat to the United States, he was also able to indulge in the fantasy of how revolution might come to America. This work first appeared as a series of essays in *The Dial* in 1919. They were then published as a book entitled *The Engineers and the Price System*.

In the early chapters of the book, Veblen describes the current state of the economy. He then describes the response to Bolshevism:

> Bolshevism is a menace to the vested rights of property and privilege. Therefore the Guardians of the Vested Interests have been thrown into a state of Red trepidation by the continued functioning of Soviet Russia and the continued outbreaks of the same Red distemper elsewhere on the continent of Europe. It is feared, with a nerve-shattering fear, that the same Red distemper of Bolshevism must presently infect the underlying population in America and bring on an overturn of the established order.[10]

Veblen says that the most effective way to counter the threat is by adopting the British method of "gentlemanly compromise, collusion, conciliation, and popular defeat" and avoid overreacting.[11] No revolutionary plan can succeed in America unless there is an organized group who can take over the running of the industrial system immediately upon the removal of the present absentee owners. But there is no such organized group in America. The nearest approach to such an organization is the AFL, but that is clearly incapable of any such action.

There are several factors, Veblen says, that make the Vested Interests vulnerable. One is the ever-increasing integration and articulation of the industrial system. At present the system is so productive that it is capable of providing sufficient quantities of goods to meet the needs of the general population; indeed, the problem of business is to restrain production sufficiently to avoid swamping the market. And the system is able to do this despite the extensive use of sabotage. But as the integration and articulation of the system increase, sabotage becomes more effective, and one can foresee a time when sabotage could bring about the collapse of the entire industrial system. A second factor is the amount of waste that the system involves. Not only are goods provided that have no function beyond satisfying conspicuous consumption, but business practices such as salesmanship, in all its forms, contribute nothing to the well-being of the community. One half or more of the prices paid by consumers go to fund the various practices of salesmanship. If and when the general public becomes aware of the degree to which they are being bilked by business, they should be receptive to the Red distemper. Third, the current system of business is competitive; it sets one business against another, constantly disorganizes the industrial system, and produces unemployment of men, resources, and equipment in efforts to get an advantage for each business over its rivals. This "goes to persuade apprehensive persons that the regime of business enterprise is fast approaching the limit of tolerance."[12]

The competitive order of business creates a duplication of firms competing in the same market, and disruption of the industrial system as firms seek advantages over each other. One route to industrial peace has been consolidation that brings many businesses into a single holding company, thereby eliminating competition among the component corporations but even this has not eliminated competition between businesses and consumers, nor has it eliminated "the competition between captains of industry and the absentee owners in whose name and with whose funds the captains do business."[13]

Nor does Veblen believe competition can be eliminated from business. "The incentive to all business is after all private gain at the cost of any whom it may concern."[14] This sort of strife will go on within holding companies and between holding companies as long as business lasts.

The owners of current businesses – at least of large businesses such as those in the key industries – are absentee owners. Their expertise, if any, lies in pecuniary matters – they neither know nor understand the technology that runs their businesses and for the most part, they have but a limited understanding of the businesses they own. They own, but they do not manage these business; the management of the businesses is entrusted to hired managers who are experts in the pecuniary affairs of the business, but these hired managers have little understanding of the science and technology that actually runs the industrial plant. Those who do understand the science and technology are the highly skilled technicians – those Veblen calls the "engineers"; these are the men who actually operate the industrial plant.

> They now constitute the General Staff of the industrial system, in fact; whatever law and custom may formally say in protest. …The chances of anything like a Soviet in America, therefore, are the chances of a Soviet of technicians. And, to the due comfort of the Guardians of the Vested Interests and the good citizens who make up their background, it can be shown that

anything like a Soviet of Technicians is at the most a remote contingency in America.[15]

What would be required to bring about a revolution? As Veblen has insisted, there would have to be an organization ready and able to take over the operation of industry immediately upon the launching of the revolution. Clearly, what Veblen believes could do this is a Soviet of Engineers. These men actually run the industrial system now; they could do so after the revolution but they would have to be won to the cause and organized for action. At present, Veblen says, they are scattered across the country as employees of various business. They would have to be recruited to the cause of the revolution. That would require an extensive educational campaign, accompanied by publicity. Veblen believes that the older engineers probably could not be won to the cause; they have served business too long and may have pensions at stake. It is the young engineers who would have to be recruited. A detailed script would have to be prepared specifying who would do what, when, and where.

Suppose this done. Still success would require the support of labor; if not of all, at least of the workers in the key industries. This would require extensive campaigns of publicity, a large program of adult education and persuasion. All of this would, of course, be observed by the business leaders who can be expected to defend their property rights. Veblen equivocated on how the absentee owners would respond. He thought at times that they might give up without a fight; at other times, he considered armed combat likely. How such a public revolutionary campaign could actually be carried out he does not say.

The actual overthrow of the existing system, Veblen thought, could be brought about by a general strike. Given their strategic position in industry, the engineers would be able to shut the system down, if they have the support of the workers – at least the workers in the key industries. Assuming that this plan worked, a revolutionary government would have to be ready to take over at once. Veblen says that since it was the failure of the business system to meet the economic needs of the people that sparked the revolution, the new "directorate" must be concerned chiefly with the economy. He proposes a directorate with three main foci – production, transportation, and distribution.[16] He assumes that there will be some sort of representative body – a chamber of deputies perhaps, but the details are not spelled out. He refers to "subcenters and local councils,"[17] and says that the directorate will require a large staff, including consulting economists whose "place in the scheme is analogous to the part which legal counsel now plays in the maneuvers of diplomats and statesmen."[18] But there is one restriction on which Veblen is insistent.

> To avoid persistent confusion and prospective defeat, it will be necessary to exclude from all positions of trust and executive responsibility all persons who have been trained for business or who have had experience in business undertakings of the larger sort.[19]

Veblen believed that such persons would have been "irretrievably biased" against any plan not drawn in terms "of commercial profit and loss and [that] does not provide a margin of free income to go to absentee owners."[20]

If Veblen's sketch of the revolutionary order is vague, there is one point on which he is very clear. Absentee ownership is to be abolished. Veblen spells out just what that means.

> By absentee ownership, as the term applies in this connection, is here to be understood the ownership of an industrially useful article by any person or persons who are not habitually employed in the industrial use of it. In this connection, office work of a commercial nature is not rated as industrial employment. A corollary of some breadth follows immediately ... An owner who is employed in the industrial use of a given parcel of property owned by him, will still be an "absentee owner," within the meaning of the term, in case he is not the only person habitually employed in its use. [A further corollary follows]: Collective ownership of the corporate form, that is to say ownership by a collectivity instituted *ad hoc*, also falls away as being unavoidably absentee ownership, within the meaning of the term ... To be sufficiently explicit, may be added that the cancelment of absentee ownership as here understood will apply indiscriminately to all industrially useful objects, whether realty or personalty, whether natural resources, equipment, banking capital, or wrought goods in stock.[21]

The only exception Veblen specifies, beyond office work, is property held in joint ownership by a household group. However, if the property is not used by the household group or is only used with hired help, then it is absentee ownership. This is one of Veblen's clearest statements of the meaning of absentee ownership, and it is sweeping. Just how and by whom property confiscated under this rule is to be used, Veblen does not say.

Such a revolution would obviously be radical. But Veblen says there is no chance of it occurring, "just yet." Veblen says, "Absentee ownership after all is the idol of every true American heart. It is the substance of things hoped for and the reality of things not seen."[22] Furthermore, "by settled habit, the American population are quite unable to see their way to entrust any appreciable responsibility to any other than business men."[23] There is, Veblen says, no popular support for such a revolution; there is no evidence of revolutionary fervor among the engineers or any other significant group in the country.

"There is nothing in the situation that should reasonably flutter the sensibilities of the guardians [of the Vested Interests] or of that massive body of well-to-do citizens who make up the rank and file of absentee owners, just yet."[24] The "just yet" was meant to keep the guardians from sleeping too soundly. But Veblen's reassurance had no effect on those who feared that the Red distemper would reach America. And so the Red Scare mounted in intensity.

Typical of the Red Scare was the career of the Lusk Commission. Acting on a recommendation from the Union League of New York City, the New York legislature established, on March 26, 1919, a committee for the investigation of seditious activities, chaired by Representative Clayton Lusk. Working with the Bureau of Investigations, the forerunner of the FBI, the Committee carried out raids, subpoenaed witnesses, infiltrated organizations, and, with the aid of local authorities, managed to make arrests. Its activities led to convictions and deportations as well as ruining reputations. In its report to the legislature, the Committee recommended legislation to repress seditious activities. In 1922, the legislature passed such bills. But in 1923, Governor Al Smith signed the bill repealing both Lusk laws and commented, "They are repugnant to the fundamentals of American democracy."[25]

In 1922, Veblen published an article entitled "Dementia Precox."[26] It had been a great mistake, Veblen now said, for America to have entered the Great War. He had supported our entrance to the war even after we went in, but his views had radically changed.

When the whole adventure is seen in perspective it is evident that the defeat of the Germans was decided at the battle of the Marne in 1914, and the rest of the conflict was a desperate fight for negotiable terms on which the German war-lords hoped to save their face at home; and America's intervention has helped them save the remnants of their face.[27]

American intervention, Veblen said, ended the war too soon. Without our intervention, the war would have continued until Germany was exhausted, at which point they would have had to surrender unconditionally. Had we not intervened, we would have avoided most of the war debt and the taxes. "There is at least a reasonable chance that, [had we not intervened] there would have arisen no 'American Legion,' no Ku-Klux-Klan, no Knights of Columbus, and no Lusk Commission."[28] There would also have been "little of the rant and bounce of Red-Cross patriotism; no espionage act, no wholesale sentences or deportations for constructive sedition, and no prosecution of pacifists and conscientious objectors for excessive sanity."[29] In short, we might have avoided a national state of Dementia Precox.

"Dementia Precox" is not a household word. As Veblen describes it, the condition produces illusions of persecution and a derangement of the logical faculty. It creates a "fearsome credulity" including fears that one may be subject to atrocities. The patient believes himself to be the victim of plots and conspiracies. The "predisposing cause" is thought to be exhaustion due to excessive strain or shock. It is a condition, Veblen says, that can afflict either sex and any age, but it is thought to be most common in adolescent males. It is fairly obvious that the conditions created by the Red Scare fit the profile almost exactly, and Veblen clearly believes that the hysteria that characterize the Red Scare was responsible for bringing this affliction on the nation.

America entered the Great War to "make the world safe for democracy."[30] There is no call to impugn the motives of those who took us to war, but the consequences of that event have not been what was expected. Chief among these, Veblen says,

> Has been a certain fearsome and feverish credulity with which a large proportion of the Americans are effected ... They are predisposed to believe in the footless outrages and odious plots and machinations – "treasons, stratagems, and spoils." They are readily provoked to a headlong intolerance, and resort to unadvised atrocities as a defense against imaginary evils.[31]

There has been a revival of animistic belief, including magic and odd religious notions. The Reverend Billy Sunday has become the rage in religion; Fundamentalism has become a power in American religion; and attacks are now being launched against scientific theories as being inconsistent with the biblical text.

> Even a man of such signal good sense and humanity as Mr. [William Jennings] Bryan is joining forces with the Rev. Billy Sunday in the propagation of intolerance, while the gifts of so engaging a raconteur as Sir [Arthur] Conan Doyle are brought in to cover the flanks of this drive into intellectual twilight.[32]

The Red Scare passed. Bryan suffered a disastrous defeat at the Scopes trial even though Scopes was convicted. Whether Veblen came to a different view of the Soviet Union we do not know but so far as I know, he never changed his view of the Treaty of Versailles and the war. He was not alone; many came to share his belief that we should not have entered the war, but most for different reasons than Veblen's. According to Dorfman, "Six months before his death in 1929, Veblen said in substance to his neighbor, Mrs. R. H. Fisher, 'Naturally there will be other developments right along, but right now communism offers the best course that I can see.'"[33]

I am not sure what to make of this passage. To say, "Someone said in substance..." usually means that what follows is not what was actually said but rather the gist of what was said. But putting a passage in quotes usually means that the quoted passage is exactly what was said. The construction "'said in substance, blah blah...'" is self-contradictory. Given Veblen's long standing animus against private property and the communists' view that private property should be abolished, its attraction for Veblen is obvious. But what if anything he actually said about the Soviet Union remains not clear.

Probably the best evidence we have of his final attitude toward the Soviet Union comes from an interview with his ninety-two-year old stepdaughter, Becky Veblen Meyers:

> He wanted to visit the Soviet Union, but Stalin, whom Veblen already regarded as politically dangerous, refused to let him enter the country. John Reed, radical journalist and author of *Ten Days that Shook the World*, had attempted earlier to persuade Veblen to go to the new home of revolutionary socialism, but by the time he finally decided to make the trip Lenin had died and Trotsky had fallen from power. Veblen had seen much in early Bolshevism that was positive and he admired both Lenin and Trotsky, especially the latter because he had "more brains" than Lenin.[34]

Yet Tilman remarks, "Veblen's comments on Bolshevism, despite praise for the new worker controlled and socially owned industrial system that had emerged, give evidence of grave concern over the future of Bolshevism and considerable evidence of recognition of the bloodshed and suffering that the revolution brought about."[35] That is probably all we can reliably say about Veblen's view of the Soviet Union.

Coda

Thorstein Veblen was born in 1857 in a rural part of a country still largely rural. The Civil War began when he was four; it ended when he was eight. What lay before him was an era in which the country and the lives of its people were to be profoundly changed. Domestic life in America in 1870 was little different than it had been fifty years or a hundred years before. By 1940, electrification, running water, indoor plumbing, and central heating worked a greater change in domestic life than anything that had occurred in the previous millennium.[36] Nor was domestic life all that changed; the culture as a whole was transformed by technology – most notably by electrification and the internal combustion engine.[37] Technological change was everywhere. The industrialization of America swept away older ways; the geography of the land was changed by the railroad and the automobile. Business corporations grew almost beyond comprehension into trusts and holding companies. By the time Veblen was forty, huge business organizations dominated America; the robber barons ruled the land.

Veblen's early life was spent in a world of growing protest against these changes. Farm movements like the Grange and the Alliances, labor movements like the Knights and the AFL, political movements like the Populists, the progressives, and the Socialists were gaining strength, and industrial conflicts like the Homestead Strike and the Pullman Strike were redefining industrial life. For Veblen, coming of age in this period, it was obvious that transformative changes lay in store, and no one knew what the outcome would be.

Confused by this technological world, people sought to find ways of explaining for themselves and others what was happening. But many pillars of intellectual life were falling in this storm of change. Religious certainties, economic doctrines, political faiths – all were under stress, and the scientific revolution of the time, particularly the theory of evolution, confounded traditional beliefs. Veblen was caught in the middle of this hurricane. But for him, Darwinian evolution was not the threat it was to so many others. Rather, he thought it the key to understanding the chaotic world around him.

To say that Veblen was a Darwinian is to say very little, for who was not? But Veblen was a Darwinian in a more extreme sense than any other social theorist of his time. Veblen accepted the notion that societies evolved; so did institutions and so did human individuals. But just what that meant depended on what one took human beings to be. In Veblen's view, human beings are a combination of instincts and habits. He held that human instincts were fixed by mutations that had created the present version of human nature in the neolithic period, a version that had remained unchanged since then. But habits were learned and so changed with circumstances and experience. Habits or habit clusters that became established in societies Veblen called institutions, and these too were subject to evolution. So institutions were changeable, but they could, and often did, persist over long periods of time. They thus embodied the knowledge and ways of acting that were passed on from generation to generation. Individuals born into a society grew up in a social world of institutions that carry the culture of the past embedded in them. One learns the social institutions of one's society because they are the social environment to which one must adapt to survive. Institutions thus change and form individuals, and individuals change institutions when they change their habits. There is thus a constant interplay between institutions and individuals. For example, one is taught what items constitute food for people – this is a matter of learned behavior. But the great immigration of the nineteenth and early twentieth centuries brought people who ate things as food that Americans did not. The result has been a radical change in foodways during the twentieth century. Institutional change consists in people changing established ways of thought and action, and many factors can produce such changes. This is not simply a matter of acquiring a new habit since institutions are held to be right and good by their society. So internalizing the institutions means internalizing the norms and standards they embody. The norms and standards that the Leisure Class internalized in the members of the society created the aspiration to attain the standards of living of the classes above their own. So Veblen believed that the experience of working eight to ten hours a day with machines would lead the workers to adopt a materialistic view of the world that would undermine their beliefs in anthropomorphic entities and doctrines such as ownership. And here he went wrong.

Veblen overestimated the amount of cognitive dissidence that industrial work would produce. Of course the workers must acquire at least a working knowledge of how the machine operates – an understanding sufficient to allow them to operate the machine. But a knowledge of how to operate a machine does not require an understanding of the theory underlying the machine. Most people can drive an automobile quite adequately without knowing how an internal combustion engine works. And factory employment exposes the worker to more than the machine. The dominant experience of factory work is that one is working on equipment owned by someone else and subject to rules and standards set by the owners. For the worker the dominant fact about his employment is obedience to the boss, however much he may hate him. Veblen was led by his mistaken notion of the power of the machine discipline to anticipate a course of events that did not occur.

But if Veblen was wrong about the development of labor, he was right about the development of business. He saw very early that mechanization would lead to ever larger business organizations and ever larger concentrations of business ownership. He also saw that although in the early days these organizations were run by buccaneers, they would inevitably evolve into bureaucracies. He was of course not alone in this insight; many others saw this too. But his focus on technology allowed him to see something else. Veblen's division between industry and business was a division between the making of goods and the making of money. Traditional economics joined the making of goods and the making of money. The possibility that business might concentrate on making money without making goods and services was not considered. But Veblen saw that this was a clear implication of the control by what he called "the Captains of Solvency." The games played by financiers – the stock manipulations, the consolidations and mergers of businesses, the growth of trusts and holding companies – showed that more money could be made by manipulating stocks than by making goods. The recognition was new in Veblen's time, but he made the point very clearly that the interests of the financiers were not only those of ordinary businesses but were often antithetical to those of ordinary business. How right he was only became clear with the turn to the twenty-first century.

In an early article, Veblen endorses the system of "modern constitutional government."[38] But this favorable view of constitutional government did not last. Veblen soon came to the conclusion that the American government, and those of western Europe, were controlled by business interests. It was businessmen who were elected to run these governments and business interests that determined their policies. This was not only true of domestic policies but equally true of foreign policy where governments acted as agents of business organized to protect and advance their operations abroad. International conflicts he interpreted as clashes between business interests. But Veblen was also a social theorist who held that nations evolved in their governance as well as their technology and economic organizations. When the Great War began, Veblen took the position that Germany was a dynastic state whose newly acquired technology was being perverted to serve the dynastic ambitions of the state. It was therefore an archaic barbarian society bent on war and conquest but wielding modern weapons. The nations of the Entente, on the other hand, were modern business organizations bent on their profits and power but which still allowed more freedom and self-determination than the dynastic state. Given the choice, Veblen took the side of the Entente.

Veblen viewed the Great War as an unmitigated catastrophe. It marked, he held, the collapse of the modern business culture. So disastrous was the war that he thought it would be obvious to all intelligent observers that a radical reconstruction of the modern point of view was essential – an institutional revolution that would make the recurrence of such a cataclysm impossible in the future. It was for this reason that he wrote his book on peace and threw himself into government work to support the administration.

It was all for nothing. The elder statesmen paid no attention to his writings. The peace that emerged at Versailles Veblen considered an attempt to reinstate Victorian culture in the post-war European order. The elder statesmen had no intention of making any significant change in the old order. And the old order continued along the lines that Veblen had foreseen. Within a few years of the end of the Great War, business had so consolidated its hold on the American economy that Veblen concluded no breakdown of the economic order was in prospect. The One Big Union, including the Federal Reserve, had control of the nation's credit resources and could prevent any business crisis from happening.

He had predicted monopoly; he got oligopoly. The difference was trivial. He saw that the concentration of business control of the economy was being superseded by the rule of the financers whose interests were not consistent with those of the general population or even those of ordinary business. He was right, although it took a long time for the crippling effects of financial rule to become apparent; a new millennium dawned before the takeover by the Captains of Solvency was widely recognized. He predicted the transformation of major businesses into stifling bureaucracies, and that came to pass. And he foretold the reduction of labor to the status of the bacteria used in fermentation, and that too came to pass.

Veblen's hope had been that the discipline of the machine would alter the perspective of the working men sufficiently that they would mount a movement that would fundamentally reform the American economic system. More and more men worked with the machines, but Veblen watched in vain for signs that they were becoming disenchanted with ownership or the prevailing economic order. Veblen never gave up hope that the discipline of the machine would produce the results for which he waited, but he was forced to conclude that the change would not come soon, or in his time.

By the late 1920s, Veblen was deeply depressed. His warnings were ignored. Capitalism was clearly in command; the world order gave no signs of revision. Imperialism was barely altered; Germany lost her colonies but no other power did, and no steps were taken to end the exploitation of the victims of colonization. The only glimmer of hope that he could see came from Russia, but just what the Soviet experiment might become was far from clear.

Veblen had grown up in an era of business turmoil, labor strife, growing reform movements, a rising Socialist movement – a time when real reform had seemed probable, if not inevitable. He had watched the Populists, the Progressives, the Socialists, all striving to bring about a major transformation in the culture of the United States. But the Great War appeared to have ended that. The Socialist Party collapsed, the IWW was destroyed, the anti-Red campaigns drove protest underground. The 1920s had little to offer Veblen but disillusion and defeat.

Had he lived a few years longer, the Great Depression would have lifted his spirits, but not for long. The rule of business continued, despite the disaster that it had brought upon the nation. And once the New Deal was in place, it was clear that there would be no second American revolution. On August 3, 1929, Veblen died, a bitter and disillusioned man.

Notes

1 Joseph Dorfman, *Thorstein Veblen and His America* (Clifton, New Jersey: Augustus M. Kelley, 1972), 372.
2 Thorstein Veblen, "Editorials from 'The Dial,'" in *Essays in our Changing Order*, ed. Leon Ardzrooni (New York: The Viking Press, 1945), 460–461.
3 Thorstein Veblen, "The Economic Consequences of the Peace," in *Essays in our Changing Order*, ed. Leon Ardzrooni (New York: The Viking Press, 1945), 462–470.
4 Veblen, "Consequences of Peace," in *Changing Order*, 464.
5 Veit Valentin, *The German People: Their History from the Holy Roman Empire to the Third Reich* (New York: Knopf, 1946), 645.
6 Veblen, "Consequences of Peace," in *Changing Order*, 467–468.
7 Dorfman, *Veblen and His America*, 426.
8 Thorstein Veblen, "Between Bolshevism and War," in *Essays in our Changing Order*, ed. Leon Ardzrooni (New York: The Viking Press, 1945), 441.
9 Thorstein Veblen, "Bolshevism is a Menace – to Whom?" in *Essays in our Changing Order*, ed. Leon Ardzrooni (New York: The Viking Press, 1945), 404.
10 Veblen, *Engineers*, 83.
11 Veblen, *Engineers*, 87.
12 Veblen, *Engineers*, 119.
13 Veblen, *Engineers*, 125.
14 Veblen, *Engineers*, 129.
15 Veblen, *Engineers*, 133–134.
16 Veblen, *Engineers*, 143.
17 Veblen, *Engineers*, 144.
18 Veblen, *Engineers*, 145.
19 Veblen, *Engineers*, 146.
20 Veblen, *Engineers*, 146.
21 Veblen, *Engineers*, 156–157.
22 Veblen, *Engineers*, 161–162.
23 Veblen, *Engineers*, 150.
24 Veblen, *Engineers*, 169.

25 David Colburn, "Governor Alfred E. Smith and the Red Scare, 1919–1920," *Political Science Quarterly* 88 no. 3 (September 1973), 443.
26 Thorstein Veblen, "Dementia Precox," in *Essays in our Changing Order*, ed. Leon Ardzrooni (New York: The Viking Press, 1945), 423–436.
27 Veblen, "Dementia," in *Changing Order*, 425.
28 Veblen, "Dementia," in *Changing Order*, 427.
29 Veblen, "Dementia," in *Changing Order*, 427.
30 Veblen, "Dementia," in *Changing Order*, 428.
31 Veblen, "Dementia," in *Changing Order*, 429–430.
32 Veblen, "Dementia," in *Changing Order*, 431.
33 Dorfman, *Veblen and His America*, 500.
34 Rick Tilman, *The Intellectual Legacy of Thorstein Veblen: Unresolved Issues* (Westport, Connecticut: Greenwood Press, 1996), 122.
35 Tilman, *Intellectual Legacy*, 122.
36 Robert Gordon, *The Rise and Fall of American Growth* (Princeton: Princeton University Press, 2016), Ch. 4.
37 Gordon, *Rise and Fall*, 374.
38 Thorstein Veblen, "Some Neglected Points in the Theory of Socialism," in *The Place of Science in Modern Civilization*, intro. Warren J. Samuels (New York: Cosimo, 2007), 306.

INDEX

Note: T.V. = Thorstein Veblen